Upon the Somme, 1916

Upon the Somme, 1916

Two Personal Experiences of British Soldiers in the Battle of the Somme During the First World War

A Subaltern on the Somme in 1916

Mark Severn

The Adventures of an Ensign

Valentine Williams

LEONAUR

Upon the Somme, 1916
Two Personal Experiences of British Soldiers in the Battle of the Somme During the First World War
A Subaltern on the Somme in 1916
by Mark Severn
The Adventures of an Ensign
by Valentine Williams

FIRST EDITION

First published under the titles
A Subaltern on the Somme in 1916
and
The Adventures of an Ensign

Leonaur is an imprint
of Oakpast Ltd

Copyright in this form © 2016 Oakpast Ltd

ISBN: 978-1-78282-531-9 (hardcover)
ISBN: 978-1-78282-532-6 (softcover)

http://www.leonaur.com

Publisher's Notes
The views expressed in this book are not necessarily those of the publisher.

Contents

A Subaltern on the Somme in 1916   7
The Adventures of an Ensign   133

A Subaltern on the Somme in 1916

Contents

Introductory	13
July	15
August	30
September	56
October	71
November	89
December	115
January 1917	126

To "Johnny"
Who
Sang in all weathers

Introductory

Odd the pranks that Memory plays. Odd the features of the past that stand out when we look back over an abyss of years.

Of those now living who assembled at Charing Cross Station soon after nine o'clock on a morning in mid-July 1916, to make the journey that had for its end the Battle of the Somme, are there many to whom the memory of that tremendous occasion prompts the question: "Did we, or did we not, then shave the upper lip?" That one, at any rate, did so speculate may as well be confessed at once; for the reactions to experience this book intends to present must be as candid and truthful as the writer can make them, or authorship on such a subject as the European War will, in his case, be valueless.

The Powers that Were in those days (*facilis descensus!*) have already committed themselves to much educative print, showing us the why and how of high politics and strategy as they affected the fates of some millions of the world's citizens; and we are grateful to them, on the whole, in proportion to their candour. But the lack of candour, in just those places where our curiosity is most piqued, is common to such works, and there is nothing more distressing to the honest listener than to be told, by one who knows more, only the discreet truth. As the lives of great men all remind us, Time has a passion for the indiscreet truth. It is therefore not surprising that, from the great men's records of the war, the scraps of candour which fall from their tables are what we most hungrily devour. Might it also be that a record of experiences which befell one of the least in those days would not be without interest if the writer were capable of telling the simple truth?

That is no small task. Yet even supposing the possibility of such a chronicler, he should be warned not to deceive himself. Many of his experiences were doubtless common to millions, and if it is their attention he would engage, then something other than the bare record of facts will be required. Facts are mere accessories to the truth, and we do not invite to our hearth the guest who can only remind us that on such a day we suffered calamity. Still less welcome is he who would make a Roman holiday of our misfortunes. Exaggeration of what was monstrous is quickly recognised as a sign of egotism, and that contrarious symptom of the same disease which pretends that what is accepted as monstrous was really little more than normal is equally unwelcome. All that is sufferable in the way of reminiscence must be truth expressed through personality. And that is art. It gives us pause.

There comes to our rescue the thought of those among us, who will soon be men and women, to whom the war is not even a memory—nothing but a great adventure just missed through an unlucky accident of birth. They'd like to know, they say; and their children's children rise in vision plying our ears with questions easy to be answered now, but unanswerable when the moss is thick on our graves.

July 1916

CHARING CROSS

Charing Cross Station: A sombre, sunless place, crowded with khaki figures thinly interspersed with civilians, mostly women, dressed in sombre colours. The figures in plain khaki are listless, but those decorated with ribbons, and still more those with red or blue tabs, look animated with the bustle of busy self-importance. Today the heavy lugubrious atmosphere that often seems to pervade a London terminus is lightning-charged, so that the air vibrates with repressed emotions, felt all the more intensely because no one gives them relief. The hopes and fears of all are the same; but they are not shared: each one bears his own.

Beyond the barrier lie the trains: long black sleeping snakes. We disregard them, as if they were not. They are public servants that have become our masters. We turn away from them because we know that in this scene they are the chief instruments of destiny.

I am hideously self-conscious. One half of me is tunic, belt, *puttees*, badges, revolver—a figure hoping it presents an approved appearance in the public eye and faintly flattered by the sense of voluntary heroism; the other is a mind seething. This mind has become like a cloud brooding above my body, so full of violence and revolt that constant effort is required to keep it suppressed. Its impulses suggest the maddest actions. Now, as my young wife and I weave an outwardly nonchalant way through the crowd (she does not touch my arm: we know the etiquette), I am on the point of proposing that we walk straight out of the station, get into a taxi and drive and drive and drive till the car breaks down. Even the thought brings a sense of relief, for it opens a *vista* upon a garden of old enchantment. I draw a shutter across it violently. We go upstairs and drink coffee in the gloomy buffet.

One glance round to see there are no officers of one's own regiment here, then heart's ease for a moment. We can smile to one another. We do not speak. There is nothing to say now. Twenty-two months ago we saw this hour. We were reading *The Globe* after a little dinner at a place near the Marble Arch. We looked up, and as our eyes met we saw this day. That was a lifetime ago; but from that hour every step has been towards this chasm. Then, the rumble of earthquake bringing foreknowledge as clearly as if the red printed page had announced it: now the event, so many times lived in imagination it is difficult to realise it as fact. We look in each other's eyes to reassure one another of reality. The look implies: "You are you. I am I. Nothing else matters."

For all the months of grace between then and now we are not ungrateful. We have reason to give thanks. Love's embodiment now lives. I listened to the flutter of his heart as he lay on my arm last night. Kind was the fate that had kept me from going sooner; for had it been otherwise one victory over death might have been lost. We are free from double dread. For that my heart sings a song often to be sung again in strange places.

We must go. Back through the khaki whirlpool: up the long platform. Ah! There's Brunning the South African, and Zenu the bright, blond beauty, and Leonard the weed, and some more.

Brunning has a full-dress introduction. He is that timely relief, a natural humorist. Besides, he has served in German West Africa, where he lost his right ear. We see in him sound proof that war is not all death. Fat and smiling—Brunning, you're our man for today. We'll keep pace with you, though we ride Rosinante.

There is something like a dozen of us in this odd saloon-car with its large, broad windows. We take our places like guests at a conference.

Now the last fierce moment comes. "Step inside, please." Your hand. "Goodbye. Might be back in a fortnight: you never know. Goodbye. Never goodbye." The train moving: a girlish figure running beyond the end of the platform waving, all sadness gone, still waving. . . . Snap! The cord is broken. Back through the window, and here's this collection sitting round like the figures in the poem, "all silent and all . . ." Well, you never know. Some will come back: some won't.

Already I am away in my mind. I know it clearly enough; but the sickly Leonard is sitting beside me starting a whispered confidential burble. It appears he also has an affair of the heart and therefore presumes we must feel alike. He has a grievance, too. It is that younger men than either of us are still at the training-camp. 'They've no such ties as we have, and Roberts has been fairly crawling round the old colonel to be kept on as adjutant. Roberts is a perfect swine. He has been chortling about the number of fellows he sent out who were killed on the first of July. When he signed Leonard's papers he sniggered over "another death warrant." The whole bloody war was rotten. Of course, it didn't matter to fellows who had no ties. But even if they did get back, who could say what might happen in the meantime with all these crowds of slackers about? The damned Huns! They ought to chuck taking prisoners—that'd soon end it. How long did I think it would last? It couldn't last much longer. Had I been on the musketry course at Catterick? He ought to have gone—ought to be there now—would have been, but for Roberts. It would be good if we got in the same company, wouldn't it? So few fellows understood.'

Feeling much dislike for Leonard and his comparisons, I respond in monosyllables. Yet I am sorry for him, and when at last he stops, I find that his hang-dog misery and petty resentments have been good for nerves stretched, five minutes ago, almost to breaking-point. At least there shall be no grovelling. Well enough I know that I shall never be the real soldier. He lives on pinnacles of indifference I have long decided I shall never reach; but at least one can die decently: at least I've resolution enough for that. Whether I have sufficient to look a man in the face and then blow out his brains with this revolver remains to be seen. What I shall experience at the sight of a bayonet entering my own vitals also remains, possibly, to be known. Now there is no knowing—only possibilities to be faced. Yet a thousand less ghastly things might happen: honours, wounds, hospital, leave, peace. God! Peace itself will come one day. Fancy living to see it! One might.

There is peace outside, there in the fields of Kent. Nature here knows nothing of the war. Through the window I see the fruit-trees dancing in the sunlight. Now they are changed for the rich ranks of hops, bobbing as we pass; and now again the clustering apple-trees. That green and lovely world is at peace; and though the very sunlight seems at times an insult, one would not have Nature lose her loveliness. The mere knowledge that beauty somewhere still persists is relief.

The Channel
Oh ye! who have your eye-balls vex'd and tir'd,
Feast them upon the wideness of the sea.

It is in its happiest, most bewitching humour. There is just enough movement to show the sea has a life of its own. The sun shines down, master of the dance. I have not seen the sea for nearly two years. This might be a summer holiday, except that astern there's a deadly-looking little destroyer: our escort, I suppose. Mines, torpedoes—the sea is full of man's filth: there is enough to provide a remote possibility we might never reach France. Well, the sea looks bewitching.

A man comes up by my side at the rail. He is a captain in a line regiment, and looks elderly for his rank. His large, mobile features do not suggest the army. He is certainly not of the regular army, for captains in the regular army do not begin conversations with subalterns. He devoutly hopes he is not for the Front this time: he has done his share of fighting in Gallipoli. He believes there's a good chance of his being appointed Director of Entertainment Parties for troops just out of the line: close up, of course, but not actually under fire.

I wonder at his frankness. Somebody's got to do the fighting. Is everyone in France quite as ready to leave it to somebody else? He explains that he is over forty, and after Gallipoli rather thought they might give him a job at home. He is an actor and went to enlist straight from a London theatre on the day war broke out. Oh yes! Of course; now I remember him. I am pleased and flattered by his geniality, for in the theatre he is a person of importance. Who'd have thought, that day when I sat in the pit, I should next see him here? He talks to me now, I suppose, because most men become sociable in time of misfortune.

Boulogne

What a change has come over Boulogne since August 1st, 1914! It has been converted from a guest-house into a workshop. As we steamed up the harbour on the day of France's mobilisation nearly two years ago, cheers greeted us from the pier, blue figures on the quay waved their flags and a band played. Boulogne was French, and full of French excitement and cordiality. Today, as we silently drifted in like cargo, and like cargo lay waiting I know not what formalities before we could land, I felt that Boulogne had been Anglicised. Now, after lunching at the British Officers' Club, as I drift about the town waiting for the train that is to take us to Étaples, it seems as if the French element had retired to its fastness before an invader. The place wears a big British mask, and the mask shows the broad commercial features of John Bull. Boulogne is busier than it has ever been; but it has lost its character in the exigencies of war.

That the war is not very far away I am made conscious as I enter the station. An ambulance-train has just come in and suddenly "walking cases" appear, their heads or arms swathed in bandages. They look like men let out of prison, so much bustle and vigour they have: so much anxiety to get along. The blood still stains their dressings and shocks by its gross reality. The hours of idling in Boulogne made an anti-climax in our journey: we seemed to have missed our way to the Front. Now these bloodstained heads come as a sharp reminder of our destination. Quite surely we are bound for the places these men have left.

ÉTAPLES

Dusk is falling as we detrain at Étaples. We have been a long time making the short journey, and are glad to shake our limbs after being wedged tight in those uncomfortable wooden carriages. We drop out by the side of the rails and scuttle up a sandy slope, where we report and receive details of our quarters for the night. We wander through a sea of canvas, our valises following, and now by the light of a candle unroll them on the wooden floor of a bell-tent. Zenu, Hill and two others share this tent with me. They are soon asleep. Even the longest day comes to an end at last. A gramophone at a Y.M.C.A. hut some way down on the side of this sandy hill is playing tunes from *The Maid of the Mountains*. It stops. Through the door-flap of the tent I can see the stars. Hill snores loudly as I get into my bag. What a release to feel alone and free from military busyness! Passionately I try to send waves of something deeper than thought across the estranging miles, and in the effort fall asleep.

"THE BULL RING"

It is nine o'clock on a day that promises heat. We are on our way to the Bull Ring: two hundred of us, officers who have not been to the Front and are therefore due for a course of intensive training till some battalion of our regiments shall require us. Here we are, slogging along under the command of a captain, back in the ranks again, carrying rifles. This appears to be an indignity to some of these fellows; but it does not trouble me, for I have no gift for the assertion of authority, and find it easier to obey army orders than to give them. The responsibility of command is an effort which diverts thought from what are much more natural, if useless, channels.

These huts to our right and left are hospitals. And what is that, looking like an ungrown hopfield? A British cemetery, Lord! How many have died already! The ground is smothered with wooden crosses. We march on in the heat till we come to a great open sandy arena. Out on to this plain we file, and now we are put through physical jerks by officers who have risen from the regular ranks; and now are drilled by sergeant-majors who have been chosen for this duty presumably by virtue of the harshness of their voices and the austerity of their manners. It is hot work, and there is a fierce, vindictive atmosphere about this place which makes its name of "Bull Ring" intelligible.

Later we climb up among the sand dunes on the other side of the road, and there practise firing rifle grenades and throwing those small egg-shaped cast-iron missiles known as Mills' bombs. Here too we learn more of the methods of gas attack and defence, and practise the art of shoving our heads quickly into the clammy flannel bags that are dignified by the name of P. H. helmets. We finish the morning's work by running obstacle races over a prepared course back on the arena.

In other times, all signs of our activity banished, these sand dunes must make a place of delightful holiday. Even today one's eyes wandered instinctively toward the blue estuary that lay below us, where the tiny white sail of a yacht moved slowly upstream.

Gramophones

The tents in this camp; are uncountable. All the way down this sandy slope, up the next hillock and down over the other side, beyond, away and on all sides they stretch, interspersed here and there with more solid buildings: canteens, army ordnance depots and Y.M.C.A. huts. It is a city of canvas whose inhabitants are always changing. Men and officers, they are here today and gone tomorrow. We are all waiting. A batch of Somersets arrived last night. Today they belong to the Black Watch and have gone up the line in kilts. The casualties since July 1st have been too heavy to allow every draft to go to its own regiment.

Off parade there is little to do. We write letters: eat and drink in the mess: talk or play cards in the hut. And whether we like it or not, we listen to the eternal gramophone. At every hour of the day, and half the night, some gramophone is going. Up the slope the pitiful wail is carried on the breeze:

If you were the only girl in the world
And I were the only boy,

A pathetic hymn before battle. Yet it serves as a reminder that, under many layers of treacly sentiment, the human heart still beats: even this war cannot remove that organ. Nero did well to play the fiddle: the gramophone is our best substitute. And that pathetic tune, who knows but its terrible popularity is due to the subconscious craving in every one of us here for his own suspended individual life?

Paris-Plage

We might be in England. Someone has had the good taste to open a tea-shop in Paris-Plage that, but for its military customers, puts the thought of camps and army routine a thousand miles away. The *cretonnes* about the windows are in strong simple colours, and the china might have come from a Cottage Tea Room. Half a dozen of us have walked and trammed to Paris-Plage solely for the luxury of feeling English civil ease again. What creatures of environment we are! We could buy the same food in the mess for half the money; yet no one would mistake us for dilettanti.

There is little attraction about Paris-Plage itself. The front is deserted: the normal life of the place is suffering war repression. Like every English seaside town during the war, Paris-Plage wears by daylight the fancy dress of last night's dance. We wander round and the time hangs heavy on our hands. Nothing is more desolate than forsaken gaiety. Let's jump on the little tram and go back to camp.

On the road to Balancourt

We are on the road from Longprès to Balancourt, Zenu, Hill and myself, marching at the rear of a motley detachment made up of men belonging to three regiments. They are being drafted into the battalion of the line regiment we also are joining today. Leonard and Brunning have already been posted to this battalion, which was badly cut up on July 1st, and is now our on rest, being re-formed.

Conversing at the first halt, we discover that these men have come from all directions. Some are little more than boys and have yet to see fighting: some have come *via* hospital from Gallipoli; others from Egypt; and they vary in ages from seventeen to forty-five. It is a close afternoon: they seem to be badly out of training, and those from Egypt suffer with soft feet. We have not done more than half the six miles when one of the boys faints. He lies in the dust, his face red and puffy, while I undo his tunic, wondering why he should have collapsed.

The reason is soon obvious. He is wearing one of those much-advertised body-shields, a thing that in the trenches might stop a very tired bullet, though here its only purpose has been to impede the lad's breathing and overheat his body. I wonder what pathetic history attaches to this unhappy life-preserver. Some anxious woman has obtained a promise from the boy to wear it. Alas, the thrusts of death in this encounter are not quite so easily parried as the merchants of this pitiful armour would have you, good mother, to believe.

JOINING THE REGIMENT

I had formed a mental picture of how a subaltern joined his regiment. First he met the adjutant, who took careful particulars of training and special qualifications. Then, with due ceremony, he was taken into another room and formally introduced to the colonel, who deigned to extend his hand and wish the young man luck. Then the colonel would follow this with some details of the battalion's immediate history, a footnote on esprit de corps and the honour of the regiment, and finally give a few words of fatherly advice. The subaltern saluted and returned to the adjutant, who now gave the junior particulars of his company, told him how he could obtain an orderly, what were the regimental messing arrangements and any other local details.

But it does not happen like that.

As the draft reaches the top of the last hill, we are met by a sallow-faced cadaverous-looking young man on a horse, who in a Cockney accent shouts directions to the troops. He tells Hill and me we are for C Company and will report to Captain Rowley. We inquire the way of men on the road and are directed to a farmhouse standing beyond the midden that fills the courtyard of a French farm.

We pick our way across the dung-heap and enter a room that seems to be fulfilling nearly all the purposes of human habitation at once. There are two large wooden bedsteads and two camp-beds, unmade; dirty water in a tin washing-basin, unemptied chamber-pots, unwashed linen, food, whisky-bottles, glasses, papers, bedding, equipment strewn all over the place. Captain Rowley lies fully dressed on the sheets of one of the unmade beds, dozing. We tell him who we are and he replies in a mild friendly voice, but hardly takes a look at us; he is evidently very tired.

Another subaltern comes in. He is a bright, fresh-faced youth, fair-haired and slim, with the down still on his upper lip. He tells us he has been with the battalion a week or two, having seen service in the trenches last year with one of the London territorial regiments. He has a public-school accent and a sly, half-humorous expression. His name is Hardy.

A moment later another subaltern, Mallow, the bombing-officer, comes in. He begins to hold a conversation with Rowley which is one of the frankest I have ever heard. It appears that on the previous evening they rode into a neighbouring town where they spent the night with women of easy affections, and now they proceed to recount the details of their adventures and discuss the possibilities of similar entertainment, with a coarseness which is without reserve. They drink big tots of whisky, but seem too dissipated to raise more than a mirthless laugh. Hardy tries to join in, but meets with only tolerant patronage. The whole scene strikes me as a study for Teniers.

Two of a Kind

Hill and I stroll out of the village: our dignity is offended. We are neither of us prudes, but the obscenity was too rank. Moreover, Hill too had cherished some idea of being decently installed in the regiment, and is very sore about our reception.

We come to a bank overlooking a cornfield and sit down. The lush green of the earth, the colour in the evening sky and the songs of birds in the thicket behind us make the peace of twilight like a presence felt. It begets confidences, and the shy Hill hints at a love-affair and gives me an address he would like me to write to if anything should happen to him. He tells me of his home and his life as a shipping-clerk in the City. It is all very ordinary; but just now the knowledge that another human being here has lived an ordered human life with its natural affections is welcome by its contrast. I realise that we are just a pair of homesick children.

The Sergeant-Major

On the first parade of our company one figure stands out. It is Company-Sergeant-Major Steel. He is a tall, thin, dark man of about five-and twenty, with a long hooked nose and a slight stoop. He wears the D.C.M., but his manner is casual, and there is nothing of the parade sergeant-major about him: indeed, I wonder at first how a man of such weedy appearance can have attained his rank. But when Rowley introduces us, I see a couple of keen, intelligent eyes looking abnormally bright, like eyes that have seen too much. As we step aside, Rowley describes him to me as the bravest man in the regiment, who obtained his distinction by bringing in fourteen prisoners, single-handed, on July 1st.

In days to come I am to see much of this man. Many a dreary hour in the trenches we shall wile away together, talking of his home in the West of England where he used to be a confectioner, and where his young wife and child wait for him. There's strange galvanism in this man, for he can pull the whole company together with a word, and yet his natural habit of mind is soft and reflective. Already he is utterly sick of the war and many a time he is to tell me, in response to some chaff about his ribbon, how gladly he would exchange it for a week's leave.

The C.O.

It is the second day after our arrival. Word comes round while we are at breakfast, "All officers to the C.O. at 8.30." Now I shall see the colonel. At present I don't know who he is. Officers, many of whom I have not seen before, crowd into a small room, each one saluting as he comes before a grey-headed, red-faced man, wearing a Scottish uniform, who sits writing at a table. Standing by his side is another Scotsman, tall, raw-boned and of very sour expression. He is our medical officer. The faces of the two men offer a contrast in red and grey; but they both look unpleasant.

Without preamble the colonel begins:

> The discipline in this battalion is damnable. Some of you officers don't know your job at all. You think the men will respect you just because you wear a belt. They won't, and I don't blame them. You've got to command these men before they'll respect you, and the sooner you make up your minds to it the better. I see officers talking to men as their equals. I won't have that. If there isn't an alteration at once I intend to make it devilish hot for you. I don't know what you've learnt at home. I don't know who sent you out here. Some of you fellows have only just come out. Well, you may as well understand, this isn't a picnic. If you don't know your job and show a very different idea of discipline, I'll have you sent back and reduced to the ranks. You think you've come to France to loaf about. You'll find your mistake. There's got to be a drastic alteration, or back you go. I'll not allow the men to be under the command of inefficient officers. Just understand that.—You can go.

We salute and file out. This seems a strange introduction. What does he know about our efficiency? The majority of us have only been with the battalion a matter of days. Why should we be cursed by a man who has never set eyes on us? We are volunteers; most of us joined in '14, and our prospects of dying for our grateful country are the brightest in the world. Is this the way the modern commander spurs his men on to victory? As a matter of fact, Hill and Zenu, I happen to know, are particularly good responsible officers, and Brunning is no chicken.

I am stung with resentment. Rowley sees this and smiles indulgently. He declares it is all "eyewash," prompted by the doctor who regards every man who was not in France before July as a skunk. But the knowledge of what I have given up to come out here is too strong for my sense of humour, and my anger, at what seems to me studied insult, seethes.

Captain Rowley

I am getting to know my captain. He is just a good-natured fellow, with any amount of pluck, whose morals have been damaged by the war and its whisky. The amount of whisky he and Mallow, the bombing-officer, can drink is astonishing. Every time Mallow reaches for the bottle he repeats the parrot phrase, "This war will be won on whisky or it won't be won at all," apparently intending to float home on whisky himself. Mallow is a pretty coarse-fibred creature; but Rowley is of different material. There's been tragedy in this fellow's life and it has knocked off his rudder. His hair is prematurely grey; his complexion ashy; and although there is still a twinkle in his eye, it is fading, and in repose his face wears the expression of an injured animal. Crossed, he shows a streak of cruelty, but at heart he is full of kindliness. He carries out his duties as a company commander with a queer mixture of punctiliousness and slackness. I wish his conversation was not quite so filthy, for temperamentally I believe we are friends.

Moving up

We are marching out of Balancourt, and for the first time I am at the head of my own platoon, number eleven. Hardy has number nine, Hill ten, and twelve is at present in charge of a sergeant. It is the glorious afternoon of a perfect July day. The sky is flecked with white clouds whose shadows chase across the undulating wooded country. The tall corn is ripening, and between its stalks poppies and cornflowers glow with colour. Through the valley we are descending a noisy stream finds its way, and on the hills beyond, great elm-trees stand like wise men brooding. It is a lush green country, full of beauty. The war seems far away.

How this natural beauty soothes the mind! Where beauty is, life and death are not estranged; they seem, as now, treble and bass of the same harmony. War breaks that harmony; but only for a time, and who could not endure the pause with scenes like this deep-dyed upon his memory?

"Left, right! Left, right! Keep closed up! By your right!" I shall gain the confidence, and more—the affection of these men. What do I care if they now think me green? What does it matter if they are a mixed lot, mostly undersized? We are all men. We shall see it through together. If I can mitigate the hardness of their lot, that's my job. I loathe their beastly packs and rifles as much as they do. Cheerio! my hearties. We'll see it through together. And I fall to wondering what number eleven and its officer looked like a month ago.

SOUTH AFRICANS

We are approaching Condé when a small company of Scottish troops appear, coming along the road towards us. We halt together, and they prove to be the pioneers of the South African Scottish. Their major comes over to Rowley to inquire where we are bound for. We show him our newly issued trench-maps of the country round Martinpuich, and his comment is that we've got a long way to go. His battalion has had a terrible time in Delville Wood. More than half are casualties, and he doesn't yet know which of his brother officers are dead or alive.

CONDÉ

I hear Rowley shouting from the next room that it is time to get up. We are sleeping on the red-tiled floor of a farmhouse at Condé and it is still pitch dark. We draw ourselves out of our valise-bags and dress in the shadows of candlelight. It is still dark as I go down the street to see my platoon which has slept in a barn. Dark figures move about with lanterns as we form up in line ready to move off. "Form fours! Right! By the right, quick march!" Here and there heads are poked out of windows as we tramp out of the town.

The dawn breaks pale and misty. We are halted beside a railway embankment, waiting to entrain at Hangest for some station near the battle-line. Rowley smiles grimly as we discuss our prospects over a cold breakfast. He has seen Hooge and Ypres. "All you poor beggars (only he never said "beggars") will be dead in a week," he says cheerily. "Three hours' bombardment and you'll break the bones of your legs with your knees knocking together. You're in for a bloody fine time, I can tell you. Cheerio! Let's have that whisky. You'll want whisky when you get into those trenches. And by the way—no prisoners. If any of you come back with prisoners to me, you'll be in for it. We're not taking any more prisoners in this regiment, and the Hun knows it. Shoot the beggars. If you bring 'em to me, I'll shoot 'em—and you, too."

I remember the jibe of a London cabman, "Brave words off a weak stomach," and laugh, saying I shall certainly bring in any prisoners that come my way. There is a waver in his eyes which puts me quite at ease, though he, not certain whether he is serious or not, repeats the threat.

Prisoners' Cages

While we are forming up outside Méricourt station I see for the first time a prisoners' "cage." Surely this is the foulest insult to mankind the war has begotten. The cage is like a poultry-run, only laced in disordered strands with wire that is "barbed" after the pattern of the crown of thorns.

A sentry stands at the gate with fixed bayonet, and his smart and soldierly appearance stands out in terrible contrast with that of the creatures who loll about or sit on the bare ground within, hatless, ragged and lousy.

A viler invention than barbed wire was never conceived: it is the perfect symbol of cruelty. The man who first devised it must have received a peerage in hell. And here it is used to provide a place of rest and habitation for the lords of creation. These "lords" have sunk below the status given to the monkeys at the Zoo; and certainly, in their decrepitude and dejection, the inmates of this cage cannot compare with the nimble beasts whose cages have no barbs. I cannot get by without a shudder. This is the bottom of degradation. Call them Huns if you like: there remains a limit to the indignity judges may impose upon criminals without grave moral damage to the judges. These cages pass that limit. We should show more natural feeling if we lined these poor devils up in a row and shot them. That at least would acknowledge their manhood.

I should like to be allowed to go inside and apologise, explaining that the beastly necessities of the times have driven us to means we abhor.

Dernancourt

We are bivouacking on the side of a chalk hill about a mile west of Dernancourt. The wide valley of the Ancre stretches out before us, the sluggish river itself running where those pollard willows stand, two hundred yards from the road that passes at the foot of this hill. Albert lies hidden about a couple of miles north-east, and the battle-line is now somewhere beyond those hills on our left.

The boom of the guns is continuous. We are not far from our destination, for we can see the absurd sausage-balloons that are let up on their cords into the sky and slowly drawn to earth again when observation is over. Aeroplanes, too, are busy, usually flying singly; the red, white and blue rings of the Allied planes just distinguishable in the sky. Occasionally two or three German machines will penetrate our line as far as this, and then there is a clatter of anti-aircraft guns and puffs of white smoke form little clouds around the hawk-like objects in the blue that have the white Maltese crosses on their breasts. The "archies" make it too hot for them to come far, though we never see a hit.

The road below is a highway to the battle. Day and night a continuous stream of traffic trundles by; guns, limbers, wagons, lorries, they flow along. Destruction has a big appetite and feeds incessantly.

On the hillside, kits are set out in rows just as the men were halted, and there they sleep in the open, for the weather is gloriously fine. We officers of C Company prefer the open to a tent and have planted ourselves under a bank near the crest of the hill. Now it is afternoon and the men have gathered in circles to play a game, new to me, known as "House." It seems to be a strange game, for it is accompanied by a lot of shouting on the part of one who presumably acts in the capacity of "bookie," counting and shouting all the time.

Other men sit on their ground-sheets addressing those highly coloured silk-sewn cards that will one day adorn many an English cottage mantelshelf. These cards, with their bright hues, sentimental messages and French character, are very popular: they supply a compendious want. They also save platoon-officers from the business of censoring, which tends to become irksome whenever the men have much time on their hands. Censoring letters is an unpleasant, impertinent duty, to be hurried over and treated as formally as possible. By constant repetition it becomes a deadly bore.

Occasionally there is a patch of rich unconscious humour, but the formula is almost unvaried. The writer is in the pink, in spite of everything: a condition he hopes is mutual. He believes there's a war on, so we must keep smiling. Hopes and fears for leave are always expressed, and promises of battle-souvenirs are usually remembered. There is the inevitable P.S.:

> The cakes were all right, but a bit smashed, and I'd like some Woodbines: the fags they serve out here are rotten.

Ugly punishments

There is a boy from D Company doing Field Punishment No. 1. down by the road this afternoon. His outstretched arms are tied to the wheel of a travelling field-kitchen. The regimental-sergeant-major has just told me that the boy is there for falling out on the march. He defended himself before the C.O. by saying that he had splinters of glass in his feet; but the M.O. decided against him. Quite possibly the boy is a liar; but wouldn't the army do well to avoid punishments which remind men of the Crucifixion?

And these two men being marched up and down in the blazing heat, under the raucous voice of the provost-sergeant, they disturb all peace of mind. I do not know from what offences they are doing "pack-drill," but it is depressing to see them, loaded with rifles and full packs, going to and fro over a piece of ground not more than twenty yards long, moving like automata under that awful voice.

Volunteers going shortly into battle! It is not a pleasant picture. It calls to mind too vividly those propagandist posters of the "bonny boys." Besides, surely this war wants all our energy. The most fearfully arduous task, if it served some purpose, would be preferable to these senseless evolutions, designed merely to fatigue. Volunteers going into battle! I think with almost physical sickness of the legends that sustain our armchair patriots at home.

August

Castlereagh and others

I am getting to know the men of my platoon. About a third of them, the pick of the bunch, are miners from the north of England: short, tough, reserved men, used to hard work and not given to "grousing." More than half of them are married. Collins, with the mild voice of a curate, is a widower, and by religion a Methodist. Burt stands next him on parade. He is the platoon Hercules: a hard drinker with the neck of a bull. He wants me to issue a boxing challenge on his behalf to anyone in the regiment. Spencer is a tall, red-faced lad, awkward but intelligent. I presume the pits have given him that incurable stoop. These are among the miners.

The trades of the rest make an extraordinary list. Labourer, wheelwright, railway storekeeper, farmer, platelayer, cabinet-maker, rag-conditioner, oil-presser, painter, shoe-salesman, driller, grinder, wool-sorter—what occupations a civil world provides! Then Barlow calls himself a "horseman," and, being the platoon fool, can give no more explicit description of himself. Anyway, it is unlikely that he will be wanted for the cavalry: and I should be sorry if he were, for he is an unconscious comedian. Jenkins again is an "interpreter"—of languages, perhaps; but I rather suspect the description as being designed for purposes of reference when those "chits" from the orderly room come round, promising comfortable billets for men of strange trades. I suspect this because Jenkins shows himself a cute student of his own well-being in other ways.

That little wisp of a man, Jackson, who has been to India with the regular army, is something of an enigma. He is smart enough, but he wears a bored expression and seems strangely reticent and unresponsive. Today, when I told him I wanted him to take a stripe, seeing that in point of service he was nearly the oldest soldier in the platoon, he replied that he would rather not. Well, he must, for there's nobody else.

Corporal Neal, who escaped injury on July 1st with the old battalion, has lost his nerve, if he ever had it. He is demonstrative in his authority; but I do not like his stupid, shifty eyes or his subservient manner. Still less do I like the sergeant I am saddled with by the colonel. He has a criminal look, and why he should suddenly be promoted from the ranks to full sergeant I cannot imagine. He has served in Gallipoli, but we do not know his record. Like Neal, he is too servile, and I am a bad judge of men if he proves trustworthy.

Another from the batch that joined the regiment with me I have taken for my orderly. Herbert Castlereagh (better known to his mates as "Erb") is a dark undersized Cockney with a switch of black hair that the company barber ought to see to. His personal cleanliness is an item he forgets, and his speech is difficult to understand; but he has a comical face and there is a good deal of the faithful spaniel about him. He says he is twenty-one: he doesn't look more than sixteen. With a true Cockney's ability to make shift, he found some sticks and rigged me up quite a tolerable bath this morning; and though the performance entailed mild censure for indecent exposure, I'm pleased with Castlereagh, and we shall repeat the trick.

An orderly has a few privileges, and, after Gallipoli, it seems only human to save such a brat from as much hardship as possible. He is the butt of the other orderlies, but in his old serio-comic fashion he is quite able to defend himself. He has a marvellous stock of righteous indignation that he displays like a coster if I, or another, happen to swear at him. A queer self-contained bit of old humanity, I like him, and believe he likes me.

Nearing the Beginning

We have been on this hillside ten days, getting in all the training possible, adding to our strength, shaping up the companies and, not the least pleasantly, bathing in the river below. Hardy has been made acting-adjutant. The new colonel has arrived, and we are determined to like him because he is a regular officer of this regiment. I am afraid it will be hard work, for he has fishy eyes and a weak chin; still, everybody is glad the old Scotchman has gone. Other new officers have arrived, among them Smalley, who has taken over number twelve platoon of this company. He is an Englishman who came back from Australia at the outbreak of the war and has seen service in the ranks of the Guards: an excellent fellow who knows his job and is without frills or outstanding vices. The battalion is still considerably below strength, but I hear we are moving forward tomorrow.

What a strange emotion all objects stir when we look upon them wondering whether we do so for the last time in this life! I catch myself having a fierce desire to rivet impressions, even of commonplace things like the curve of a roof, the turn of a road, or a mere milestone.

But at my back I always hear
Time's winged chariot hurrying near;
And yonder all before us lie
Deserts of vast eternity.

THE PANORAMA

The sun is setting over Albert.

I have wandered out alone to the top of this hill, learning that a view of the battle-front may be had from this spot. Nearly all the rough ground hereabouts is taken over by some department of the army; dumps and camps are littered about everywhere like a child's toys strewn over the nursery floor. But here, for a few hundred yards, where the scrub is clear, poppies and cornflowers stud the ground about my feet and glow bright as jewels in the evening light. Behind the ruined spire of the cathedral, torn as if some beast had mauled its flanks, the sun goes down in a blaze. Banners of the richest and palest hues float out and flutter there in long and narrow waves that ebb in the receding light. From palest green to deep blood-red they blend their harmonies. They ravish the eye and melt the heart.

I turn from them to look out over the east.

The sky is purple dark and all along the horizon gun-flashes quiver as if some fearful *aurora borealis* were continually appearing. Every now and then huge explosions send up pillars of smoke, as though the internal fires of the earth had broken through. Nearer, the darkness is pricked by lesser lights that rise to fall and fade successively, like matches thrown into the air; and to all these ominous illuminations there comes the continual accompaniment of roll and roar: the grind and belch of guns and the shock of countless explosions.

It is an inferno. Can anything live in that? Heaven on one side: hell on the other. One should not hope to come out of that alive. It is a continuous earthquake.

Well, life must end somewhere. One wouldn't have chosen it there. But how to be rid of this ceaseless resentment against being pulled back by death just as one had one foot on the threshold of life? How to die whole?

That wholeness seems best found in praising what has been. Yes, life has been good; rich, sweet and good. Seen now through memory's prism it glows with colours rich as the sunset's. And with that to fortify the will there must be no bitterness, no unassuageable regret.

There is peace—even joy if we can only release our hold with childlike gentleness.

NEAR ALBERT

We have moved another step forward. This field by the cross-roads, where we sleep in the open, is called Belle Vue Farm, though I see no farm. As to the *belle vue*, that has been spoilt. The town of Albert, which lies below us to the north, has been raked with shell-fire and looks half ruins. Some chimney-stacks still stand. They sway beneath the gilded figure of the Mother and Child. That figure once stood triumphant on the cathedral tower; now it is bowed as by the last extremity of grief. Troops still occupy the cellars of the town, but shells drop into the place every day. I woke just now to an eerie watery sound, followed by a long whizzing rush, and then a thud: shells falling behind us. I did not recognise them at once, their watery gurgle through the air as they passed overhead seemed so slow and tame.

THE OLD FRONT LINE

Hardy and I are off to Pommiers Redoubt, Mametz, where we are to report that the battalion will arrive this evening. We descend the long hill leading to Fricourt, dodging about the stream of traffic that stirs the dust of the road to a thick haze. Near the bottom of the hill we come upon the old front line of July 1st. The country here is stricken waste: the trees that formed an avenue to the road are now torn and broken stumps, some still holding unexploded shells in their shattered trunks, others looped about with useless telegraph-wire. The earth on both sides of the road is churned up into a crumbling mass, and so tossed and scarred is the ground that the actual line of the front trenches is hardly distinguishable.

On the far side, in the face of a steep rise, we see the remains of what were deep German dugouts; but everything needs pointing out, for the general impression is of a wilderness without verdure or growth of any kind. To our right we notice a ruined cemetery. It looks as if it might have heard the Last Trump. Graves are opened and monuments of stone and beaded wire lie smashed and piled in heaps.

Now, as we near Mametz, we come upon guns hidden under the

banks of the roadside and camouflaged above by netting. The road through Mametz is still under enemy observation; so we turn sharply to the right to go round the back of the rising ground that faces us. All that remains of the village of Fricourt is a pile of bricks; there appear to be just about enough to build one house; and Mametz Wood is nothing more than a small collection of thin tree-trunks standing as if a forest fire had just swept over them. On the right of the sunken road we have now taken is a mound of sinking freshly-turned earth. It marks the grave of the Devons who died in the capture of Montauban.

A little farther on we come upon all that remains of a German field cemetery: two or three painted triangular wooden crosses; the other graves will now go unmarked for ever. Here we leave the road and begin to climb over the forsaken trenches. Barbed wire, bombs, bully-beef tins, broken rifles, rounds of ammunition, unexploded shells, mess-tins, bits of leather and webbing equipment, British and German battered steel helmets, iron stakes, and all the refuse of a battlefield, still litter the mazy ground. I come across a skull, white and clean as if it had lain in the desert.

We can only move slowly over this confusion of forsaken trenches running in every direction, but at last we are clear of them and mount the hill which is our objective. It broadens out to a wide plateau. Little holes are cut in the ground just big enough to shelter one or two men and presumably give them cover from observation. The large old German dugouts are not at first visible. We report at one of them and return along the hot road by the way we came.

Trenches on the Somme

We are going to the trenches. That little knot of men two hundred yards ahead, just disappearing over the barren crest of the rise, is Hill's platoon. Two hundred yards behind us is Smalley's. This afternoon the sun glares down on earth that has lost its nature, for, pitted everywhere with shell-holes, it crumbles and cracks as though it has indeed been subject to earthquake. Up here we can be seen by the enemy; but there is no hurrying, for we have to keep distance between platoons. Hill has halted: we must halt, too. The men behind me swear with nervous irritation and mutter about being stuck out here to be fired at, I turn to look at them. Standing loaded up with boxes of bombs and sandbags of rations, how utterly unlike the red-coats of romance they appear.

We are off again, now traversing the slope that leads to the valley of Longueval. "Death Valley," it is nicknamed, and it has earned its title, for everywhere there are signs of death: an inverted bottle with a bit of paper in it: a forage-cap hung on a stick: a rough wooden cross bearing the pencilled inscription, "To an Unknown British Soldier." These signs recur: pathetic, temporary memorials; will they outlast the war? In the bottom of the valley lie broken trucks and the shattered rails of a tramway. As we come to the end of the tram-line we have to pass the body of a dead horse, foul and distended, poisoning the air. Suddenly, like a rat, a human figure comes out of the earth. Who would have thought there were dugouts here? As quickly it disappears and we pass on. We march in silence, broken occasionally by a jest that fails to catch on, or by an irritable rebuke from one jogged by his companion. There is no singing now; 'tis as if we moved under an invisible cloud.

We halt for a moment in a chalk-pit where the M.O. has his dugout, and then follow the narrowing sunken road that leads up St. George's Hill. By the time we have reached the top we are moving in single file round the horseshoe bend of the trench we are to occupy, pushing by the troops that wait for us to relieve them.

This is an old German trench that has been reversed and now forms part of our second line facing High Wood, just distinguishable as such, about five hundred yards away on the hill opposite. We have hardly entered the trench before we come on a stretcher lying on the ground. It bears the body of a boy: the face quite black. He has just been killed. It appears there was an old German latrine close to the parapet of the trench; two boys had gone to it when a shell came over and killed them both. As we push along I find that this particular sector falls to my platoon. The shell has made a big breach. Tonight we shall have to repair it and clean up the mess which is beyond description.

The men are posted and the relieved troops scuttle out. In this narrow gap between two deep walls of clay we shall spend the next four days. The air is tainted with the sickly-sweet odour of decaying bodies. At certain corners this odour intensified by the heat, becomes a stench so foul the bay cannot be occupied. Just now I tripped over a lump in the floor of the trench. It was necessary to get a shovel and quickly cover the spot. Literally we are the living among the dead.

Shelling is incessant. There is not a moment when something is not passing overhead; but the fire is not upon this trench, it is meant for the batteries now crammed up close behind on the rearward slope of the hill. Our batteries are replying, shell for shell. Somewhere very close to my sector a French seventy-five barks deafeningly.

I look for a place to lay my ground-sheet and rations, and find a hole burrowed in the side of the parapet and a new German saxe-blue coat lying on the floor. This hole will give cover from shrapnel and serve to deaden the noise if there's any chance of sleep; but it would prove an ugly death-trap if a shell dropped near. I lay my things in the hole and turn to see Rowley and the company-sergeant-major coming along to inspect.

We go round together till we come to a spot in a traverse behind my sector where the smell of decay is so strong they are convinced there is a body lying out. Sure enough, just behind the parados, the dead body of a gunner lies on a stretcher evidently left in haste. Both shin-bones are broken, but otherwise the poor fellow looks unhurt. We have the corpse carried out along the narrow trench: a difficult, awkward business.

I see Jackson considering the gap in our parapet and speak to him about it. He has the whole thing sized up, and without any fuss makes himself responsible for a particularly filthy job, telling me just what he proposes to do as soon as it is dark. He seems more at his ease in the trenches. I shall like this man.

Wondering how Hill fares I go down the trench to see him, and we decide we shall have to spread out our platoons, that are much under strength if we are to keep in touch. I am just returning along the unoccupied gap between us when rapid rifle-fire suddenly starts in the valley below. What does it mean? I get up on a firestep and peer over. There's nothing to see, but the firing continues, causing a cloud of smoke that begins to fill the air. Are they coming over? If they do—well, I've this bit of the line to myself. I pull out my revolver, load it and wait, wondering ironically what anyone would give for my chances.

If they come as soon as this, it will have been quick work. The firing continues so that the smoke obscures all view. Then to my relief the sergeant-major comes along. He too is wondering what is going to happen and we wait together silently. Gradually the firing dies down. It ceases. We go back to my platoon and beyond to see Smalley on the right. He has put his men into their P.H. helmets, mistaking the smoke for a gas attack. "*All's well that ends well.*" But we do not fail to chaff Smalley about his precaution.

Night in the trenches

Night has fallen. The stars shine brilliantly and (these trenches facing north) I gaze at The Plough dipping towards High Wood. What joy it is to know that you in England and I out here at least can look upon the same beauty in the sky! We've the stars to share. Look at them! They have become seers—images of divine stability—guardians of a peace and order beyond the power of weak and petty madness. Upon what havoc and ruin have they looked down in days of Greece and Rome and centuries beyond! Still they shine and keep their calm serenity. They, at least, will outlast the war and still be beautiful. We cannot shoot the stars.

If only those two guns on the horizon beyond High Wood could stop! They flash a pair of devilish eyes and we, trembling, wait the result; for they are firing on us. Already they have knocked the trench in twice, luckily at unoccupied places. It's all because of that damned machine-gun that keeps hammering away on our left. Why on earth do they want to keep firing into the dark like that?

Hill and I think it our duty to find out. After some difficulty we discover the machine-gun and ask the gunners if they can't stop for a while. Sorry, but they've instructions to carry on overhead fire all night on a road beyond the hill which it is reported the Germans use every night.

We come back to my burrow and crawl in, drawing the groundsheet across the opening so that we can strike a match and by the light of a candle eat and smoke.

This is the first time in the trenches for us both, and we marvel at the continuous shelling, wondering if it is ever going to stop. Hill falls asleep and with friendship's pity I look upon his sleeping face. Then a whiz-bang bursts just above us and he wakes, scared like a child. We climb out and parade, for the rest of the night up and down the trench.

Dawn over Delville Wood

Morning breaks shrouded in mist: pale pink veils in the sky above announce the coming of the sun. We shall have seemed to have lived another day before the inhabitants of England awake. These hours between dawn and noon are the longest of the twenty-four. At home we breakfast at eight and try to cram in a day's work before six. Here we breakfast at four or five, and the clock goes round on leaden wheels over the hours of our enforced idleness: the day's work is never begun or ended.

The shelling goes on, now heaviest over Delville Wood. We go and look down over it, from the horseshoe bend in the trench on Smalley's right flank, as the mist begins to clear. We can only guess very roughly the lie of our own and the German trenches: not a living thing is to be seen. The wood itself is just a collection of stakes stuck upright in the ground, looking like the broken teeth of some vicious beast. Shells drop everywhere, making little Etnas as they burst, but we cannot tell which are the hits.

Shelling in trenches

I've a prescription for anyone who wants to know what being shelled in trenches is like. Here it is.

Dig a hole in the garden fairly close to the house, a few yards long, six feet deep and about four feet wide. At night go armed with a popgun and stand in this hole. Then persuade the members of your family to throw into the hole from the upper windows of the house every utensil and article of furniture they can lay hands on: crockery, fire-irons, coal, chairs, tables, beds, let them heave the lot at you, not forgetting the grand piano, just to give you an idea of a nine-inch shell. You must not leave the hole, but while the bombardment is going on you are quite at liberty to march up and down, eat, sleep, remove the debris that doesn't hit you, and generally to pretend that nothing unpleasant is happening. Remain there for a few days or you will evade the trench-dweller's worst enemy, boredom; and if you want to be realistic, add heat, shortage of water, stench, shortage of sleep, and give yourself the actual possibility of being killed every moment.

It would give some idea. Of course you would miss the noise. But you would know the sense of futility which being shelled in a trench produces. At the end of your "tour" I think you would understand how sage a comment on the experience was that made by a poor scared fellow I met on Pommiers Redoubt. He had just come out of trenches where most of his companions had been killed by shelling and, looking at me with wide, staring eyes, he said, "Why, this isn't war at all. It's bloody murder!"

"A soft time"

We seem to have been here for weeks: actually we have been here three days. It has been what is called "a soft time," too, for the only casualties in the battalion have occurred in the company behind us, and there they have only had about half a dozen killed and wounded. We hear the batteries have suffered heavily, and small wonder, for so far the shelling has never stopped.

This afternoon, frayed out with the incessant noise, I went to see Rowley in his miserable little dugout for the sole purpose of asking him whether shelling ever did stop. He smiled and inquired what I expected, adding that it was "a bit steep," but we ought to be thinking ourselves damned lucky we weren't getting it. I was immensely grateful to him, for he was friendly and not in the least superior. I shall owe him something for that kindness as long as we are together.

Digging in front

As dark comes on we are filing out to dig a new communication-trench down in the valley between the front line and our own. Passing a dump, the men draw picks and shovels alternately. It is strange and exciting to be in the open again. The men are extended in line while the tape is being laid. They begin to chatter—too loudly it seems, for half a dozen whiz-bangs come fizzing right among us, glaring red as they burst. The men flop, and I, knowing no better, do the same. Down along the line comes Rowley cursing the men furiously.

"What the hell do you think you are doing lying there?"

I get up feeling badly chagrined, and the work is begun. For a couple of hours it is continued, practically undisturbed. Then we file hurriedly back to the trench, learning as we enter it that we are to return to the work in the morning.

Half-wounded

Another perfect day; but against the blue sky beyond High Wood an observation-balloon hangs ominously. If we were shelled in the dark, how shall we fare in such daylight as this with that balloon hanging over there?

Anyway—merciful and delicious relief!—the shelling here has ceased at last.

At moments there is real silence. To our tired ears this absence of sound is positive and acute pleasure: we drink it like wine, loath to break it even with conversation.

Wondering what will happen, we file down the hillside. To our surprise the silence continues. Out in the bright sunlight the trench is deepened and widened and not a shot is fired at us, though looking across the valley we can see shrapnel falling, ironically enough, on the trenches we have left.

Soon after noon we return, very hot, to eat our bully beef and bread, sitting on the fire-step. Castlereagh, bright lad, has made me a drink of tea, which I am thankful to accept even from his mess-tin. But while drinking it, I feel a smack on the neck and look round to see who is throwing earth about. No one looks guilty, and putting my hand up I find my neck bleeding; and there at my feet lies an inch of shrapnel I had not seen before. Luckily it must have been the flat side that hit and split the skin. Hill ties me up and we laugh over our first "casualty." Then Rowley comes along and, brushing my ridicule aside, insists that I must report to the M.O. for anti-tetanus inoculation. I can get on at once with Hardy's sergeant, and afterwards, on behalf of the company, "take over" at Pommiers Redoubt where the battalion is due again tonight. We shall pass the dressing-station on the way out.

That greasy-looking M.O.! Rowley says that he covers his skin with the fat of bully beef to save washing and keep off the lice, and though that is probably gross libel, unfortunately it looks true. I suffer his attentions, wondering what devil of malice he must house to make him scornful of our easy spell, and together the sergeant and I go into the fearsome valley.

Suddenly those black-bursting shells known as "coal-boxes" begin to fall. They come with terrifying explosions, and we scuttle in search of a deep communication-trench there should be hereabouts. At the far end of the valley a limber is moving along the road. A shell comes over, and when the cloud of smoke clears, the wagon is gone and the horses are bolting down the road. A moment later and we are mopping our hot faces in the comparative security of the deep trench.

The doctor

My platoon arrives at the Redoubt as twilight fades. The sergeant reports "all correct," except that Brown, a youngster among the Gallipoli men, is "bad." I find him lying on the ground breathing heavily and apparently unconscious. He should not have been given that box of bombs to carry. I loosen his tunic and try the ordinary restoratives without effect. This is a case for the doctor. After searching for some time, I find him at mess in the Headquarters dugout; so I send down a message. He comes up, evidently annoyed at being disturbed, and I apologise as we go to the boy together. The doctor bends over him for a moment, and then, rising, shouts with astonishing fury: "You damned young scrimshanker, get up! What the devil do you fancy you're playing at? Think you can swing the lead on me? Get up, or I'll have you in the guard-room."

He pushes the boy with his foot, but the lad does not stir.

"Don't you think he is ill?"

"Ill! There's nothing the matter with him at all. Just 'wind up,' the bloody young coward. Leave him there if he doesn't get up, and don't call me again. I don't waste my time over these damned scrimshankers."

He turns and goes back to the dugout.

This strikes me as callous brutality, and for a moment I am at a loss to know what to do. The men around come to the rescue. They pick up the boy, assuring me they will look after him. As they carry him off I hear them murmuring, "Brute," "Swine."

"He had the fever in Gallipoli," the sergeant explains, "and he gets these attacks. I think he'll come to after a bit, and then we'll get him something warm."

During the next two months it is distressing to watch this boy's efforts to carry on. With the help of the sergeant-major, he is given all the easiest jobs and most comfortable places available; but the marching is always too much for him. He carries his pack like the burden of Atlas. In the end he has a similar attack after a long march, and the battalion having now changed doctors, I send for the new M.O., who orders the boy to hospital on the next day.

STILL ALIVE

It is marvellous to be out of the trenches: it is like being born again. The cloud of uncertainty that hung above us every moment while we were under fire, putting its minatory query before the least anticipation, is lifted, and we are free to say, "In an hour's time," without challenging Fate with the phrase. When freedom to anticipate is being persistently challenged, one understands as never before how much man lives by hope. To be deprived of reasonable expectation—even of the next moment—is the real strain. I had not thought of that. Certainty, even of violent death, would often come as a relief. It is the perpetual uncertainty that makes life in the trenches endurance all the time. "Stick it" has become a password: intelligibly the right one. We have to forget "I shall." It is this constriction of hope that depresses men in the trenches. "If" stands before every prospect, and it is no small "if" in this war.

But here we are, alive again, like men redeemed from the grave. We have left the trenches behind.

Instinctively we feel as if we have earned the right to go home. We gave Death the chance. Death did not take it and we've escaped alive. What about it? Isn't the war finished—at least for us? Some of these men have put their lives in pawn a hundred times. Haven't at least they earned the right of respite? Surely you who live walled round by safety would not demand of these men that they shall keep on offering Death their lives till he accepts? Surely, despite your grey hairs, you'd rather leap from seats of assembly and run into the breach yourselves? I hope you would, but now I am wondering whether you've imagination enough to know what's happening.

I should like to remind army commanders, cabinet ministers and other members of parliament, that soldiers only respect those in command over them who are themselves willing to hazard their lives. Napoleon knew this. It behoves them to remember. If they are content merely to prescribe our fates, let them be assured that their share in the honours of posterity will be the award of contempt.

Anyway we are alive again for a time—most probably—though three men have been killed in a cook-house that was standing here when we left, but has since been shelled out of sight. Peace will come some day, bringing to some men, if not to us, its almost unthinkable reprieve. Peace might even come today. Who can tell?

Battle instructions

Peace has not arrived. On the contrary, I've just come from a meeting of officers before the C.O., at which he told us we are going back to make an attack from Orchard Trench.

He was needlessly emphatic about the word "Retire" and its deletion from our vocabulary. We haven't come out here to retire. Even so, if an officer did use the word, I doubt if we should obey that strict injunction to shoot him. We shan't win this war shooting one another. And all those details about battle police being appointed and instructed to shoot loiterers: are they necessary? Anyone would think we were criminal conscripts.

Alas for the old romantic pictures of the colonel leading his men into the fray! His last words to them now are these scarce-veiled threats.

If only the romantic British public knew! Yet, in the words of our battle-hymn, "They'd never believe it."

Under fire

Cheerio! "For it again," as we say. Here's the latest order:

> Two half-companies under the command of two subalterns per half-company will report to the officer of the Royal Engineers for digging on the communication-trench at St. George's Hill this evening.

The lot has fallen on Smalley and me. My cut in the neck hardly pities me, but I would have dodged that inoculation had I known; for now, at the height of its effect, it produces headache and drowsiness.

We parade at dusk and trail back to the deep trench that Hardy's sergeant and I were glad to find yesterday afternoon. Here we stop and wait. An hour goes by; we are still waiting. At last word trickles down that there is heavy shelling on the trench we are bound for: we have been waiting for this to hold up. A little later we file along, and after much stumbling over wire and other obstructions come out near the old horseshoe bend.

What's all this confusion? Suddenly I see, silhouetted against the moonlit sky, the figure of a man borne high on the shoulders of stretcher-bearers. He is waving his arms and in a hoarse voice shouting and crying for water, like a man in a tragic melodrama. The bearers tell him to be quiet and lie down, but he takes no notice of them, and as we pass I see blood half covers his face. Round the corner of the trench a boy sits moaning. "He wants his mother," whispers the man tending him. "He's been hit in the stomach." The boy gives a sigh and dies as we pass.

We stumble on down the valley and into the shallow trench. All is quiet now. Smalley and I run along the top, setting out the men about a couple of yards apart. The engineer officer comes along and courteously asks me if I will please count the men in the trench. I have nearly finished when a machine-gun out of High Wood starts firing on us. I jump into the trench among the men. It is not more than two feet deep, and we have to lie flat, for the gun is traversing and the bullets mow like a scythe. The earth drops on our faces as the stroke passes and again as the sweep returns.

The man at my head is in mortal terror. "They're coming over! They're coming over! My God! We're for it now!"

The man at my feet is perfectly cool. "Jerry's got the wind up," he remarks slowly. "I reckon he's got the wind up, don't you, sir? He needn't fret himself."

For my part, I wish my heart would stop thumping.

The machine-guns have not ceased before shelling begins. That at least means they are not coming over yet; but to be shelled in a bit of a ditch like this is terrifying. Over and over they come, now short, now beyond, now so close a red glare fills the eyes and a wave of heat scorches the face. This lasts about ten minutes, and as it dies down, the machine-guns begin again, sweeping the top of the trench with fiendish accuracy. Now, worse than all, heavy shells are dropping. *Crump! Boom! Thud!* The storm rises to its height with shells of all calibres.

On and on—light, heat and sound, in agonising confusion. This surely must be the end. I suffer the last torment of fear, and then, as one who has already passed through the gate, concentrate every faculty in the effort to focus life to this point. I am ready; but Death fails to come. To my surprise the moments lengthen: the firing begins to die down. Like a sick man coming out of delirium I hear it growing less and less. It stops. I am amazedly alive.

We get on our feet; but the men of the battalion posted farther up the trench, frightened by their casualties and swearing in their fear, come blundering past, pushing and tearing their way out of the trench. As soon as they have passed we begin to dig, but we have not been at work long before the engineer comes up, and after thanking us with the same courtesy, tells us we may go.

The men assemble on the hill, excited and pleased with their luck. We hurry away, and in our haste miss the communication-trench. A cold mist comes down making the task of finding it in the dark impossible. We wander on through the night seeking the way; the men are apparently too glad to be alive to complain. Morning breaks cold and dank, when we at last discover the plateau.

Brunning sits down

Another reprieve. The attack is not coming off. We are going right out, to come back in another part of the line. What luck! Now we shall get letters.

I've just met Brunning, who was with B half-company last night. It appears he was blown up, but came down again, sitting. Being fat he suffered no damage beyond bruises. Today he waddles like a duck, for the first time in his life cannot see the joke; which is not surprising, seeing where the point of it lies.

It's just what would happen to Brunning.

Lice

This morning I slept in a big German dugout to which Rowley had moved while Smalley and I were out last night. It would have been wiser to have slept on top, for that filthy old place has left me a legacy of lice. People at home are horrified at the thought of lice, but they seem a very minor ill here. Apparently no one who sees much of the front line is altogether free from them. They are a curse when the body becomes heated. New underclothing seems the best remedy; which means that men must suffer more than officers in this respect, as they undoubtedly do in many other more serious ways.

On the March

We are on the march, now twenty miles from the line as the crow flies, making for the little village of Bonniers, about eight miles northeast of Doullens. We returned by the road we had come, as far as Méricourt, bivouacking again at Belle Vue Farm, and stopping for a couple of days at the old chalk hillside near Dernancourt. From Méricourt we trained to Candas, and since then have been making zigzag tracks about the country, presumably to get out of the way of troops going up to the trenches. Last night we stopped at Le Meillard.

It is good to leave the guns behind and get back to the comparative quiet of these long white roads, lined with tall trees. The country is mildly picturesque, and now everywhere one sees the French peasant at work on his harvest. He is usually an old man and most of his helpers are women; but he is getting the work done—the solid, satisfactory, primary work of harvesting the grain. On the road outside the farmhouse stands the thresher. The sound of threshing is good music. I could listen to it and watch the corn falling into the hopper for half the day. As we march past the peasants scarcely trouble to raise their eyes; they have probably seen too many of our kind already. We are intruders upon their work; however necessary just now, still intruders.

We are marching as a brigade, and strict march discipline is observed. Each regiment of the four takes its turn at the head of the column; and no small difference does it make on dusty roads whether you happen to be at the head or the tail of the column: not merely (as the uninitiated might imagine) because of the dust, but chiefly because of the concertina movement between the files that almost inevitably occurs when a large body of men marches over an undulating surface. Bad marching increases the amount of this "play," till the men In the rear seem to be running and halting by turns; but even with the best going, since men are not automata, those at the tail of a column always feel they have farther to go.

For this reason one's chief duty, as a platoon commander on the march, is to see that the men keep properly closed up, taking no more than their correct amount of road-space either way. We halt regularly for ten minutes every hour, and "fall out" on the side of the road to rest and adjust our burdens. No drinking is allowed except by order. If a man falls out on the march without orders, or is guilty of any other breach of discipline, he is called to account on the following morning, and usually gets some extra duty by way of punishment, such as extra guard, or digging latrines with the pioneers.

At present we have no band: not only the bandsmen but the instruments were lost on July 1st. However, I hear the colonel is keen to raise something in the drum-and-fife line, and the men will welcome it, first with jeers and then with cheers, like every innovation. They whistle and sing anything but *Tipperary*, which, I suppose, died out here at Mons. Every now and then a strange song crops up with a local dialect, sometimes bawdy in its details; but that is by way of variety, when the platoon humorist happens to feel fresh. Our regular repertory is made up of last year's musical comedy with *I want to go Home, The Long Trail, Tennessee*, and hymn-tune parodies. They love the "sob stuff," and roar out those inexplicable lines,

And roses round the door
Make me love mother more

(they sing "makes") with fervent gusto. When singing dies down and there's no more whistling, one knows they are tired or coming under fire.

At Bonniers

This old farmhouse is a very comfortable billet. It stands in a shady lane under huge walnut-trees, as if it had slept for centuries. The woman of the house, too, is very agreeable, and last night cooked us a delicious dish of omelets. Rumour says we are staying awhile. I hope it is true. I should like an hour or two to write letters. Hardy reads sixpenny novels. I envy him, for all literature seems to me like a voice from another planet—desirable and beautiful perhaps, but like an echo from the farthest horizon. Hardy can even read while Rowley discusses sex.

There were some ugly feet at my parade for foot inspection this evening—another reason why I hope we shall stay for a bit. These fellows seem to have a very elementary idea of how to look after their feet. Since "sore feet" is an ill that can be avoided, I am keen on these parades and insist on regular washing, which surprises and even amuses some men. Still, they are beginning to appreciate my administrations from the grease-pot. How a man can march with the flesh raw on his heel, like Bowler's, I can't imagine. I will get some spare socks sent out.

Going east again

Companies will parade on the road facing H.Q. in full marching order at 8.30 a.m."

This "chit" from the orderly room came round to Rowley at midnight. Here, indeed, we have no abiding city, and if we seek one to come, its name is never known to subalterns or men. We breakfast while in the same room the servants pack our valises, Castlereagh creating his own merry din over a strap he fancies someone has stolen. Belts are cleaned, tin hats found, and we hustle on to parade to find the men drawn up. The sergeant reports "all present and correct," and by nine we are on the move again, back along the road by which we came here yesterday.

It is a glorious morning, dew is still heavy on the ground, and the air is clear under a cloudless sky. Our first halt is by a wooded bank on the outskirts of Frohen-le-Grand—an idyllic spot with a stream running down one side of the road. Frohen itself is a charming place.

Now we take the road through Mézerolles to Doullens. It rises and falls along the north bank of the River Authie that is sometimes hidden by thick foliage and sometimes the foreground to an enchanting wooded landscape. This constantly changing scene makes the march go easily to me, but some of the men are beginning to find the heat oppressive. We halt just before Doullens, and then proceed to clatter through the town. After the trenches and the many villages we have passed through, Doullens has the air of a city, with its cobbled stones, large public buildings and many civilians. Now we turn into what appears to be a manufacturing quarter of the town, and are ascending the steep hill on the eastern side.

The dust hangs in a cloud about the rear of the battalion, and it is hard work to keep some of the men going. Their rifles have to be carried for them, and still they seem distressed. The songs have ceased, and complaints come down from the colonel about spreading over the road. Frayed and hot, we make the top of the hill and pull ourselves together for a last lap. A couple of miles on we turn sharp to the right and descend the hill leading to Halloy.

It has not been a long march, only sixteen miles, but in the ranks, on a hot day, with several days' marching behind you, with forty pounds on your back and a long column in front, it wants endurance. 'Tis easier to do twice the distance under civil conditions.

Some Portraits

All places that the eye of heaven visits
Are to a wise man ports and happy havens.

This orchard on the outskirts of Halloy is certainly one. While the eye of heaven looks down upon these flimsy canvas shelters in the orchard, their simple accommodation is very pleasant. We might be camping out in a country garden. Officers have primitive beds of canvas stretched over rough frames. The men sleep on the ground, but there is plenty of room and I should think they prefer those quarters to the barn, stable, or forsaken and dilapidated room they usually get for a billet.

Halloy has evidently been used as a rest-camp for some time. It has a town-major. A town-major is a kind of military mayor whose duty it is to regulate the occupation, sanitation and general economy of the place. Town-majorship is usually held by an officer of the rank of captain, and is regarded as a safe and comfortable job, though it must be full of petty annoyances, for he is the disposer of billets and has to mediate between the natural wishes of the inhabitants of the town and military requirements.

Taylor, a captain who had one of the companies before the 1st of July, has returned to the battalion and taken over the adjutancy. He is a tall, lean, well-educated man, with a superficial ease and grace of manner that must be welcome to hostesses. A perfect diplomat, his stimulated vivacity in the presence of his superiors leaves him at other times with that look of weariness so typical of the tactician. I see him as a slave of the desire to please, and even while I despise him for it, feel an innate sympathy with him.

He sits at the far end of this shelter, drinking with Rowley and Simpkins of D Company. He drinks a lot, fidgeting all the time. Obviously his nerve has gone.

Simpkins is the fool-who-knows-his-job type of officer. Short and heavy featured, he has the colourless air of one whose intelligence never reaches the study of human nature. He jokes like a hippopotamus; wakes to vitality in the presence of the colonel, but shows a dull, boorish eye to subalterns and men. They say the interior economy of his company is the best in the battalion. I wonder now whether, as a fighting unit, he is preferable to the no-fool-who-doesn't-know-his-job type—the type one so often met among the stray Jews at the training-camps in England? Maybe; but there's a lot wanting in a commander of men who is without intuition.

Wilson of A Company is the shining light among the captains. He is about forty-five: a short, red, fair man with eyes that twinkle under long brows, a gentle paternal manner and a secret well of good spirits that quietly bubbles over. A very strict disciplinarian, I should think he might have been a schoolmaster. His wrath is fiery and short-lived: his discipline effective, because he seems to insist upon it as though it were a form of natural good manners that had social service and amenity for its end, and not a tyranny that is an end in itself. Wilson is no prig, but I wonder whether his subalterns do not find the paternal air a little oppressive. Anyway, it is obvious that the men have respect and affection for him. Men are lynx-eyed for character.

Lilley of B is the dandy of the regiment. With his dark curly hair and apple complexion, he is a regular Adonis. His name suits him too well. The war becomes a vulgarity at the sight of Lilley—all this disorder around a perfectly-turned-out specimen of English good-looks; and in a Cromwellian tin hat, too, that looks ridiculous on the head of one who is obviously a cavalier born out of his time. He is much too well-bred and handsome for this ugly war, and ought to be given a job at the War Office. Just to see him marching down the Mall would be an encouragement to the folks at home.

Meanwhile those three at the end of the shelter are getting to the bottom of the whisky-bottle. Their conversation is not edifying: that old rascal Rowley sees to that.

Sailly-au-Bois

We have reached the deserted village of Sailly-au-Bois, three miles behind the line at Hébuterne. The men are in cellars of the forsaken houses, for the place is shelled occasionally. Our company headquarters is an imposing farmhouse that stands back from the road, walled-in, with a large clean cobbled courtyard in front. It has a cellar we can hop into in case of trouble, but we prefer to sleep on the ground-floor where there are still one or two pieces of furniture. A six-inch gun hides in the orchard at the back, firing rarely.

On the march yesterday we halted at Souastre, turning into a field that lay in a hollow where the field-kitchens were got to work cooking us a meal. While we were thinking about moving off again, shells began to drop in the town. They came as a great surprise, for the place had not been shelled for weeks, and gave us a sharp reminder of our whereabouts. Thence on to Sailly the cloud of apprehension seemed to hang over us, making the men quiet and producing the unmistakable signs of tension. Now we shall live under that cloud more or less consciously for—how long?

The post-boy

Shells have been dropping in the village. Going out to see that all was well with my little crowd, I met the company post-boy, who has been in France for over a year. He was looking white but extraordinarily pleased. His right hand was bound up and his arm was in a sling. A shell dropped on the road while he was going his round with the letters, and before he could find cover he had lost a couple of fingers. That finishes the war for him. He knows it, and his delight is undisguised. He will start for England when we start for the trenches this afternoon. I envy him keenly, but my envy is mixed with a peculiar pleasure at the thought that this boy, now actually here, will form a link between us and the land of heart's desire. I could make garlands for him to take back.

Hébuterne

We are going in by platoons. Hardy and Hill have already moved off. We are waiting our five minutes' interval under the trees that arch over the road. Time's up. "Number eleven platoon! 'Shun! Slope 'ipe! Form fours! Right! By the right, quick march!" The shortest way to the line would be by the road, but it is under observation of the enemy from the rising ground at Gommecourt, so we pass through a gap in the trees and take the open track across fields that two years ago grew corn. The detour is just sufficient to hide us, but the fields lie open as a plain the whole way to Hébuterne. We keep Hill's platoon in sight, following it for half an hour until it disappears in the village.

As we enter the village we come upon the ruined church. The roof has gone and the near wall leans over us at a perilous angle; yet within we can see images still standing on the altar. Beyond the shadow of the church we face the main street of the village which we enter, turning sharp to the right. Here we keep to the middle of the road to avoid falling masonry in case of shelling. Although knocked about, the houses stand in recognisable order, and we wonder as we pass them by whether they are beyond repair.

Near the end of the village we turn suddenly to the left and dive into an old communication-trench. It winds on interminably by the foundations of houses and through the village gardens, its walls moss-grown and worn, its floor often bricked. This brings us out at last into a maze of trenches that has been in regular occupation for a year. Until recently they were held by the French, who seem to have had a taste for a quiet life and a good idea of making themselves comfortable.

The troops we are relieving are Scots whose kilts make a welcome spot of colour in the drab trench. They hand over in a leisurely manner that is very agreeable and show us just how they have held the line, telling us that this has been a quiet front since the 1st of July, when they buried half a battalion of men in a front-line trench that has been abandoned.

Ours is the second line. A and B Companies are about a hundred yards in front. D is in reserve, occupying cellars of houses on the eastern outskirts of the town. We have a long winding sector of trench, revetted here and there with fine wire, and again in many places floored with bricks. There are no bays, so we post the men at various firing-points at fairly wide intervals and put Lewis gunners out on both flanks. Other disused trenches wind about in the rear of our line, and altogether there appear to be many opportunities for losing one's way and finding that extraordinary and sometimes terrifying loneliness which solitude in the trenches can beget.

What impresses me now, as I seek the company dugout, is the amazing quiet. Not only is there little or no shelling here, but during the last five minutes I have heard nothing but the distant rumble of guns far down on the Somme. Blessed relief! Long may it continue. Was it Ruskin who said that the upper and more glorious half of Nature's pageant goes unseen by the majority of people? Eulogising Turner's skies, I think he said something of the kind. Well, the trenches have altered that. Shutting off the landscape, they compel us to observe the sky; and when it is a canopy of blue flecked with white clouds like this, and when the earth below is a shell-stricken waste, one looks up with delight, recalling perhaps the days when, as a small boy, one lay on the garden lawn at home counting the clouds as they passed.

RATS

Our dugout is not very deep, but it's a wonderful place. At the bottom of the steps on the left there are two canvas bunks that are extremely comfortable when you have walked up and down the trench for an hour or two. Then there's a table, which Rowley naturally monopolises, and a chair, which is also Rowley's. But that's not all. Marvel of marvels, there's a great gilt mirror, big enough to reflect two or even three shaving faces at the same time. All this makes for luxury; but there's one fly in the ointment, apart from lice, of which the old place has its complement. I refer to rats.

Rats outside I saw last night at twilight. They were squeaking and gibbering all over the rough ground of the cast-up earth, and Hill and I have wasted a good supply of revolver ammunition potting at them. Twice during the night I trod on them in the trench, and just now, as I was lying in this top bunk, I noticed the strip of sacking that serves as ceiling, blobbing about, and promptly kicked the blobs into quietness. But the war on rats is being prosecuted with the fiercest determination, as they say, in the ante-room to this chamber, where the orderlies keep their gear.

Smalley sits on the chair reversed with his revolver pointed over the back. He is looking intently along the sights and his aim is at a large rat-hole. On the other side Rowley also stands armed, ready for general emergencies. The main drama, however, rests between his servant and Smalley's, one of whom holds against the wall a large piece of cheese on the end of a bayonet, while the other stands "on guard," his bayonet fixed, ready to make the movements "in" and "out," as on parade, at the first appearance of the rat. Already two corpses testify to the efficiency of the bayonet as a weapon of war.

ROUTINE AND GAS

How unmercifully slowly the days wear away! Just before dawn the order "stand to" comes round, and then everybody is wakened, bayonets are fixed, Rowley comes out of the dugout, followed by the subalterns who happened to be sleeping at the time, and in the chilly air we watch the sunrise. Looking east, we have the advantage of the Germans at dawn. I only wish both sides would agree to sing hymns to the sun, for the beauty of these autumn sunrises is very great, and it seems a pity to leave their celebration to artillerymen a mile or so behind, who come out and pop off a few rounds for our benefit before going back to sleep.

As soon as the sun has risen we "stand down," only those who were sentries keeping to their posts: the rest go to sleep again or have an informal meal. Rowley returns to the dugout to write his report, which always includes news of the wind's direction. At about seven the sergeant sends a couple of men out of the trenches to bring in dixies of hot tea from the field-kitchens which cook for us in the village; and these men go again for dinner at twelve, and again at four for more tea. In the middle of the morning a dozen or so 5.9 shells come over at regular half-minute intervals, and then the front nearly always remains quiet until "stand to" at sunset, when there's generally some rifle-firing and a machinegun in Gommecourt shows us what it can do. Desultory firing goes on till midnight, when the place is quiet as a grave.

Now tonight, if the wind is favourable, gas is going over from our front line immediately after "stand to"; or, as Rowley informed us,

"We are going to give the Huns a dose of their own bloody physic tonight. Let's hope it wipes out all the b—— in the trench."

"Let's hope it's not blown back," says Hardy, who has suffered gas at St. Julien.

We stand in the dark awaiting the effect.

Gas! I believe there's not a man among us, Rowley most certainly included, who does not feel some shamefacedness at this loathly method of war. Many times since I heard the news I have said to myself, "They started it." I wonder why I find it necessary to say it to myself so many times?

It is half-past nine. If the gas went off to time it should have reached them now. Yes, the machine-guns have begun to rattle, and there is a fusillade of rifle-fire. A rain of bullets sings above us, spattering among the trees that overhang this trench. It behoves us to keep our heads down. For about an hour this rapid fire is kept up, and the village is treated to a few extra shells which reverberate among the houses behind us. Then all is normal again, and we are left with a sickly wondering what has happened in the German line.

Coming out

All is a bustle and stir in the trench. We are being relieved. Except that Barlow has lost his mess-tin and Smith his ground-sheet, we are ready to move off; but before we are free to go we must show patience to the incoming troops and answer every question the merest lance-jack may ask about how the line is held. They are fairly satisfied at last, and we clutter along the tortuous communication-trench, moving at about double the pace we made coming in. Out on the main street the men slip into fours without any need for hustling, and there are no complaints from rear files about the pace, however much those in front step out.

Striding along, one feels a tremor run through the little band at the sound of shells falling behind us; but the pace does not alter. We are coming out. Every step is one nearer that invisible, yet instinctively appreciable line which marks the danger zone. As we round the church corner breath comes bated, for there were casualties here this morning, and it is a critical spot. We are passing.... We are by.... Another of Death's gins and traps escaped. Now for the plain! The pace is kept going: indeed needs checking; for we must keep our distance from the platoon in front. On we go. Somebody begins to whistle and the tune is quickly caught up: the spirit of gaiety is beginning to loosen its wings. Through Hébuterne, past the old billets, and now up the hill on the road to Bayencourt. Singing breaks out as we make the top of the hill. We are beyond the palsied area: almost to a yard this is where we cross the line. The cloud of foreboding is lifted: the expectation of life is free and natural again.

Quartermasters

We have been staying at Bayencourt four days: the men billeted in rooms down the village. We officers are at a starveling farm just outside. A French peasant and his wife were still in possession on our arrival and were much aggrieved at being ejected; but I suppose military necessity knows no law.

This afternoon I took my platoon down to the quartermaster's stores while Rowley was saying farewell to the doctor over a bottle of whisky. Thank Heaven, *he* is going. I hear he fell out with the colonel. It is certainly probable, because a battalion only wants one commander at a time.

I suppose we did fairly well down at the stores, but until I was commissioned, I little knew how much that important item of a junior officer's duty, "the care of his men," depends for its successful accomplishment upon the temper of the quartermaster and the subaltern's ability to keep on the right side of it. Quartermasters are queer fish. In the first place, their status is peculiar because, though it is above non-commissioned and below ordinary commissioned rank, they reign supreme in their own department.

As a class they may be described as "hard-faced." Then their job is a most complicated and all-embracing one. In practice a quartermaster is butcher, baker, grocer, ready-made clothes dealer, accountant, detective, universal provider and charity organisation agent; and it all depends on the quartermaster whether you are wise to approach him on the business or the charitable side. Most quartermasters seem to prefer the latter, and since, if you insist upon military and commercial rights, you may find yourself having to appeal to high tribunals with expert evidence in opposition, a wise subaltern falls out with the quartermaster only in the last extremity. This is sometimes galling, for, as I said, quartermasters on the whole are hard-faced men, inclined to act upon the assumption that the ideal quartermaster is he who can retain his goods on the shop side of the counter for all eternity.

If a Socialistic state meant the universal appointment of quartermasters, I should turn vegetarian and wear the garb of Adam. I could not face that music on my own behalf.

Back at Hébuterne. We are in the front line at Hébuterne, just a little to the right of the trenches the battalion held last time. Fusiliers are on our right flank; D Company on our left. The ground to our front slopes gently away for a few hundred yards, and then rises again in a long sweep. Slightly to our right we can just see the white tower of the church in Achiet-le-Petit, half-hidden by trees. To our left, standing on slightly higher ground and almost enfilading us, is Gommecourt, a sinister spot, now a heap of rubble and the bare remnants of a wood.

All day it reveals no sign of life, but under cover of darkness it becomes a venomous beast, spitting machine-gun fire. On our extreme right the ground falls away. Down in that near hollow stand the three poplars where it is reported the Germans are sapping. Beyond lies the valley overlooking Serre, and in the far distance Beaumont-Hamel. The German trenches are just behind the long roll of barbed wire that stands like a wave a hundred yards away. Those forsaken trenches, a few paces in front of us, are the graves of many of the men who held this bit of line prior to July 1st.

The lovely weather still holds: we have come to take it for granted; but the preparations now being made in this trench show foresight of coming rain. It rather looks as if the higher command had decided to hold on here for the winter. Engineers are busy on two deep dugouts that will each be capable of accommodating half a company, and the Tunnelling Corps is secretly very busy laying a mine—to blow up Gommecourt, we hope. In the trench itself, revetting with wire and sandbags is systematically going on, and the floor is being drained and covered with new duckboards, not only up here, but right down the communication-trench to the second line. Altogether these trenches offer the sharpest contrast to the rough bayless chasm of St. George's Hill, or even the comparatively formless second line we occupied last week. These must be after the pattern of the routine trench-warfare of 1915. We brought rolls of barbed wire and bundles of sandbags in with us, and tonight we shall begin our share of the improvements.

September

WIRING

Smalley and I are on top with a wiring-party. Queer and eerie the sensation of standing high above the heads of Germans in the trench just over there beyond the wire. With automatic regularity they keep firing Verey lights that rise like roman candles and reveal our silhouetted forms to one another so clearly it seems impossible at first to believe the enemy cannot see us. When the light is strong we stand stock-still. At first these moments are terrifying; then, as time goes on, one gains confidence in the darkness that covers our own trenches. Just now I was badly scared by a light that seemed to come right out of no-man's land, just behind my back. Luckily I dropped in a shell-hole before the light began to fall.

One cannot realise how hideously ploughed up this ground is till one begins to wander about over it. It is simply a succession of larger and smaller shell-holes. What a fearful job it must be to keep men in an attack, over such ground, in any sort of regular formation! Here, slowly wiring, it is simply devilish difficult to get alignment, and one takes a fantastic time getting from place to place. If we didn't live in momentary fear of those machine-guns suddenly starting again out of Gommecourt, the efforts of some of these fellows would be comic. As it is, it is infuriating to find one man tying himself up in his own strand of wire and another going pell-mell down a deep shell-hole; or to hear two fools cursing each other in loud tones that will give us away if they are not silenced.

We wire badly. I must ask Rowley for wiring practice next time we are out of the line.

A "DUD" SERGEANT

I have twenty men with my sergeant pushing forward a bombing-post under cover of night. Getting out on top, I set the men at their proper intervals in the trench and stand by for a while before handing over to the sergeant. Coming back I find him lolling against the wall of the frontline trench, idly talking to Corporal Neal. Not seeing me, he continues this for some time; so I fetch him out on top, take him to the head of the sap and leave him there. Half an hour afterwards I go back to find him sitting where I left him, only now fast asleep. One would have thought that for the sake of his own skin he would have at least remained awake. If a raiding party came over they would come on him first. Ignorant, insensitive, snoring lump—let him stay there. Of course I ought to haul him up before the C.O., and perhaps get him shot for sleeping on duty. But what's the good? Besides, I don't want the trouble, especially as I hear his predecessor is rejoining the battalion to take the worthless beggar's place.

Watching the shells

The outstanding feature of this kind of warfare is that, practically speaking, one never sees the enemy. We know by his effects that he is there, but during more than half the day, if his trenches were empty and he himself a myth, 'twould be all the same. The exception proves the rule, and I am reminded of this by the two Germans I saw in the distance this afternoon digging and moving about on the slope behind their line. Their appearance was regarded as an impertinence asking for target practice which promptly followed. It was probably off the mark, but good enough to make them quickly disappear. They are the first living Germans I have seen beyond no-man's land.

Looking over the top soon afterwards I saw what struck me as a truly awful sight. One of our guns was firing on the German front line. I happened to be standing in the direct line of fire, so that I could actually see the shell in the air at the instant before it dived into the trench. Stated thus, this doesn't sound very terrible; and yet to watch the actual devil of destruction on its way, hurtling through the air so that it appeared like a black cricket-ball seen in its flight for the thousandth part of a second, was to me the most awful sight I've yet seen. Instinctively one contrasted the force and velocity of the thing with the human bodies it was making for.

Barrage-fire at Serre

The rumble on our right this afternoon is increasing. Looking southward over the valley towards Serre we see shells bursting in rapid succession at the foot of a promontory. Like an oncoming thunderstorm the rumble increases, now rising to a roar, while the individual shell-bursts become merged in a white line that moves slowly forward like the smoke of a forest fire. A living thing, it creeps on and on, up the side of the hill and over the crest, to the accompaniment of a sound like continuous thunder. In addition to the barrage, big shells now fall behind it, making volcanoes of earth. One thinks of the fate of Sodom and Gomorrah and wonders whether it could compare with this. From start to finish the bombardment lasts fully half an hour; and then, as we look over the stricken, still smouldering land, we wonder what has happened. We shall never know. No one, except those immediately concerned, will ever know. As we turn away, our hearts go out to the poor devils who had to sit under that fire.

Aeroplanes at sunset

As well as in their appearance, the aeroplanes are like the birds in their habits; for as birds sing at twilight and at dawn, so is the habitual singing of aeroplanes. Late in the afternoon we look back to see a squadron coming out of the sunset. Like rooks against the light they appear, gradually taking shape as the hum of their engines is heard rising and falling on the breeze. Nearer and nearer they come, till they whirl and manoeuvre overhead, remaining for perhaps ten or fifteen minutes, and then, like a flock of homing birds, back they go into the fading sunlight. They take one's desire with them, for their pilots will sleep in sound beds tonight. Man has gone to his home at dusk for so many centuries, the habit has become an instinct. Staying here, we need resolution to break that instinct every time darkness descends.

Sleeping on duty

Day and night (unless patrols or working-parties are out in front) we have three men to every bay: one on sentry while the other two rest or sleep. The sergeant changes the sentries every hour. During the day the sentry's chief duty here is to keep his eye on the periscope and report any movement or change in the picture he sees there. At night he stands on the firestep and peers into the darkness over the top, his bayonet fixed and his rifle always in his hand. Firing the Verey pistol at night is nominally the privilege of the company-sergeant-major; but at present our pistol won't act, the only cartridges to be obtained don't fit it, so we dispense with Verey lights. It seems to be a matter of no account, for the Germans keep firing enough for both sides. There are Lewis-gunners and bombers at the head of one bombing-post, and Corporal Jackson is in charge of another. Odd the way that man always seems to be the first in the trenches and the last out. I noticed, too, that directly we get into the trenches his nonchalant air disappears and he becomes keen on whatever job falls to him. When I went to see him just now, he told me in his piping, far-away voice exactly how he was holding the post and what he should do if there was any trouble, showing clearly that he had worked the whole situation out for himself. He is my best N.C.O.

At night the men seem to like being visited. The most taciturn in daylight will talk at night. Up till twelve o'clock I prefer night to day duty. Turning out in the very early hours is not exactly pleasant; but as each subaltern only does four hours at a time, it is never very arduous. The sergeant called me up an hour ago and we went round once together. Now I have dispensed with him; 'tis so seldom one can be alone out here.

Old Burt, the bruiser, looked funny when I passed him; I think I'll go back and make sure he's awake. There he is, and it certainly doesn't look like it. His head rests on his chest and his rifle is leaning against the corner of the bay. The other two men are sprawled on the firestep, sleeping. No, Burt, this won't do!

Quietly I collect all three rifles, hide them in the traverse and get up on the firestep beside Burt. Still he does not wake. Burt, my man, you must have a lesson. I load my revolver and fire it over the top, almost in the man's ear, shouting "Hands up!" All three jump to their feet feeling for their rifles and fairly gibbering with fear. There follows a short and vehement address. I return them their rifles and, pointing an obvious moral, leave them.

Somehow the scene when they awoke was too pitiable and realistic to be amusing; but I don't think Burt will sleep on sentry again. I wonder if he thinks I shall split on him?

Corporal Side

"What is the life of man! Is it not to shift from side to side?—from sorrow to sorrow?—to button up one cause of vexation—and unbutton another?"

Side has lost his kit. A 5.9 dropped in his trench, while he was absent upon a business essential to health, and demolished the bay together with all Corporal Side's worldly effects in France. He is much aggrieved. I met him round the bend.

"I hear you've had a lucky escape," I remarked.

"The beggars 'a got all my kit," he replied lugubriously.

The good fortune of being alive seemed to have escaped his notice, perhaps because he has experienced it so often.

Side is a remarkable soldier. He looks less like a soldier than any man I have seen in France, and that is saying a good deal. He is short, cross eyed, bandy-legged, and has a preference for boots and clothes sizes too big for him. In civil life I believe he is a rag-picker, and the character of his profession adheres, as it will, to the man. He joined the battalion two years ago as a stretcher-bearer, and on the 1st of July carried stretchers *under fire continuously* for twenty-four hours. Anyone who knows the weight of a loaded stretcher and remembers the heat, the condition of the ground, and what the firing was like upon that day, will agree with me that the Victoria Cross would have expressed rather less than Side's deserts. However, he for his bravery was promoted to full corporal in the fighting-ranks.

For parade purposes he really ought to be smuggled among the cooks: he would move any inspecting officer to fury. But in the trenches Side is a treasure. He is tireless and has the heart of a lion. The other day, when we were in the sap and shells were dropping uncomfortably near, some timid idiot set the rumour running that the Germans were coming over. I was standing close to Side when it reached him. "Coming over, are they?" he replied. "'Ere, gimme my rifle," and before one could say "knife" he was gone up the sap, apparently intending to put the Germans back in their places single-handed.

Yes, Side is not much to look at, but he has hold of what may be called the business end of the war.

The Major

This place is beginning to show what the newspapers describe as "*a certain amount of liveliness.*" (Why "liveliness"? Deathliness would be truer.) We are not accustomed to much shelling in the morning, but we have been watching shells fall between us and the second line for some time now.

We are still watching the bursts when who should appear round the bay of the trench but our second-in-command, Major Smythe! This is a great shock, for though Major Smythe looms very large on parade, I have never seen him in the trenches before. Out on rest he glows like a star of the first magnitude, making woe betide those who are ignorant of ceremonial behaviour; but he seems to suffer the fate of waning by exact degrees according to our proximity to the Germans. So well is this declension calculated that the star is reputed to suffer regular and complete eclipse, under cover of "officer-in-charge of the rear party," whenever the battalion is actually in trenches.

But here he is, showing Rumour in her old colours; and how friendly he is as he invites me upon a tour of inspection! I respond cordially; but he seems to be in rather a hurry—indeed, before I can show him how the land lies, he has vanished round the next bay. I follow, and he does the vanishing trick again. It really becomes hard work to keep up: who'd have believed he could move so fast? Our "tour" degenerates at last into a walking-match, and I finish a bad second by the time he reaches the dugout in the second line. Well, well! 'Tis true the trenches are no place for valuable lives, and Major Smythe, tall and thin, bears strong physical resemblance to Wellington. Perhaps he will play the great duke reviewing his troops for the cinema—*après la guerre*.

Lieutenant Hardy

A boy in Hardy's platoon has just been killed. Hardy is upset. The boy was a chubby-faced youngster and something of a wag: not much younger than Hardy himself and always ready to have his leg pulled. He was standing in a bit of the trench that can be observed out of Gommecourt, and a whiz-bang fell at his feet, killing him instantly. Hardy has gone off to find the *padre*, and is very anxious the lad should be properly buried. I didn't know we had a *padre*, but it appears there's one attached to the brigade.

Personally I should never have dreamt of seeking him now, but Hardy has great respect for the conventions; moreover, his feeling about decent burial is strong. His own, almost his only, fear for himself is lest his corpse should be left unburied. He told me the other day he simply could not stand the thought of his body being left on the wire to rot, and he extracted a promise from me to do what I could if he were killed. I made no compact with him, for I don't share his feeling, having too much concern for my living body to care what happens to it dead.

Hardy is too much of a child in many ways to make an ideal subaltern. He has what I consider a schoolboy's idea of discipline, and we rag one another on that score pretty regularly. But for pluck he is not to be beaten. If there's danger about, Hardy at once considers it his duty to be there, and he is reckless to a fault. The public-school tradition stands him in good stead, and he is an excellent example of its merits and limitations. The man who is brave by nature appraises the danger and then goes calmly into it. There is no calmness about Hardy; he can be easily scared out of his wits, wherein he shows the limitations of education by example; but where I admire him unfeignedly, and where the merits of the public-school system tell, is in the fact that being scared makes no difference to him. He is just as ready and full of pluck next time.

I find one grows to love and hate men here according as one feels that in crucial moments they will be on the spot or absent. Whatever happens I know that Hardy will be there, and this last quality of comradeship is worshipful: it seems to be the very basic test of manhood. I suppose it is because war makes that test so obviously that its old appeal has force. Courage is a social quality. Out here I see it means caring for your pals more than yourself. For me it has no meaning apart from some degree of friendship.

Fatigues

We are back in the farmhouse at Sailly. Outside in the cobbled courtyard there's a hole in the ground where a shell dropped the other day, killing the captain and two N.C.O.s of the company from whom we took over.

It is something to be out of the trenches for a while, but here, not much; for we provide fatigue-parties every evening to carry materials into the line, and work there most of the night. After a spell of the trenches a succession of nights like this becomes tiring, and my luck has been out, so that I have been on fatigue three nights out of the past four. (By the way, why is work in the army always called "fatigue"?) And here comes the adjutant again.

I protest I have done my share, but he merely condescends to ladle out soft soap about the colonel's good opinion. Well, I'm tired; but there's no saying "No" in this service, so I must rout out my unwilling men as if I enjoyed the job. The devil of it is that they are inclined to esteem an officer in proportion as he is able to dodge these impositions. They must be like him tonight and lump it. The only compensation about doing more than my share is that it lulls the fear of failure. At least I am pulling my oar.

Approaching the guns

We are off to the trenches again, and I declare it will be rest to be there, for I have been in the front line practically every night for the past three weeks.

Getting in and out of the village of Hébuterne has become too adventurous for tired nerves. It looks as if it will be unpleasant again this afternoon, for there's shelling going on in the distance. Now as we begin to cross the plain we see shells dropping near the fresh battery of guns drawn up in line on the western outskirt of the village. Our path runs between the guns, and we are watching the slow traversing of an area we shall very soon have to cross. We have a mile to march, and every step towards that barrier of fire. No wonder our pace seems to drag. If only we could tell where the shell that comes over when we pass will fall! There's nothing for it but to go on.... We are getting to the zone. The shells are falling on our left. But that one was clean on the road! ... Now we are passing. What's it to be? ... Our shell falls on the right covering us with dust. We are safe, and would like to put wings to our heels.

A prisoner

Rowley comes back from the front line, where he had been to see Simpkins this morning, with great news. Peeping over the top he saw three Germans quite close to our trenches looking as though they had been out on patrol last night and lost their way. Quickly borrowing a rifle, he covered them. Two of the men ran and escaped, but the third, an officer, who was close under the parapet, put up his hands and came in. Rowley searched him and sent him down the trench to H.Q., keeping his revolver, which he shows me, remarking that he has always wanted one of these automatic revolvers and intends to hang on to this. I fail to see why, for we've no ammunition for it. Still he ought to have a trophy, for it sounds like a fairly smart capture. We do not forget to congratulate him, and he goes up a useful peg in the eyes of the men.

Tear shells

I have just come into the dugout from wiring. All the while we were at work we heard light shells sailing with a watery whistle high over our heads towards Hébuterne. They flowed on in a stream, and we wondered what they could be, for they burst with very little noise. Now this sickly-sweet pear-drop smell, together with a tingling sensation in the eyes, shows they were what we call tear shells—shells filled with some gas, very harmless in its effects, but sufficiently unpleasant to make the eyes water profusely. They also make uncovered food uneatable and smoking beastly. Those last two effects are particularly offensive to me because my birthday fare, sent from England, lies here in the dugout wasted, and a hard smoker could do great violence to the man who poisons his tobacco.

This futile waste seems an epitome of the childishness of modern war. The kind of mind that now devises inventions for war would be kept in an imbecile home in any civilised society; such a mind is as far beneath reprobation as contempt.

Gruesome work

Of all ghastly work this digging of a sap through the ground covered in the attack of July 1st is the most horrible. Hill returned from it last night physically sick. There are men buried here four or five feet deep, their bodies often lying as they fell, with the limbs stretched in all directions. We dig among the bodies, and the difficulties that ensue when they lie deep, stretched transversely across the gap, must be imagined, for they will not be described.

Loot

There's trouble brewing over that German officer's revolver. In his examination he said Rowley had taken it from him, and on the same day a "chit" comes down from the colonel asking Rowley to hand it over. He replies that he hasn't got it. Another chit comes along to say search must be made for it and the revolver handed in at once. Rowley duly orders a search to be made—with the natural result. That doesn't satisfy the colonel, who seems to have his suspicions. Meantime Rowley, who has made elaborate arrangements for smuggling the precious weapon home, is not feeling very happy about it. His store of fairy-tales is getting exhausted. I wonder whether the storm will stay in the tea-cup.

Devilment?

Hardy reports that the colonel went round the front line this afternoon, and, not content with that, insisted on wandering about on top and compelling a reluctant subaltern to follow him. Opinion is divided upon whether the colonel was sober. It is not disputed that he starts the day with whisky and drinks late into the night, but the defence declares he is never drunk and is a man without fear. I am only convinced that whisky is an unmitigated curse in wartime. Men take to it in time of strain: the strain is unrelieved; then what are they to do? The distillers should be great patriots. I believe they are.

The patrol

It has been raining sharply, but now at ten o'clock the sky clears and the full moon makes dark the shadows of the trenches. I meet Rowley with a chit in his hand, which he reads by the moonlight. He is to send out one officer and ten men who will bring in a German prisoner, dead or alive, for purposes of identification. "And I'm afraid," he adds apologetically, "it's your turn."

The time, the moonlight and the siting of the trenches make this order as nearly impossible as the improbable can be. Rowley agrees. It ought to have been tried when the sky was dark and before patrols went in. Thinking it probable that the colonel sent the order before the sky cleared, I ask Rowley if he will have it confirmed. No. Orders are orders, even when they come in the form of plain invitations to suicide. I'd better go out and make a show, and together we'll cook the report. Here's a vile quandary. Is the colonel aware that the battalion intelligence officer went out with a sergeant and a couple of men two hours ago and has not yet returned? Besides, with ten men, across one hundred yards of no man's land, on a night when you can see from wire to wire! A first-class cut-throat might stand a chance, working alone; but even he would avoid such a night.

The mere receipt of such an order seems like an insult. I shall not attempt to carry it out, and that not only for my own sake; but I should like to see the colonel and be clear with him. That's impossible.

Sick at heart and savage in temper, I pick my men and lead them down a disused forward sap. Well away from our own trenches, it becomes uncanny work creeping along in the shadows, stick in one hand, revolver in the other, not knowing what we may confront round the next bend, I turn to see the men and find the corporal, who bragged so much about his skill at such exploits, holding back at a very safe distance. We go on. Then suddenly, out from our left, there comes a long whistle. A moment later it is replied to by a similar signal on our right. We wait and then go on again. The signal is repeated. That is enough for me. I reckon we are seen and tell the men to get back.

Down in the dugout Rowley and I write a report that is as near lying as can be without being actual falsehood. The whole business makes me angry. I suppose I am wanting in humour.

MISSING

I hear the colonel was not pleased with the report. I also hear that the other party started off from the same point, and that they still have not returned. It is presumed they are captured, as they well might have been when the sky suddenly cleared. Captured or dead, the colonel is said to be vexed with them. I wonder what would have happened had we gone on? My resentment at being sent on such a fool's errand is not allayed by this news.

Chits about the German officer's revolver have stopped at last.

Rowley is relieved.

Farewell to Hébuterne

This starry night is our last at Hébuterne. At midnight we are marching to Bayencourt, and Rowley says we are going right out on rest. It is so bright a prospect one is tempted to entertain it as a certainty; but hope mustn't rise too high while we are still in trenches; expectation must remain in the shadow a few hours longer, knowing that not an hour, ten minutes, or even a single moment, is yet within the bounds of common certainty. Still, with ordinary luck ...

Either they've decided that the support trenches are too far back, or they want reserve trenches for "kicking-off" in an attack that's impending. We are out on top between the first and second lines, and have begun digging. It is wonderfully quiet. If the Germans only knew, they could make it hot for us; but by some extraordinary coincidence they have even stopped their machine-guns tonight. This is all the more remarkable because of the distinct change that has come over the place since that summer afternoon, ages ago, when we first took over.

'Tisn't bad now, but it can be no longer called a quiet front; and those batteries outside the village seem to augur trouble to come. With any luck we shall be out of that, stretching our limbs for a while in the realms of civilisation—seeing shops and inhabited houses and the faces of well-dressed women—aware, by contact with it, that there is another world in being beside this place of fear and devastation. In the first large town we stay at I shall go to the best *pâtisserie* in the place and order *café-au-lait* and a dozen *éclairs*. Hill and I will eat them sitting on steady chairs, wearing clean clothes, in a room so fresh and bright we could eat off the floor. Then we shall ...

Wait a while! We are not out yet.

How well these miners dig! We could give points to the Guards and beat them at digging.

It is midnight. We begin to pack up. Still the quiet continues. This is a gift from the gods. Down through the trenches, under the trees. Hullo! They are not going to let us go without a salute. *Scissz! Plonk!* They are wide of the mark. We are leaving them behind. Goodbye, you damned old trenches! May you all be covered in before we see you again. Not a man of my platoon does this evil ground cover. Come on, my merry men; but not too fast for self-respect. Another "bit" of the Great War's over. Here's level ground again. Another mile or two and you will sing, if you're not too sleepy.

Going westward

It is cheering to be going westward: the farther you go in this direction the more human the world becomes. Roads in repair, trees, houses, civilians at their civil tasks, old women whitening their doorsteps, old men threshing corn—all the unmarshalled ease of common life appears again. It is welcome to our eyes as light to the blind, for every common object of civilisation looks like a work of art. I actually fell in love with a lamppost at Doullens.

Billets at Halloy

Here we are at Halloy again, but the days (or rather nights) of sleeping in thin canvas shelters are over. We woke last night to find the rain pouring through, making the uneven ground a series of pools. The men of course fared worse, and we have had to find fresh billets all round. I am ashamed to see the men in the hovel they've got. In England a tramp wouldn't sleep in it; but the town-major declares nothing else is to be had at the moment, and we are moving on tomorrow. We officers of C Company have obtained reluctant permission from the farm which adjoins the orchard to sleep in a stable. At least it's dry and has a loft for the orderlies overhead; but we are none too pleased with our host for his unwillingness to give us the shelter accorded to beasts. The orderlies repeat the old tale about having to pay for a glass of water.

Grilled chicken

The army canteen was low in supplies yesterday and army rations will never move a gourmet to eloquence; nevertheless we have just fed like princes. We have tasted the sweets—or rather the *entrées*—of adversity; for if it hadn't been for the adversity of our host, well, we might have managed the sweets, but the *entrée* would have been as Castlereagh says—"*Napoo*." When hungry men are sick of bully beef, barn-door fowls should remain in barns. They ought to be warned against strutting between a hungry man's legs. Sikes, Smalley's servant, first noticed them. He would. Rumour says he's a professional burglar in civil life. That is no doubt flattery; but Sikes certainly knows something of the fine art of poaching.

After whispering between him and Smalley, and sundry nods and smiles between them and Rowley, certain assignations were approved whereby our prospects brightened, and happy in hope we retired to rest—all except Sikes and Castlereagh, who appeared coming down from the loft with a sack. We waited and listened; but not a sound was heard, not a funeral cluck. Then back to the loft they bore them. We had grilled chicken for lunch today, and I defy Sherlock Holmes to find a feather.

OUT ON REST

Halloy to Barly—Barly to Maizicourt—Maizicourt to Caours: that has been our itinerary for the past three days' marching. Once we are on the march, things are pretty much the same. We go right into the country, billet at a village farm, where the men sleep in the barns and the officers take whatever accommodation the farmhouse will give. This of course varies. Barly was clean, Maizicourt dirty—and no wonder considering that midden. We slept eight in one small room at Maizicourt. Still, any billet is lavender after a day's march, even if it doesn't smell quite like it.

We wander on, passing from place to place, never arriving, till one has the sensation of moving in a trance. As a child I remember being worried over a kaleidoscope, because I could never determine the one pattern which really *was* the kaleidoscope. Now here the same desire to shake the frame of things till they fall into settled reality comes over me. But we go on, moved like pawns in a game of chess, by minds that do not declare their intentions, to fates which even the players do not know.

Now we are at Caours and rumour says we are staying for sixteen days. Abbeville is only three miles away, and just to walk into a town outside a marching column and have a bath and a meal served will be luxury and adventure. Here, too, we can get through some much-needed training with those new drafts that have recently been dribbling into the regiment.

This is a fairly large village—suburb perhaps it should be called—yet we had difficulty in finding billets. The French people are not hospitable to English troops, and naturally there's a good deal of soreness on that score.

Yet I can see the picture from their angle. English soldiers are not the finest exponents of delicate manners. Dourness and hoggishness easily appear after a spell in the trenches, and to the lips of gay-mannered folk like the French I've no doubt the adjective *bête* rises easily when they are asked suddenly to open their rooms to rough, dirty-looking herds. You have to be very charitable before you open your house gladly to officers who are a little lousy, usually none too well-bred, and sometimes quite anxious to seduce your servants. Anyway, we are not the guests in French houses we were in English billets.

The rooms of this big country house are nearly all shut up: the owner is away in Paris; but we can only have the use of two bedrooms via the back staircase, and these only because French law obliges the owner to give us that amount of accommodation. We have to pay three *francs* a day for permission to mess at an *estaminet* half a mile from the billet. We needed all our philosophy, after a long, hot march to look upon this great empty place with its walled garden and big kitchens, and then learn that our orderlies must make a camp-fire in a neighbouring field before we could have a cup of tea, and that our sanitary squad must provide for our other physical needs by digging.

Well, there 'tis; with this moral. No civil population can endure a military one for long.

Abbeville

Hill has been sent on a Lewis-gun course at le Touquet, so my jaunt to Abbeville is with Hardy and Smalley. In the town we meet Jenkins, a new subaltern who has just been attached to our company, and after a bath we have dinner together at a hotel that is crowded with officers. 'Tis strange to be treading pavement and looking in shop-windows again: so reminiscent that it tugs at the heart, and in a second one is wondering why one wanders here so idly when across only a few miles of water lives another—perhaps at this very hour wandering in London—whose living presence is all one lives for: whose living form one may never see again.

To banish the thought we buy trinkets and trifles, and then go to the beautiful Gothic church. What centuries of deep religious purposeful life raised these arching pillars and made this form and beauty! How deeply it impresses, though the spirit that animated the life of those people is fled! How those history-books of successive wars traduced the life of the past! Places like this were not built by hands that knew war as we know it. We and our khaki are out of our element.

Let's get away. Besides, there is little inducement to stop; for a service is on, and from the pulpit a villainous-faced priest is repeating a litany in Latin that must remain unintelligible to all but initiates, since it sounds like nothing but a rapid and nasal repetition of the words "*Daily Mail.*" Spoken by other lips, in other tones, in other times, who knows but this very litany was a thing of awe and beauty. Why seek we the living among the dead? The spirit of the old religion is now to be found in its churches only when they are empty.

What now? Shall we go back? Jenkins scoffs at the idea. He is a fat, comical figure, oddly possessed of a very nimble brain. He has no intention of going back without enjoying some sort of feminine society. Ah me! And what wouldn't I give for my sort! But any sort? And that hired? I try to persuade them good-humouredly to return with me. They smile too knowingly; so I jog back alone.

There are other pities in the world beside this war, and of all I know, this war-begotten waste of feeling now looks heaviest.

October

"The offensive spirit"

My new sergeant has taken over. He is a dapper, intelligent little fellow—rather young to be a sergeant, but a welcome change from that lazy old ruffian. I would have preferred to remain with the company just now; but courses seem the order of the day. Not only Hill is gone; Smalley is on a bombing course, Hardy attached to some sort of tunnelling section, and I have begun a bayonet course.

I wonder how Hamlet would have fared with a bayonet? He must have been no bad hand at rapiers.

The course is laid out at a field two miles away, and there we cultivate ferocity before sacks once again, and learn most ungentlemanly ways of dispatching our enemies. From the standpoint of realism a good deal is wanting, and as the week goes by the sergeant-major in charge of the course has difficulty in preventing our exercises from becoming a mere sporting competition as gaily undertaken as a rugger match. We are inclined to go over the track too much like children playing at Indians in search of scalps. I am convinced the proper spirit of animosity cannot be inculcated by such methods. They are too direct. Any newspaper editor could teach the army more excellent ways. The army seems dimly aware of this. It does its best, though very clumsily I think.

Yesterday the whole battalion marched out to a quarry not far from here and, in the natural amphitheatre, heard a lecture by a Scottish officer on "The Spirit of the Bayonet."

From a purely military standpoint it was excellent. Why, indeed, should we spare a fat German just because he throws up his hands and shouts "*Kamarad*," when, as the lecturer says, if we let him live, he may become the father of ten more Huns? Killing is the job for infantrymen, and if we don't like killing, why did we join the infantry?

The bayonet is the logical conclusion of all fighting: there you get to the real thing; and a proper lust for blood is what you need to use a bayonet. What sapient fool thinks he's going to do his country credit without it? But we mustn't overdo it. Three inches is enough. Don't go and bury the muzzle of your rifle in your man and then find you can't get your bayonet out, no matter how hard you stamp on him. "In," "out," and then ready for the next, is the way.

Yes, I've no doubt this kind of instruction is quite necessary, and it is futile to start wondering upon what terms this bloodthirsty incarnation of hate lives with his wife. As has been said, "There's a war on." But I cannot help wishing all the parsonry, who so kindly praise our noble Christian sacrifice, could have a little of this tonic. They might then, with the Bishop of London in command, be sent on a bayonet charge. "The stern reality" looks so different when you make a trade of wrapping it in a phrase.

The effect of the lecture was probably different upon different hearers. For my part, I confess to a weak stomach.

TANKS

We are still out "on rest," but it isn't quite so restful as it sounds. Last night, 8 to 11.130:—a night march on a compass bearing. Today, 6.30 to 8:—adjutant's parade. 9.30 to 10.30:—close-order drill. 10.30 to 11:—walk out to brigade bayonet course. 11 to 2.30:—bayonet fighting and returning, 3.30 to 5:—assistant officer at pay of company. 7.30 to 9.30:—walk to Brigade H.Q. for lecture on Tanks and back again.

The lecture on Tanks was a little disappointing. We were all agog to hear about these new land-caterpillars that, according to the papers, have done such marvellous things in the recent push on the Somme, knocking down houses and trees, careering over trenches and frightening the Germans out of their wits. But the Tanks' officer put rather a damper on our hopes.

He started off by pooh-poohing the newspaper reports as exaggerations of the patriotic imagination, and explained that tanks have to go very carefully, or they get stuck in T-places where communication-trenches join the line. He also said they were quite vulnerable underneath and on top, and instead of painting the glowing picture of infantrymen marching in their wake triumphantly to Berlin, he cynically told us our chief duty in regard to the tanks would be to provide a squad to march in front of them and drag the wounded out of the way: a none too healthy job, he added, as of course a tank draws the enemy fire. Finally he reminded us that of course tanks were too heavy to use on very soft ground, and, with the winter coming on, their general employment would probably be delayed till the spring.

Now rain is falling heavily again, and the weather seems to have broken up. Thank God we're not in the line yet, though we are moving soon. I wish people who talk cheerfully about the campaigns of next spring would lecture only to the folks at home. A day at a time is enough for us out here.

"Fed up"

We are on the march again, now going east. It rained heavily almost every day of our last week at Caours. The winter has begun.

Last night we slept at Conteville: now we are at Frohen-le-Grand, and again it is raining. I suppose I am depressed by the weather, but quite possibly by the fact that we are on our way to that place of desolation again. I wonder how, in God's name, we do go on with this life! Looked at from an individual standpoint it is the very insanity of slavery.

This endless hideous life of the automaton—I shall never get used to it. I am too old. Perhaps if I were seventeen I shouldn't mind. I should know so little that was different, and this would only seem a perpetual, rather unpleasant boarding-school. I should have less memory and be less inclined to reflect. I shouldn't be carrying about a heart that's fixed: it might easily be the bladder on a fool's stick. But now sometimes the thought that I may never again know any other life than this affects me like a madness. My God! I understand desertion. A man distraught determines that the last act of his life shall at least be one of his own volition; and who can say that what is commonly regarded as the limit of cowardice is not then heroic?

But the job out here's not done. The Germans are still in France. While that is so, who can talk of peace? Truly there's nothing I'd sooner be doing than helping to push the Germans out of France. Why can't the devils go of their own accord? It would settle everything. If they only retired to their own frontier, for my part the war would be over tomorrow. But they don't; so all the loathsomeness of this life is swallowed up in the consideration that the work is fundamentally good to anyone who is fit for it. I am fit. I shall go on, even gladly. But it is hell.

The new Captain

Our old Don Juan, Rowley, is on Paris leave, which has been instituted because the U-boats have weakened the Channel service and stopped home leave for the time. In his place we have Captain Lancy, who has been out in France a long time, though he has not seen the trenches recently, being lucky enough to hold a town-majorship for a goodish while.

We shall be glad when Rowley comes back, for Lancy is snivelling and pernickety. Having no natural authority, he adopts a disagreeable air as a substitute, and while he is competent enough from the orderly-room standpoint, the men dislike him: when the nondescript of weak character poses as the strong man of discipline they are not deceived.

Hardy and Hill are back, and now we meet Lancy at the billet to receive news which is to be given us in great secrecy. Lancy can hardly bring himself to deliver it, so great is his sense of importance while he holds information we lack. After pledging our silence he begins: "There's going to be an attack at Hébuterne very shortly, and you fellows are going over with the company. Number nine platoon will take the German front line, 'Fall.' Number ten will go on and take the support trench, 'Fame.' Number eleven will go over both those lines and take 'Fate.' Smalley as our company bomber will clear the communication-trenches and help you to consolidate when he comes up. That's the bare outline. Of course you'll get details, but we're going to practise this stunt on ground marked out at Halloy; so the C.O. thought it as well that you fellows should know what you are practising for. You're not to tell the men anything—not even the N.C.O.s."

"And where will you be?" I inquire.

Lancy smiles with satisfaction.

"I shall be in our front line to receive messages; and, by the way, don't forget: you send a runner back as soon as ever you've taken the trench. I shall want to know at once."

Nothing more is said; but his obvious pleasure at taking a back seat in this stunt does not raise him in our esteem. As to the "show" itself, only Hardy is pleased with the prospect. He declares he is sick of "arsing about the trenches waiting to get pipped. Now there'll be a chance of a good 'blighty.' Death or glory, and a good job too. If you're killed that finishes it."

I remember that German wire and wonder what sort of bombardment can ever cut it enough to give us a chance; for their wire is not like ours; it is heavily stranded and has barbs about an inch long.

In any case an attack is bound to be a foul business. In the way of personal fighting, I devoutly hope I shan't be too hideously involved.

Back to Halloy

A day of sun and cool wind, perfect for marching, and the luck to be at the head of the column, immediately behind our newly formed drum-and-fife band, made the march to Halloy a pleasure. The noble band is only eight flutes, six bugles and six drums; but a little band goes a long way to shorten the road: even its failures, greeted with cheering, help men to keep their eyes off the "Boots-boots-boots-boots movin' up and down again!" They've a rotten billet here again: a tumbledown old barn, with no straw in it, and a stinking midden just outside. I've had the midden cleared and given them inner relief for external discomfort. Tins of fish, tinned apricots, five hundred cigarettes and some sweets. Lord! what a mixture; but it was all that could be had at the engineers' canteen.

We are back in our barn, and whatever is thought, nothing is said about those fowls lately deceased.

Practising the attack

We have been at Halloy a week, drilling, training and practising our stunt. First we did it by spoken orders in daylight: then by the watch: then by spoken orders at night: finally by the watch at night. Out here, where there are no shells dropping about, where we have to imagine our own barrage-fire and all the enemy elects to put up in reply, we can do it perfectly, and a pretty tame affair it looks. It would be howled out of the arena at a military tournament. No dashing, hell-for-leather, with wide throats and bayonets extended: just men getting up for no apparent reason and going forward at a slow marching-pace in extended order for a given distance, followed by others doing precisely the same, time and distance being almost everything. Over and over again we have impressed upon us the necessity of keeping close up to the barrage: even if we have a few casualties from our own fire, we are told that our only chance lies in keeping close up.

Hardy is getting dead keen, and with Hill and Smalley coming too, one couldn't be better accompanied; but what lies at the back of my mind all the time is the recollection of that German wire. I believe they might shell it for weeks and still we should get hung up.

Odd, and yet not so odd, the weeding out that's already gone on among the little crowd that left Charing Cross with me three months ago. Brunning and Leonard are both back with rheumatism. Zenu had the bad luck to break his leg practising bayonet-fighting. Another one of them has gone into a venereal hospital. Altogether Hill and I are the only two left. Poor Jenkins! It will be some time before he sees fighting. The morning he returned from Abbeville he told me he had spent the night with "a perfect artist." Now he too is in the venereal hospital.

THE DREAM AND THE BUSINESS

I haven't *solved* the Front. By that I mean imagination and actuality are not yet at one; and in handling any problem it seems to me you haven't the whip-hand of it until imagination and actuality are at one. Whenever I see the Front in the light of what made me join the army—whenever I think of the whole business as a task, then I welcome the Front and feel I can eat fire easily. Imaginatively I have it all right. But when I shrink to little actuality and think of watery trenches, sinister-looking crump-holes, barbed wire, machine-guns, bombs, and most of all big guns and intensive shelling, then the whole place becomes a land of foreboding, even of horror, where blind Death keeps groping hideously. It becomes a place I would give anything to keep out of, as you would a house that threatened every minute to fall about your ears.

But these two images have to become one before you have solved the Front, and in my case I know that can only come about when actuality has been wholly swallowed up by imagination. Then there will be unity, and I shall no longer be perpetually passing from one extreme state of mind to the other.

Somehow I must get hold of a sense of true proportion and be able to keep it, and not let the first law of Nature, or any other individual consideration, play old Harry by setting up a dualism which destroys the dream in the misery of the business.

When I can do that I shall have solved the Front. It is like focussing the lenses of these field-glasses. There is a spot where you get perfect sight with both eyes; but it takes finding.

CINEMA FILMS

I've just come across a bundle of old newspapers giving accounts of the film of the Somme battle now being shown at the Scala in London. Those "cheery columns of men going into action" were unwittingly a little deceptive, I fancy. Not that I would say a word disparaging the men. Heaven knows. But, in the first place that comfortably seated audience should be told that a camera out here is a phenomenon and a reminder of home which any men anywhere would greet with cheers. And, in the second, I should like to insist that men going into action are usually frightfully depressed at first, so that they grouse, curse their luck, and then become silent and brooding.

Later, just to keep their courage up, and because they feel something has to be done, they start singing "Pack up your troubles in your old kit-bag," get excited, and feel their troubles *are* over—until a shell bursts near. Then the silence is grim. Here and there a fatalist is gay because he believes he is "booked for a blighty"; but men are not such fools as to be glad to be going into the hell of attack.

The cinema can show some things, but, great Heavens! what a gap lies between looking *at* war on a screen and being *in* it.

WAR HISTORY

There's another cutting from these newspapers here which is amusing to me. It also goes to show how hard it will be for anyone to write the true history of this war.

The report says that on one of the nights when we happened to be in the line at St. George's Hill, the Germans were seen leaving their trenches, but were driven back by the Allied barrage-fire before they could reach our line.

Now the true history of that little episode is this. There were strict orders at the time that S.O.S. signals were only to be used in extreme emergency. A certain company-commander (close to us, but not of our battalion) became unnecessarily alarmed and sent up his S.O.S. rockets. The concentrated fire was given, and the Germans, apparently thinking we were going to attack, replied in kind just in front of the British trenches. Absolutely nothing else happened. On neither side did the men attempt to leave their trenches. But the company-commander had to save his face. Hence the report; received no doubt with enormous armchair satisfaction. Probably the German version was precisely similar.

CHANGED PLANS

The attack at Hébuterne is cancelled; no one knows why. The colonel has gone on leave, and tomorrow we march south. It looks as if we were bound for the Somme again. The only one who is not pleased with the news is Hardy. He is genuinely disappointed. "Now we shall be here for the whole bloody winter," he remarks.

I wonder.

BEAUQUESNE

We are at Talmas, a village lying midway between Doullens and Amiens. After heavy rain last night it has been a delicious day, and the landscape between Beauquesne and Talmas, wooded and hilly, looked entrancing in the still, clear, autumn air. I had a fine opportunity to enjoy it, for I was orderly-officer for the day, which meant that I came on two hours after the battalion, bringing with me the twenty men who were left behind to clear up the billets. At Beauquesne we passed some large country houses that are said to be in use as army headquarters. One could not help admiring the command's taste.

Méaulte

For the past three days we have marched about ten miles a day. Last night we halted at Franvillers: today we found ourselves back on the old road, passing our hillside at Dernancourt: now we are billeted in Méaulte. I hate this place. It lies low, near the Ancre, and has the dejected utilitarian air of a poor industrial town. It is one of those waste places that are neither in nor out of the line. Shells still come over occasionally, as if to show their contempt and complete the dilapidation. Méaulte has a hang-dog look. Almost every house is used by troops for one purpose or another, and all the country round it is strewn with dumps and the refuse of the army scrap-heap. On its churned-up roads, over which the stream of traffic never ceases to pass, pitifully miserable-looking German prisoners work, scraping and sweeping. In their dirty ragged clothing they look more woebegone than the inhabitants of any slum. They are passed by like dogs by everyone.

Our billet is as cheerless. It is a matchboarded upper room without door or fireplace. Its dirty floor and scribbled walls appear to have been used by troops since the beginning of the war, and of course there is not a stick of furniture in the room. Down below is a dirty little grocer's shop. A woman actually keeps it on. Why she is allowed to remain I cannot think. Rowley, who is just back, no sooner heard of her than he vowed he would make her close acquaintance.

To crown all, the rain drizzles down.

The concert

We have now had three days of rain in this place. Rowley decided yesterday that something must be done to cheer the fellows up; so we had an impromptu concert in a large outhouse, big enough to hold most of the men. As a concert it was not a success. We had no piano, and our stock of choruses soon ran out. Before the evening was half over, every officer, and then every humorist of the company, had taken his turn at speechmaking, and finally we fell back upon the inevitable improper story. Even that didn't raise much merriment. Impropriety should be served as a savoury: it needs the background of polite society to give it relish; but we had no background, so the sharp contrast which makes humour was lacking, and we were forced back on grossness, which is dull. Still, we had beer, a full barrel of it, and all the cigarettes we could lay hands on; and certainly we wished each other well. I suppose I am a rank idealist, but Lord! how far this was from what one would wish to give these men.

The sentence

We parade to hear the sentence of court-martial on a boy who has been found guilty of refusing to obey the order of a corporal. Between the armed guards stands the prisoner, bareheaded, without rifle or belt. The sentence is forty-one days' Field Punishment No. 1. The boy receives his helmet and belt and returns to the ranks. He will begin to expiate his crime—(if he is still alive) when we next come out of the trenches.

The story behind this little drama is as follows. The corporal has been recently promoted. He and the boy were pals in the ranks. They failed to adjust the old relationship to the new conditions, and the corporal, being proud of his dignity, asserted his authority rather heavily. Finally the army, if appealed to, has to maintain the authority of its officers. But forty-one days' No. 1!

Well, the army only pretends to rough justice. Sometimes it seems very rough.

To end war?

"*A war to end war.*" I used to wonder whether it wasn't possible: whether by demonstrating the impossibility of reaching a decisive issue, this war would not convince the nations of the futility of war. Today I came across this:

But vain the sword and vain the bow
They never can work war's overthrow.

I see it is absolutely true. No policeman ever yet improved the world's morals. There's no hope from negation. War is like the rash of a disease—bound to come out if the body politic is not healthy. The patient pities himself when the fever is on him; but not by self-pity nor antagonism to disease will he escape infection.

There were two more lines to the quatrain:

The hermit's prayer and the widow's tear
Alone can free the world from fear.

What does that mean? *"The hermit's prayer"* I think must mean thought energised: thought that is more than thinking. And *"the widow's tear"* I take to be an image of the deepest pity of love.

Deeper thought and deeper pity. They are both beyond the sentimentality and hard-faced government between which weakness alternates.

One cannot imagine a future for the kind of government that makes its final arbitrament the placing of vast numbers of men in an area of flying iron. Common-sense repudiates that. That is not government, even by force.

Is there any other way of raising the ethical standard of government other than by the example of individuals? I suppose that was Tolstoy's idea. Conscientious objection to war seems a blind alley; but then every affirmation implies a negative. To contemporaries the Crucifixion must have looked an utter negation.

A TENT IN THE MUD

Another move forward. We are now in tents at Mansel Copse, which lies between Mametz and Carnoy. When we arrived, just before midday, the troops we were relieving still occupied the tents. We therefore waited an hour or so on the hillside opposite. The road below us was no-man's land on July 1st, and again we looked over the desolation of the old battlefield. Under a grey sky the place was hardly recognisable as that which Hardy and I first saw on that hot morning in August. The desolation now appeared even greater, though the whole area was as active as an ant-heap.

When they did go, the outgoing troops were too hurried to clear up their own refuse; and what with the mud and their muck, friction occurred between our companies over the disposal of the tents. Rowley, who is not given to complaining, was rather badly aggrieved to find C Company short of room. Even with sufficient room, tents on the bare soaking clay, at this time of year, would not be very desirable places.

However, we have made shift. As far as the officers are concerned there are five of us in a bell-tent, with heaps of boots, clothes, books and food piled up on our valises, until we do indeed look like an expeditionary force. Judged by appearances we might be bound for the North Pole. It is very cold, so we have rigged up a stove in the centre of the tent. This stove is a marvellous contrivance. It consists of an old petrol-tin for base: a big piece of pipe with holes knocked in it for a brazier, surmounted by a damaged steel helmet; and finally on top of that a bit of stove-pipe to serve for a chimney. This juts from a hole in the helmet out of the tent-door. Not all the smoke can be persuaded to leave the tent by the chimney; but though we occasionally weep and choke, we are warm.

The doctor drops into the *mêlée*. He is a genial young to middle-aged man. We rag him; but, after endangering his life by knocking him into the stove, make room and welcome his yarns.

"Feather beds"

All officers are required by the colonel, who returned in time to bring the battalion out of Méaulte. Never having been wanted by the CO. in a body except for a "strafe," there is much speculation as to what can be the matter now. We bundle out of the tent into the mud, and plough our way to the small marquee that adjoins the orderly-room tent.

It is at once evident that the colonel is under a misapprehension. He understands officers made a general complaint about their own quarters this morning. Of course they did nothing of the kind. The feud, such as it was, had been simply an intercompany matter over the question of disposal. He makes his mistake unpleasantly clear, and we hear his comments with as good grace as possible, till he remarks ferociously that, if we think we have come to France for nothing but feather-beds and women, he will damn well show us we haven't.

I don't know how this vulgarity affects the others, but it fills me with a desire to plant my fist in his face; and this for more reasons than the fact that I have not had a bed since I landed. The jibe comes from the wrong quarter. While I hear him talking sullenly about the shell-holes we are going to occupy up the line tomorrow, I find myself wondering, all the time, whether the choice of regular officers to command line battalions is confined to gentlemen of this quality.

No: it is sheer bad luck; for I call to mind the colonel of another regiment in our brigade, a rather elderly officer who walked over to the German trenches on July 2nd, accompanied only by his orderly, just to prove (what was not believed) that the trenches were empty—and I see a kindly, sober, humorous English gentleman.

A piteous appeal

Rowley has received a pitiable letter, signed by two or three influential people in a Northern town, setting forth the case of a mother nearly demented because she has had two of her three sons killed in the trenches since July 1st, and is in mortal fear of what may happen to the sole surviving member of the family, a boy in our company named Stream. They are petitioning the Prime Minister for his release to less dangerous duty, and meantime ask if we can do anything.

Rowley is helpless at the moment, but he has shown the letter to the colonel, who promises to see what can be done next time we are out.

A bad start

We are on the road to Montauban in the grey morning following a wet night. We can only march very slowly, with frequent halts, for traffic blocks the way and the road is being covered with loose granite. Returning troops face us, and we have to "form two-deep" to let them go by.

Good Lord! That captain's face was a sight! Grey-green, like the cheeks of the dead, and his eyes fixed and staring. The men following him are smothered in mud. They are hardly by when a boy in my platoon, newly arrived with one of the fresh drafts, falls down in a fit. I get my cane between his teeth and, as he lies foaming on the ground, wonder how this child of the factories, an obvious epileptic, can have slipped through the doctor's fingers. He soon comes round and is returned to the nearest dressing-station. On we go. It is an unpropitious start.

The Major shines

The battalion is halted at midday on sloping ground above Trônes Wood, waiting while the cooks at the field-kitchens do their best, in the drizzling rain, to make us a hot stew. The colonel has gone on with company-commanders to take over at the trenches. On this slope there are a number of tarpaulins stretched tentwise over the ground to provide low shelters, and into these the men scramble out of the wet. Each one is overcrowded by half a dozen men. Others go down to explore the dugouts in the wood below, and then return to recount horrors to be seen in that gruesome place. 'Tis bad enough here when someone's heel catches a lump in the ground and reveals a man's putrefying arm.

The cooks signal that they are ready, and the men troop across the field with their mess-tins. The company has not been handed over to me, and I am unaware that I am in charge of it; but while the men are returning word comes that I am required by Major Smythe. I see him on the other side of the field: march across and salute. He wants to know what the hell I mean by allowing men to go for their meal in that manner, and pauses imposingly for an answer.

I have been soldiering long enough to know one does not answer the rhetorical questions of superior officers, more especially when the officer happens to be a figurehead. So I take my cursing in silence, half amused to note the change that has come over the very amiable and hurried gentleman I once pursued round the bays at Hébuterne. But I reflect, as I return, what an incorrigibly unsoldierly unit I must be; for even had I known I was in command, it would never have occurred to me that the men needed marching.

Desolation on the Somme

In the dusk of a leaden afternoon we march away from Trônes Wood through Guillemont and Ginchy. On the eastern side of the tiny village of Ginchy we are suddenly confronted with a wide, rolling, open plain over which there is no road but only a single "duck-walk" track. Slowly the battalion stretches itself out in single file along this track, and one by one the men follow each other, till the trail extends like the vertebrae of an endless snake.

On either side lies the open plain. Not a sign of life is anywhere to be seen, but instead there appear, in countless succession, stretching as far as the eye can pierce the gloom, shell-holes filled with water. The sense of desolation these innumerable, silent, circular pools produce is horrible, so vividly do they remind me of a certain illustration by Doré to Dante's *Inferno*, that I begin to wonder whether I have not stepped out of life and entered one of the circles of the damned; and as I look upon these evil pools I half expect to see a head appearing from each one. Here and there the succession of pools is broken by what appear in the fading light to be deep yawning graves, and over these our duck-walk makes a frail and slippery bridge.

On and on we go. Jog, jog, jog behind one another, till slowly the merciful darkness shuts out all sight of this awful land of foreboding. But now the difficulty of our march increases, for many of the laths of these duck-boards are broken, and in the darkness a man trips and falls, pitching his sand-bag of rations or box of bombs into the mud that lies deep on either side of the track. Whenever this happens, the rest of the battalion behind him has to halt while he picks himself up, recovers his load and steadies himself on the track again before trying to make good the gap between himself and the man in front.

Despite the cautions passed along the file a hundred times: "Look out"—"Mind the gap"—"Hole there," these mishaps constantly occur, till we in the rear wonder why in the name of Heaven long halts should be needed when those in front must still be miles from the trenches. At last the men in front move, and on we go again. On and on, till it seems we must be seeking the very end of nowhere, for still the Verey lights, which will show us the line of the trenches, do not appear. Every now and then shells drop, sometimes near enough to spatter us with mud and make us shudder to think what kind of death we should meet if one dropped near enough to lift us into the watery, muddy depths of a shell-hole. But even the shells seem to be wandering, for they come fitfully, as if they were fired from nowhere and had lost their way.

On and on we go. It is getting towards midnight now. The duck-walk ceases and we come out on high grass-land, where the going is good so long as we keep to the crest of the hill and pick a careful way between the shell-holes. Now we are turning and gently descending the hill. The waspish flight of whiz-bangs is heard quite close. We must be near the line at last, though it is still out of sight. Now we drop into mud ankle-deep. A man shouts it is up to the knees where he stands. New voices are heard. The company is no longer extended. There is Rowley. We have arrived.

Across twenty yards of quagmire rough trenches are dimly visible. They are the reserve trenches—ours. The men clamber into them and wrap themselves in their ground-sheets. We have reached the mud.

The little dugout

"Cheerio, Rowley! This is all right."

"Yes, bloody awful, isn't it? You've got the rations?"

"Yes. Do you know how long we're here for?"

"Two days, they said; but I expect it'll be four. Come down the dugout if you can find room. I must see this fellow off. Lilley's down there and Collins. Collins'll have to turf out. We've got no room for damned Lewis-gunners."

I follow him down a dozen steep slippery steps; water runs down them, but in spite of this Collins is sitting on the bottom step. The air below is hot and thick: the dugout is not more than six feet square, and there are now six of us. The captain of the company we are relieving accepts another drink, and wishing us luck climbs out. We take off our equipment, but the quarters are too close for anything like comfort. Lilley sits on a case of German soda-water which he opens and finds is full.

Fancy Lilley being in such a place! The sight of him brings home and beauty to mind, and we are soon talking about both. Lilley, it appears, was married on his last leave, so the conversation veers round to the institution of marriage. Rowley thinks it a failure, Lilley a dream. My view is summed up in the wish that my wife were here.

There is little to be done outside, so we talk the night away and discuss civilisation as if it still existed for us, dozing between whiles, eating raisins, drinking whisky and taking the air when the fug becomes unbearable.

Near Lesboeufs

Here, by daylight, outside the dugout, there is nothing within sight to give an inkling of where we are. The front line is said to be over the crest of the sloping ground on our right, about a thousand yards from this spot, but nothing of it is to be seen, and on all sides nothing but open rolling downs. A map is the only guide, and that instructs us we are between Gueudecourt and Lesboeufs, rather nearer Lesboeufs than Gueudecourt, though both villages are out of sight. The map declares a windmill once stood here. There is not a trace of it now. Facing the line, H.Q. dugout is forward on our left, hidden in a sunken road, and the second line runs somewhere just beyond it.

The trenches our men occupy are negligible hastily-thrown-up dykes, and as we are practically unsighted there is no harm in moving about on top—indeed there is no alternative. Ploughing through the mud I find many bodies lying about still unburied. How unreal they look! They merely remind me of the gruesome newspaper pictures of the dead on battlefields. Yet looking on them now I reflect how each one had his own life, his individual hopes and fears. Individually each one was born dead, they come back to individuality.

A fatigue-party in the mud

It is dark again. We are waiting for the mules to bring up rations. There has been little enough to do during the day, beside cheer the men up and get them to rub their feet and change their socks, and so, if possible, ward off what is miscalled frostbite. Rain has been falling off and on all day, and once or twice a great silt of mud outside the dugout looked as if it intended to close up the entrance. We dug hard to prevent it, and though the water still runs down the steps, the mud seems to have stopped shifting.

The mules are late: but that's no wonder; what is marvellous is that those small-footed beasts should ever be able to drag their feet through the miles of mud that lie between us and Ginchy. No horses could do it. That this is a fact is now borne out by the quartermaster-sergeant, who, unused to marching, arrives fagged out to tell us that the doctor's horse has slipped into a shell-hole up to the neck and had to have his load of rations cut from his back before he could be pulled out. Those rations are now at the bottom of the shell-hole. Somebody will have to go short in consequence, and Rowley very properly decides that the company in reserve must be the losers.

Mallow, who is now attached to B Company, has his party of five-and-twenty men waiting in the darkness and mud outside the dugout. The rations arrive and are apportioned: the men loaded up with the bags and old petrol-tins filled with water. A priceless jar of rum is given into the charge of an N.C.O. The business of getting the party off is not made easier by shelling which comes presumably because a lantern carried by the transport-party has been observed.

As soon as the ration-party has moved off, Hardy and I parade thirty men and two sergeants and set out for brigade headquarters in search of sandbags. We have no guide, and after going steadily for about an hour realise we have lost our way. This is not surprising considering the country and the darkness, but we must of course find the brigade headquarters if we spend the rest of the night in search. Batteries are firing in the hollow. The men behind those gun-flashes will be able to direct us; so we make for the flashes and in time arrive at the gun-pits. An Australian battery puts us on our track.

It is no simple path. Time and again we are climbing over deep, waterlogged, disused trenches, tripping over telegraph wire, and tearing rents in our clothes on barbed strands; but before midnight we reach the deep dugouts. There, after waiting some time, we load each of our men with as much as he can carry. Slowly we make the return journey, going well until we pass our own reserve line and encounter the four hundred yards that separate us from battalion headquarters. Here the mud is often knee-deep. The men are tired and hungry. They get stuck in the mud and have to be pulled out; but after any amount of wrenching and pulling, falling and swearing, we do get the sandbags delivered. Precisely what purpose they are to serve we cannot think, for anyone who has tried to fill sandbags with mud that is like glue knows he is performing the task of Sisyphus.

Coming back to our trenches more men get stuck, so that we form a straggling procession as we come in. Returning to see that all have arrived, I find Corporal Jackson half-carrying a big fellow who has wrenched and twisted his leg. Jackson himself is as cheerful as a cricket. It is moving, but now unsurprising, to find this little man playing the Good Samaritan with all the good will of his prototype and even more good humour. Jackson behaves as if he liked difficulties.

SHELLS AND MUD

We have been here two endless days. Day and night the shelling is more constant than it was at Hébuterne, but less concentrated than at St. George's Hill, and certainly shelling seems less terrifying in this weather than it did when the ground was dry. There is less noise and the area of danger is more confined. The fellows were surprised when I said I preferred this to Hébuterne. Of course, as far as conditions are concerned, Hébuterne was luxury by comparison; but it maddens me to stand in a perfectly constructed, sandbagged and revetted trench waiting for the 5.9 that will not miss. I prefer the open, where movement is possible, even if there is more metal flying about. The more civilised the conditions, the more intolerable shelling becomes. Honestly I would rather be here than straying about a London street while Zeppelins went overhead. Out here we know we are in it up to the neck, and there is satisfaction to be derived from that so long as activity of some kind is possible.

Mallow had a bad time with his ration-party last night. They lost their way, had two killed and two wounded, and only got about half the rations into the line. It was almost light before the party returned. Let's hope Smalley has better luck tonight, or those poor beggars up in front will be hungry. They say the mud up there is appalling.

We stand outside the dugout watching a wonderful sunset after another wet day. Our friends the aeroplanes come out of the sunset to wish us good night. How beautiful, orderly and civilised they look above this devastation! They are our sole reminders here of a world behind this: our only visitors and the only signs of life visible from this spot. As they wheel to go, we would fain give them messages to take back to the civilised world.

Darkness falls. Shells like devils of darkness come from over the hill and spit up the mud. We dive down our rat-hole, where a candle is guttering, and express the hope that a big crump will never drop right overhead.

CRUEL FATE

Our regular company-sergeant-major is taking a course in Paris. Sergeant Brown, who is acting on his behalf, comes to the mouth of the dugout to report that a big shell dropped right in the trench, killing one man, though who it was he doesn't yet know: the body was blown to pieces. No one else was hurt. Rowley tells him to go back and find out who it was.

The sergeant has come back to the top of the dugout. He now reports that he has found the man's pay-book and identity disk, adding "so that's all right." The name is Stream.

Stream! Good God! That's the boy about whom Rowley received that letter. Only one casualty in the company all the while we've been here, and that, this boy blown to pieces so that there is literally nothing left to bury! What will it mean to the lad's mother? We feel a weight of gloom as if Fate and the Devil himself were one.

November

A RATION-PARTY IN THE MUD

Hill is not up on this tour: he remained with the rear party under Major Smythe. Hardy is in charge of his tunnellers, occupying a trench near by. It is my turn to take the ration-party up tonight, and the rations must arrive somehow, for Smalley's journey was only a little better than Mallow's. Four wounded and again rations lost.

By the way, fairly heavy casualties are occurring in the line, and today I had to find men from my platoon to act as extra stretcher-bearers, the regular bearers being insufficient and exhausted owing to the conditions. I asked for volunteers, and got them without the least difficulty. As might be expected, the best, but not always the most physically fit, volunteered. I should like to have shaken hands with those fellows, for they knew what they were letting themselves in for, and they went, almost shyly, without a semblance of heroics or thought of recognition.

The sergeant brings up the fatigue-party. I talk to them as they stand in the mud, waiting for the mules, telling them that every man has got to do his damnedest, because the fellows up there are short of grub, and no matter what happens every ration must be delivered. I appeal to them as good sportsmen not to let their pals down.

We must see this job through, for it is a humane one and worth doing.

Loaded and ready, we start off in single file and trudge to headquarters, where we have to report to the adjutant. 'Tis a very dark night, but luckily there is no rain. We enter the sunken road. The conditions here are terrible. The road itself has become a broad river of mud, in places two feet deep. On the right there seems to be a deep bank, and movement by it tells me there are men huddled there. They are using the bank for cover, as a trench at this level would of course be flooded.

On the left is the entrance to the dugout, and near its mouth runners, signallers and orderlies crouch together in knots to keep themselves warm. As my party has to stand in the liquid mud while I go down the dugout to report, I hurry off, and doing so stumble over a bundle and very nearly fall headlong down the steps.

"What the devil . . .?"

"Look out, sir! That's a dead man," comes the response in injured tones. Shuddering, I realise I have kicked one of their number who has just been killed.

The scene below is palatial compared with the gruesome swamp up above. This is quite a respectable place partitioned into two rooms. It is pitiful to think there is actually plenty of accommodation down here for those poor devils shivering outside. The adjutant and then the colonel rub in the necessity of getting all the rations delivered, and I go out by another flight of steps and meet the darkness.

Now we are wading down the flooded road. This dugout is a mark for fire, but please Heaven they will not shell us just here, for if a man were not killed outright being wounded he might easily drown. No, the luck holds. Now we are clambering up the steep side of the road and nearing the empty trenches that presumably were once the second line. I have put the sergeant in front and bring up the rear myself because I want to make dead certain that no one falls out. 'Tis devilish hard work to get through this mud: one's very joints seem as if they will part. And what's this? a man half-lying on his back with a ration-bag at his feet.

"What are you doing?"

"Sorry, sir, I'm whacked," he replies slowly in a low voice.

"Get up! Damn you! Don't you think those poor devils in the front line are whacked?"

"Sorry—I can't—I'm absolutely done. You know, sir," and here he pauses, continuing in a whispered voice, as if he were telling me a secret, "we don't get enough to eat."

This is true enough at the moment. Moreover this man is forty and not very strong; but I have sworn we would get those rations up, and the journey has hardly begun.

"Look here," I say, "if you don't get up, it's my duty to shoot you for disobeying an order. You understand? Either you get up and go on, or I shall have to shoot."

He does not stir, but after waiting a moment replies in the voice of one turning over to sleep:

"Then, sir, I'm afraid you'll have to shoot."

I'm second-best at this encounter. The monstrous absurdity of the threat makes me feel a fool. Cursing, I pick up his ration-bag and hasten after the disappearing file to find the men standing alongside a communication-trench debating the possibility of going up it. Already three of them are attempting this, but they haven't gone a dozen yards before they are stuck fast and give us much to do to pull them out. We will have no more of that, but keep to the line of the trench, and when we believe we are approaching the end, crawl away to the right and drop into the front line over the parados.

We move on, but fearfully slowly, slipping and sliding about, circumventing shell-holes and troubled most of all by dead bodies that look as if they have been thrown out of the communication-trench. They lie about, singly or in groups, stretched in every conceivable attitude. The living men have an innate respect for the dead and avoid touching a corpse, or even walking over it, if possible.

At last we come to the front-line trench and one by one the men fling themselves into it. Shots are fired, but by the time I am in I know that no one has been hit. This trench is just a great gully, the bottom of it so deep in mud that the only way to get along is to move straddle-wise. The men holding the line are perched up on the slope of the parapet wherever there is a foothold. Toiling along, it is soon apparent that half my men are stuck in the bottom of the trench and can get no farther. Lightlier weighted, I pass them till I come to the head of the file, and then send back word that the rations are to be handed along from man to man while I report to Captain Wilson.

He sits crouched in a hole in the parados hardly big enough to contain him. He has a ground-sheet flap over the front of the hole, but it does not prevent the candlelight shining through chinks at the side.

"By Jove, Wilson! this is a rough show."

"Yes, awful, isn't it? But we're coming out tomorrow. You brought all the rations? That's good! Do you think you could take a couple of casualties back with you? I've two boys hurt. They can walk, but they can't get back without help, and I've no one to send."

"Right-o!"

"See the sergeant-major about them, will you? I won't come out; one of my feet has gone groggy with the wet. Yes, it's beastly painful and I shall have as much as I can do to get out tomorrow. Pleased you've got all the rations up: we've been very short."

He smiles his friendly old smile and pats me on the shoulder like a father as I drop the flap. Goodbye, Wilson!

I do not know that this is the last time I shall see him: that he will go into hospital for a while with his foot: that (owing to his age, long service in the trenches, and sickness) he will be offered a job at the base which, though a newly married man, he will decline, saying "he knows the men so well now"; and that finally he, the best company-commander I ever met, will be killed in the trenches, dying without honours. But so it is to be.

After seeing the sergeant-major, who sends along the wounded boys, I go back and find most of the men have extricated themselves and are lying behind the back of the trench waiting to return. But there is a lad here, Bird, the fat boy of Hardy's platoon, stuck fast and unable to move. Obtaining a shovel, we lay it across the trench, tell him to kneel on it and pull. He kneels and the shovel sinks, but Bird remains if anything now deeper in the mud. He looks, "I told you so," and stands motionless as if to prove the hopelessness of his case.

Fidgeting on parade is Bird's especial vice. He cannot fidget now. "Well, Bird," say I, "you're not on parade, but you're standing still at last." He sees no humour in the remark, and I am afraid he is going to start blubbering. Something must be done. Shovels are useless: the only thing is to drag the pug away from his legs with one's hands, and this I proceed to do, encouraging him to pull as I loosen one leg. After twenty minutes of this business I get sick of it, and still more sick of his feeble efforts to help himself. I give it up.

"There it is, if you can't get out, we shall have to leave you. You'll have to stay there till the rest of the company comes out, and," I add vindictively, "we've brought no rations up here for *you*."

He looks at me aghast.

"Then I'll have nothing to eat!"

"No, nothing."

The horror of this prospect puts demons of energy into him. He pulls and pulls till it looks as if his foot will come off; but at last, with a mighty squelch, it appears. The rest is easy. Bird is saved by his belly.

Two or three of my men have gone on with the casualties: the rest of us now follow. Halfway back I meet a young subaltern belonging to one of the regiments in our brigade. He is in great distress. He has lost his men—the whole platoon. He left them in a trench all right while he went back to a dugout to get some cigarettes, and when he returned the whole lot had gone. What do I think he ought to do? Of course, he'll be court-martialled for leaving them. Will I give evidence that he was honestly trying to find them again?

I suggest he must have mistaken the trench and that they are still there. No. He is certain about it. They have "done a bunk" and he'll be "for it." I do my best to console him all the way back to battalion headquarters, where I have to report again. There I leave him.

At the bottom of the dugout stands the colonel, smothered in mud from head to foot, a pole still in his hand. He has been trying, the adjutant tells me, to get up to the front line; but the mud was too much for him.

Out again, we lug ourselves over the last long lap. Our journey of three thousand yards started at seven: it is now two o'clock. I stumble down into the little dugout on legs that feel as if they were made in two pieces of cast iron. What matters? We have delivered the rations without a casualty.

The deserter

The quartermaster-sergeant has brought up rare news of Sergeant Griffen, who was my platoon-sergeant at Hébuterne. While we were at Méaulte he was sent with about half a dozen men to rail-head, then near Mametz, to unload bombs. He had to make billeting and rationing arrangements, for himself and the men, with the town-major of Méaulte; so that, for the time being, he and his party were detached from the regiment. Apparently he went up with the men once and returned, reporting to the town-major that the bombs had not arrived and he had been instructed to wait at Méaulte. There he hung about for a week, drawing rations for the men and himself all the time.

At the end of the week the men began to suspect something was wrong and at the same time Sergeant Griffen disappeared. The men returned to find the battalion in the line and themselves apprehended for desertion. They explained their case to the C.O., who withdrew the charge and sent them on to the trenches. Meantime it appears that Griffen donned the uniform of a sergeant-major, forged a cheque for a thousand *francs*, and was last heard of at Amiens. Quite obviously he is asking to be shot if he is caught, and I would not stir a finger to save him; for if he is skunk enough to want to dodge these trenches himself, that doesn't excuse him for very nearly having half a dozen men court-martialled for desertion. It sounds as if the man must have gone mad; but knowing him, I suspect that he guessed what these trenches would be like and thought he would take his chances elsewhere. I doubt if he escapes.

Nothing doing

Like the prospect of paradise is the thought that we are coming out of these trenches tonight; but now at midday come tales from the company runners of our wounded lying about through insufficiency of stretcher-bearers and want of someone to organise them. This is obviously my job, and I tell Rowley I should like to take it on. Rowley says it can't be done: we might be wanted at a moment's notice in case of trouble. I point out that the conditions make that highly improbable: that it's absurd we should be hanging about doing nothing while some of our fellows are being worked to death and others dying owing to delay. I ask him if he'll let me go to the colonel about it, seeing that I reckon myself an expert at first-aid. Rowley declines, and I am much disgruntled. He might at least let the question of military necessity be decided by the C.O.

Coming out

Heaven knows where we shall finish up tonight! We have trailed the whole length of those rickety duck-boards, marched as a company to Trônes Wood, and now here we are, marching and counter-marching in the darkness as if nobody had an idea where we were bound for. I trust we are not merely manoeuvring to fill up time, for to a man we are fagged out. Smalley says we are looking for a rest-camp where we can get hot tea before going back to Mansel Copse. For my part, I should like to lie here on the hillside for the next two days. We are then due to return to those unspeakable trenches.

Rest

Back in the old tent with the smoky brazier. It is Sunday. Thank God, I'm not orderly-officer. I trust no one will ask me to move for the next twelve hours. I'm too tired yet even to get clean. Lord! What a march! The men are still straggling in. About three-quarters of the company arrived with the column this morning, and I honestly believe half my platoon would have dropped out if it hadn't been for Jackson, who simply wouldn't let them stop singing. That little man is a marvel. I have never seen such pluck.

Trench-feet

I have been talking to one of my stretcher-bearers. He has a foot swollen to three times its normal size: a great shapeless bright pink lump. He has been stretcher-bearing over that awful ground almost the whole of the four days. Changing his socks did no good: the water came in over the tops of his boots as soon as he started bearing again. He is an excellent fellow and genuinely disappointed at having to leave us. Poor beggar! I shall be surprised if he doesn't lose that foot.

BACK TO THE MUD

We have tramped through Montauban, Bernafay, Trônes Wood, Guillemont, Ginchy and across the plain again. We have passed our old trenches and the battalion dugout and now stand, at midnight, stuck in the communication-trench. There has been no rain for two days; we therefore hoped to find this trench passable. Rowley is at the head of the file. I wonder what he is doing, for we have not advanced for nearly an hour, and still we do not move. My patience gives out. I climb on top and go up alongside the row of sacking-covered helmets till I come to Rowley standing at the junction of the two trenches. I am kneeling down talking to him in low tones, when "*Phut!*" "*Ping!*"— one shot falls short in the mud and another glances off my tin hat. In double time I heave myself over into the mud.

Whoever it is we are relieving, they have gone already. The trench is empty. In the watery moonlight it appears a very ghostly place. Corpses lie along the parados, rotting in the wet: every now and then a booted foot appears jutting over the trench. The mud makes it all but impassable, and now, sunk in up to the knees, I have the momentary terror of never being able to pull myself out. Such horror gives frenzied energy, and I tear my legs free and go on. Turning sharply round a bend I come upon a fearsome sight. Deep water lies in a descending right-angle of the trench, and at arm's length from me a body has fallen face downward in the water, barring the way. Shall I push the body aside and wade, chancing the depth of the water, or shall I get out on top and double across the corner?

There is a sunken road here: that is why the water stands, and ten to one a German sniper is hiding on the forward slope below. If I try the water it may prove too deep; even if it isn't, I shall be wet to the thighs, and there are four days to go; besides that body.... If I go over the top and the sniper hits, what a kindness he might do me! I am up now, running and dodging. Twice the sniper fires, but I am more troubled to dodge the bodies than the sniper's aim. Now over, and slap into the trench; and that is past, with not only a whole but a dry skin.

RAIN AND MUD

Rain, rain, rain! It has rained all day. We are all in the trench at last, though some of the men remained stuck on the way till long after daylight. While the trenches are in this condition we can neither get to the Germans nor they to us. Both sides are glued where they stand, so that Heaven alone knows what purpose we serve here, or whether we shall ever get out again. Like so many grotesque monuments, the men sit huddled under their ground-sheets at their places beneath the parapet. I wonder how many of those rifles would fire? I wonder how they are ever going to get them clean again? To move fifty yards along the trench is, at present, half an hour's work. If it goes on raining . . .

The runners have the worst time. We've two splendid fellows who will go anywhere that is humanly possible. It takes them hours to get to and from battalion headquarters, and they risk their lives every time. They have brought back chits instructing us to get the men to work clearing the trenches and putting the place in repair. Noah might as well have given such instructions to the dove.

When it stops raining we shall see what can be done. At present, even to move is only to churn up the pug and make further movement impossible. We simply haven't the tools to clear this stuff; shovels are perfectly useless.

Rowley replies, smiling grimly as he writes, that the instructions are noted. I foresee trouble here, and beg him to be frank with the colonel and tell him clearly how matters stand. Ask him to come and see for himself.

The whole duty of a soldier, as Rowley understands it, is to receive orders and carry them out—as and when possible. In vain do I point out that nobody besides ourselves *can* know what this place is like. Rowley is adamant, and the "eyewash" goes its way.

We have been here twelve hours and have not yet got into touch with the battalion on our right. There's an impassable gap between us. At night it may be possible to get out in front and go round; but even that is very doubtful.

All this wants saying elsewhere. I cannot believe Rowley does well in keeping this kind of thing from the colonel.

Meantime here we sit, Smalley, Rowley and myself, in a hole in the parados, six by three by three. German rifles and their bayonets, covered by German ground-sheets, serve for a roof, and another ground-sheet makes a flap that covers us in front down to the knees. Our feet stick out in the mud and are sometimes uncomfortably trodden on. I came into the trench with a nice long Burberry, long enough to keep one's knees dry, but by the time we arrived it was caked to the waist, so I have cut off the skirt and it now looks like an Eton jacket with frills.

THE LIMIT

Rain has been falling almost continuously for two days, and if it goes on much longer we shall indeed leave these trenches, being washed out. Chits continue to come detailing the work expected of us, and Rowley continues to reply that instructions are noted; but little or nothing is done, for the simple reason that the Deity has not yet constructed men able to make or repair trenches when the earth at every step holds them immovable.

Last night Smalley and a sergeant went out to get in touch with the regiment on our right, but after being half-drowned they had to return. There are portions of the earth's surface that under some conditions remain impassable by unaided man, even though he learns from his commanding-officer half a dozen times a day that it is imperative they should be passed. That is the fact; but I am sure this pretence that we are doing the impossible is a tragic game.

Shelling is sporadic. Soon after dark last night we had a lot of shells uncomfortably near. Luckily not one fell in the trench, and so far all our casualties here have occurred through sniping. Last night the ration-party coming up lost its officer, shot through the head, and a fellow in my platoon and two others in the company have been killed in the same way. We should like to get at those snipers, but with the ground like this it would only be suicide to send patrols out into no-man's land. This is where a retiring enemy scores.

Hill came up with a message from the second line this evening reporting about a dozen casualties back there. He was wet to the thighs. Half the officers of the battalion seem to have gone sick.

Thank goodness I brought six pairs of socks. Morning and evening we make the men take off their boots and rub their feet; but it isn't much good: they simply cannot keep them warm or dry under such conditions, and some of them are already badly frost-bitten.

This is the very limit of endurance.

In front of Le Transloy

Thank Heaven it has stopped raining at last! The sun actually shines, and for the first time in three days we can really see where we are. We have parties of men at work trying to drain the trench; incidentally the squad under Jackson seems to have done the most useful work. The sentries are still trying to get their rifles clean.

There's Le Transloy, 1500 yards away. There's the sugar-refinery, and in front the cemetery. How peaceful and calm it all looks in the sunshine! Gazing over here, who could imagine what a hell this place has been? Now there's no firing it seems absurd to stay here. Why don't we walk over the fields and explore the village that looks so inviting?

You can bet the Germans are feeling the same. Why don't we all get out and walk away?

We seem to be here under the constraint of some malevolent idiot. In this sunshine it seems impossible to believe that at any minute we in this trench, and they in that, may be blown to bits by shells fired from guns at invisible distances by hearty fellows who would be quite ready to stand you a drink if you met them face to face. What base, pathetic slaves we are to endure such idiocy! No doubt it's good to fight when indignation and hatred boil up as they did in 1914. But these passions have long since spent themselves. Why are we fighting still?

We are compelled. We have endowed machinery with the power once confined to a man's right arm, and now the machine continues to function long after our natural impulses have spent themselves. That's what makes this war so ghastly. It is machine-made. Even our opinion is machine-made by a press suborned with fear; and we who do the fighting have no say in when the fight shall cease. Man seems to have become the slave of his own power of organisation. If all the machinery of war were now suddenly taken from our hands, I am certain the war would stop at once.

Pork and beans

Of all people entitled to praise in these times I give the palm to the army commissariat. True they cannot feed five thousand on five loaves and two fishes, but after that miracle theirs comes second. Consider it. We have been wandering about in a foreign country for four months, and never till this moment have we known what it is to feel really short of food. When I remember that this battalion is one of thousands similarly mobile, and when I see the conditions under which we ask so punctually not only for our daily bread, but our regular meals, I marvel at the organisation which can respond promptly to such a demand.

Our principal food in the trenches is, of course, bully beef and bread, falling seldom to biscuits. But this is by no means all we have. Often enough there is that excellent tin of cooked meat and vegetables known familiarly as "Maconachie": there is tea and sugar, and lately we have had plentiful supplies of good Australian jam, which came as a pleasant change from the nondescript variety known as "Tickler."

At the moment I am reminded of these blessings by their absence. Yet even now there is half a loaf going. It has suffered too many hardships since it left the bakers to make it look appetising; and muddy and wet, it must wait till we see what happens tonight before it can be sure of reaching a human interior. Still, there it is. And water? There is still a drop in the bottom of the petrol-tin.

Oh, this water! The taste of water impregnated with petrol will carry me back here if I live for ever. It is a nauseous taste, and no doubt someone ought to be hanged for not washing out the spirit before adding our water. Still, it quenches thirst.

And then there's rum. Rum of course is our chief great good. The Ark of the Covenant was never borne with greater care than is bestowed upon the large stone rum-jars in their passage through this wilderness. The popularity of rum increases, till the hour when it is served tends to become a moment of religious worship. After the divine pattern, its celebration is administered by priests in the presence of higher dignitaries. When these priests happen to be old-time N.C.O.s, they want watching, or the communicants are apt to go short, to the degradation of the priests.

There are men so devout they live for rum. I honestly believe some I know would commit suicide if the rum ration were withdrawn. And in truth the rum is good—fine, strong, warming stuff—the very concentrated essence of army-council wisdom.

But while I sit in my mud-hole dreaming of rum, a miracle of generosity happens. Robinson, a quiet stretcher-bearer who looks as if he followed the plough in times of peace, comes up to me and, with a great shy smile, asks me if I would like "this"—this being an unopened tin of Heinz's Pork and Beans. He protests he does not want it.

Permit me now to depart from the praise of rum, which all men worship, and to become lyrical upon a height where few will follow. Pork and beans shall have its song of honour. What if the beans are many and the pork is far between! What if the label on the tin should read BEANS and Pork! Hunger shall prompt the muse.

Seated today in this mud-hole,
I am weary and ill at ease,
For the aching void of a stomach
Trembles like aspen leaves;
When a stretcher-bearer named Robinson
(Long may he live in bliss!)
Comes up with a tin of treasure
And says, "Can you do with this?"
I thank him with great profusion

And would readily share my delight
With Rowley, who's also hungry,
But he turns up his nose at the sight;
And Smalley and even Castlereagh
Reply quite emphatically, "No";
So alone I will light me a candle
And prepare me my great beano.

By the light of a single candle
I am toasting the jolly lot,
Till, by dint of a little patience,
The contents are piping hot;
And now, like an Eastern monarch
Surrounded by all his queens,
I shall slowly and solemnly dine at
A banquet of pork and beans.

It may be the years will bring me
A place in the Lord Mayor's Show,
With a feast of the pheasants that follow
In the place where fat aldermen go;
But if ever I get back to Blighty
(So long as I have the means)
I shall keep in my larder a tinful
Of Robinson's Pork and Beans.

The broken plane

A solitary German plane is flying over towards Gueudecourt. "Archies" are making their white smoke-circles round it, when it begins to drop and I see one of its wings spinning like a feather high above it. The broken butterfly itself turns round and round as it flutters to the ground, looking as if it will come to earth quite restfully. It drops out of sight; but suddenly a sheet of flame leaps up, and we realise that all that soft fluttering was only the deceitful prelude to terrible death.

Luck

Turning round from gazing over the fields before Le Transloy, Rowley and I are horrified to see two of our runners coming down from the crest of the rise behind us, walking in the bright sunlight, visible to the enemy down to their feet, and looking for all the world as if they think they are out for a stroll in the country. They have lost their way. Every minute we expect to see them drop, but on they come, nearer and nearer. We try to signal to them; but either they do not understand us, or they think this is the second line; for they stroll on, right up to us, and are getting into the trench before they realise what has happened. Not a shot is fired!

A Turkish bath

I have been out in front tonight trying to get across to the regiment on our right to whom we can now signal, though the gap has never been closed. I could not get across and am soaked.

There has been pretty heavy shelling going on: we can see the flash of the gun that fires on us out of Bapaume, and the moments between the flash and the shaking of the trench are terribly nervous ones; but our luck has held. The Australians behind us have also been firing heavily. Hungry and tired and wet, Smalley, Rowley and I have just wrapped our cold legs and wet feet in one parcel of Burberry, hoping for a Turkish bath effect that will enable us to sleep.

The old soldier

We slept all right till the ration-party came cluttering in right on top of us. Some of them had drunk a good ration of rum before they started, and when they arrived they were rowdy and indifferent to cursing. Possibly as a result of their noise, shelling started again. This sobered them; but daylight came too soon for them to go back, so we have entertained them for the day. One of the party, Sawyer, an old soldier, has been alternately an anxiety and an amusement. He is a man who has been with the battalion since its formation, and seen service in the South African War. These trenches have been too much for him.

Falling asleep this morning, he lay for a long while in a state of something like coma. As time went on we became alarmed and tried to wake him, wondering what we should do if he failed to rouse himself before we were relieved. He was not drunk; but wet and exposure seemed to have numbed his brain as well as his limbs. We rubbed him, shook him, pummelled him, and shouted into his ear, for a long time without effect. At last he stirred himself a little and then proceeded to deliver a short speech full of self-gratulation and pride at being the oldest soldier in the regiment. Having wasted his strength in this eloquence, he promptly fell asleep again.

Again we rubbed and pummelled, and again he repeated his oration and feel asleep. This happened three or four times, but gradually a drowsy general consciousness returned, and now we only hope it will continue till dusk, when he is to be the first man to leave the trenches. Rowley has abandoned the idea of going out *via* the communication-trench, which is certainly impassable. As the animals entered the Ark, we shall go out over the back of the trench, scuttle a hundred yards, crawl over the crest and make for the duck-boards.

This morning, soon after daybreak, Perkins, a tall dark man of my platoon, was fatally wounded while on sentry. He must have lifted his head an inch too high: a sniper got him with a bullet through the top of his helmet. Poor fellow! He thought he was only wounded and was pleased as a child at the idea of going home. Gradually his breathing became heavy: he lapsed into unconsciousness and died in the trench an hour ago. There was no possibility of getting him back to the doctor. Thus comedy and tragedy have been jostling each other all day.

EXIT THE OLD SOLDIER

Old Sawyer is still awake. For about the fourth time Rowley is giving him his instructions:

"You see, you go up the ladder, then crawl for about fifty yards. Then nip up the hill till you're about twenty yards from the top. Crawl again till you're right over. Then take to your heels, and the best of luck. And don't stop going till you get off the duck-boards. You understand? Now tell me what you've got to do."

Sawyer repeats what he remembers and is duly corrected. "Right-o! Now you're off. And keep going."

With a little help he clambers up the steps, and we watch the huddled figure moving, slowly as a tortoise, among the pitiful dead bodies. He becomes blurred in the dusk. We turn away, congratulating ourselves on having got him to go. The next moment someone says he has stopped crawling and fallen asleep. Peering through the dusk we are convinced the old fellow is out of sight and that the motionless form indicated is a corpse, when, to our dismay, it begins to move, to turn round and crawl towards us! Back comes old Sawyer, as slowly as he had gone, inch by inch, till at last he regains the trench. Rowley meets him.

"Why the devil didn't you go on? You were more than halfway."

"I were too tired, sir, to go any farther. So I thought I'd better come back and have a rest."

Rowley remarks to me that the next time we push him off we'll have a man behind him with a bayonet and give him orders not to let the old fellow stop this side of the Channel.

The relief

The moon is getting up. The men are going out in twos when silhouetted forms appear on top of the rise. It is the relieving company coming over all at once in extended order. Shots are fired and some of the shadowy forms drop. The next minute the trench is invaded, and our successors begin to "take over." While I am waiting in the mud-hole I overhear one of them talking to himself as he struggles to move down the trench. Every word is punctuated by the prodigious effort of drawing a leg out of the mud.

"Lloyd George," he growls, "said—this—was a fight—to the finish. The b—— had better—come out here—and finish it."

Rowley and I are the last to go. For the past two days, worried by our plight and the chits from headquarters, he has been refusing food and relying on whisky; now he is as weak as a kitten, and when he falls is hardly persuaded to go on. We are sighted and shot at more than once, but the old luck holds. Struggling over the crest, we get out of direct range and sit for a long time by the side of a shell-hole which has a body lying in it. Then I persuade him to come along, and slowly we continue till we reach headquarters' dugout where the adjutant takes him down and gives him food and a hot drink.

Outside in the mud and the dark, I am talking to three of my volunteer stretcher-bearers when whiz-bangs come over, dropping among us. We disperse, but when the firing is over I can only find one of them and he is wounded.

Rowley returns. We pick up Hardy and together tramp the endless duck-boards. Posts have now been established, just off the duck-boards, where hot drinks are to be had, and but for these I question whether Rowley would have finished the journey to the rest-camp at Montauban.

"*L'esprit c'est la force*"

It is early morning before we find the camp on the hill. As we enter wearily, ominous shoutings and groanings come from all directions. These sounds tell the tale. The men are crying out with the pain in their feet. But there is nothing to be done now and, dog-tired, I am on the point of dropping into a tarpaulin-covered hole, when I remember my platoon. What can I do for them? Well, at least I ought to see how they are. Wandering round alone I come on a coke-fire burning at the end of one of the shelters. A dark figure stands by tending it. It is Jackson.

"Hullo! What are you doing?"

"Only looking to this fire, sir. I thought if I kept it going on this side, the wind 'd blow the heat through."

"Where are they?"

"They're all in there. There's only Collins and Roberts bad. The sergeant's pretty fair. He's inside. Shall I fetch him?"

"No. That's all right. How about yourself? Where are you going to sleep? Is there any room there?"

"No, sir, but I shall be all right. There's several of them want looking to. I'd as soon be here. I'm getting dry."

I bid him goodnight, and go back to the officers' shelter, thinking of heroism and wherein it consists. This is the unostentatious kind. Here's a wisp of a man with a permanently troublesome knee. He has just come from trenches, said to be worse than Ypres in 1914, where he has done two men's work, besides helping crocks out of the mud, supporting them and carrying their rifles. Under the foulest conditions his spirits have never flagged. I have heard him whistling when no other bird on earth would sing; and now, when by all the laws of Nature he ought to have dropped half-dead, he has appointed himself to the role of Florence Nightingale, and has not even left himself room to lie down. I cannot sleep for thinking of him. The Lady of the Lamp. The Gentleman of the Brazier.

A SORRY SIGHT

Here's a pitiable sight! Half a battalion being taken off in G.S. wagons because they are unable to walk. Many cannot even get into the wagons by themselves, and it is hard work carrying and lifting them in. And there they sit and stand, like victims in the tumbrils on their way to the guillotine. Some will be unloaded at the hut near Mametz, to which the rest of the battalion is moving; others will go on to the field-hospital. There's Hill and Smalley standing together in the corner of one wagon. I must go across and wish them goodbye and good luck.

This is the last time I shall see Hill, who has yet to go home, get well, transfer to the Flying Corps (knowing his feet would never stand another winter here) and be killed flying over the German lines.

The adjutant comes round, going from shelter to shelter, inquiring if there is any officer there who can walk. I tell him I can.

"Then you're for a sniping course," he replies. "You'll start tomorrow. Take your servant, and get to Pont Noyelles as best you can."

Well, well! There are many ways of choosing a marksman: eyes, hand and nerve must be considered; but this is the first time I have ever heard of one being chosen for his feet.

Meantime we parade for the short march to Mametz. Out of a company of over two hundred we can only muster fifty-two, and I note that one of them is Jackson and another Rowley—sportsmen both: they will stick it out to the end.

There is not more than two miles to it, but this is the most painful march I have ever made. We are tired out: the road is constantly blocked, and the repeated halts on loose granite, which is like glass to our tender feet, cause frenzied and impotent swearing. A little more of this and we should all drop down and cry.

How much farther? Ah! There are the huts. We are nearly there. Thank God, the camp at last. Which hut? Which hut? Not this one? Is that it? The right hut at last. Now a valise. Oh, what comfort rest on the floor can be to limbs that are really tired! And here's the sainted quartermaster-sergeant bringing round hot tea and waiting on us like a nurse.

No, thanks—nothing to eat, only sleep—sleep—oceans of it.

On the road to Amiens

They say it's about seven miles from Pont Noyelles to Amiens; anyway it will be a good walk. The commandant of the Telescopic Sniping School, out of pity for my mud-stained condition, has given me special leave to go to Amiens; so here I am on the road alone, in search of pants and *puttees*, pyjamas and most of all a shampoo, for it will take a good barber to get the mud out of my hair. Since I joined the battalion nearly four months ago, this is the first time I have been away from it for a day. It seems quite strange to be walking alone in a country road. I wonder where the battalion is now? This must be the first hour I have been really alone since I came to France. It is a pleasure. I can stuff my hands in my short "British-warm," the cane sticking out at any angle it pleases, and almost forget the war. O Lord! If only I were back in England for an hour! Well, leave will come—in time—perhaps.

Less than three days ago we were in those trenches. It's hardly credible. The weather has changed, and after sharp frost there's a sprinkling of snow on the ground, making the countryside white and beautiful. All the same, I hope the frost doesn't last. I'm too pinched and achey in the bones for hard weather. By the way, the fellows who followed us into those trenches must be glad of this frost. Two hundred odd cases of trench feet it would have saved us had it come a week ago.

Somebody ought to be shot for keeping us up there four days at a time without any precautions against trench-feet. I wonder whether the culprit will ever bear the onus of that mistake. Very likely we shall never know who he is.

I hope Rowley will get my recommendation for Jackson through. If ever a man did deserve recognition there's a case. And if, as Hardy says he is doing, Rowley puts one through for me, what shall I do about it? This I know: that I can lay my hand on my heart and say without cant or false modesty that I have done nothing to deserve it. Moreover we all know why he has done it. Didn't he vow when we met a rag-tag regiment at Halloy, with almost every officer in the battalion wearing an M.C., that somebody besides "those blighters" would be up for decorations next time we came out? I trust I shouldn't have the face to wear it; but it puts me in difficulty, for to refuse point-blank might be to let Rowley down rather badly. Let's hope the colonel cuts it out.

Those gunners in their car seem to know how to do themselves pretty well. If they are going into Amiens, they might give me a lift. Oh, luck! They are stopping and signalling to me to come along.

THE SNIPING COURSE

This school is quite good fun. It is run by elderly officers who have Bisley reputations and, like all men who are really keen on some particular branch of knowledge, they know how to make the subject interesting. If only I felt perfectly fit and the weather were not so cold, it would be thoroughly enjoyable.

We have a lecture at 8.30: spend the morning on the range: come back for lunch: then on to the range again at 2, and back again for another lecture at 5.30. The course only lasts a week and there's an examination at the end of it. It's rather ironic that I should be on such a course, for we haven't a telescopic rifle in the battalion.

We are a mixed company, Highlanders, Australians, a Guardsman, and none above the rank of captain. The Australians are very characteristic, good-natured, devil-may-care fellows, a little inclined to brag (as is customary with all men belonging to nations of recent civilisation) and good soldiers in a tight corner, I haven't a doubt. The Guards' officer makes an amusing study in contrast. He is fair, sleek, rather bald, wears a monocle and is in other respects perfectly turned out. I wondered at first how he would sort with the Australians, but in spite of his superficial manner, he is neither a snob nor a mere dandy. Best of all he has an excellent sense of humour. They get along famously, and before the end of the week the Guardsman will be the most popular man here.

The course, which is principally concerned with the use and care of telescopic-sighted rifles, includes instruction in the employment and detection of camouflage and, of course, distance-judging. Firing with a telescopic sight is a refinement of marksmanship, and in the realm of sport is a fine art which anybody with a good eye and steady hands might well prefer to golf. It is pleasant and flattering to be able to hit an object invisible to the naked eye. It is fascinating to discover the characteristics of a particular rifle; and judging the strength and direction of wind is a nice speculative study.

I begin to see that war entails many employments which are wholly enjoyable provided a certain part of the imagination is atrophied. The great seductive enjoyment of war, outside the infantry ranks, is the sense of power it confers. By means of finely adjusted guns and the use of high explosives, the maximum of effect can be produced by the minimum of effort, and this appeals to a childish instinct latent in everyone. "You press the button and we do the rest." The appeal to this instinct will sell millions of cameras in times of peace; but what is the wonder of pressing a button and seeing a photograph compared with the wonder of pulling a string and seeing as the result a dump go up perhaps five miles away?

Every sport, if you come to analyse it, depends largely upon its power of producing a big effect with apparently small cause, whether the power resides in the ace of hearts, the thickness of a cricket-bat, or the responsiveness of a golf-ball to fine timing. In war this apparent disproportionate relation between cause and effect, which confers its flattering and enjoyable sense of power upon the player, is seen at its highest. Hence, from this standpoint, war is king of sports. Only imagination can spoil the game.

I see that most clearly when, having thoroughly enjoyed practice upon a target, I begin to feel squeamish on being told that firing low is a mistake because the head is the most vulnerable part of a man. Bull's-eyes on a target are a pleasure; but when the power to make them becomes applied and we are told of the wonderful logs kept by certain snipers who recorded their bag each day as if human heads were of less account than pheasants, then a gruesome sense of mean inhumanity begins to assert itself and I think with comparative esteem of the cannibal chief and his scalps. I prefer his honesty.

Of course one does not mention this here, knowing it would be regarded as humanitarian rot. Nevertheless, it seems to me that as imagination is the great distinguishing characteristic of man, to which he has attained late in his growth, it is not improbable that when this quality in him has grown a little stronger, not only will war be impossible to man, but he will find higher uses for his energy in peace than the blind and pitiless self-assertion which at present makes so many of his activities forms of war.

Sick

We have finished the course, and the officers attending it have gone into Amiens for a farewell dinner. I am sorry not to be there; but my "innerds," which have been troublesome since we left the trenches, have collapsed and left me limp: fit only to sit over the fire in this lonely whitewashed room. It may be the effect of drinking too much petrol or—faithless thought—could it be those beans? No. I'm afraid it's the water, for I am told that others, who have no passion for beans, have been similarly affected lately.

I'm curious to see what has happened to the battalion, but otherwise sorry this little school is breaking up. We have been good company and enjoyed it, work and all.

Last night we had a mock court-martial. One of our number got up late and missed the range, so we charged him with "malingering," and formed a court over which the Guardsman presided. It was a good rag. The prisoner was remanded for medical examination at 3 a.m.; but nobody woke early enough to carry it out.

Comfort in Amiens

It is Sunday in Amiens. A lorry brought half a dozen of us in from Pont Noyelles. We are spending the night at hotels here and rejoining our regiments first thing tomorrow. We went to the cathedral this afternoon and, after wandering round, attended part of a service. Let's hope nothing befalls this lovely place. It is heavily sandbagged on the east and southern sides, though the protection looks trivial.

Coming away I met the subaltern who had lost his platoon in the mud about a fortnight ago, and was in such mortal fear of being court-martialled. I was interested to hear what had happened, for he now looked cheerful enough. He explained, rather shamefacedly, that as a matter of fact his men had never left their places: he had merely lost his way and mistaken the trench which he found again next morning.

What extraordinary luxury it is to be waited on in a hotel: to have hot baths and food served on white tablecloths with a sufficiency of cutlery! Best of all is the relief from life by order. To be one's own master, just for an hour or two, is to me relaxation beyond belief. Probably most men do not let the trivial responsibilities of regimental life hang with such absurd weight upon them. To me, just to forget time is a delicious rest.

Tonight Amiens seems all jewellers and restaurants. Many of the other shops are closed, but these seem to be doing great business. From the worst trenches to a French jeweller's is a big stride. Their common multiple, I suppose, is—us.

Now for the enormous ease of a French bed with its invariable box-mattress! French bedmakers should go to England: they could teach our manufacturers of wire racks a lot.

White sheets and a pillow for the first time for ages!

Out of favour

Lord preserve us!—for it is certain no one else will.

After jogging along early this morning in the suburban train from Amiens, I climbed the hill leading to the village of Camps-en-Amienois (about ten miles west of Amiens) where the battalion was said to be in billets. I was still feeling seedy, but pleased at the thought that I had lasted out the course at Pont Noyelles and was still fit enough to keep going. As I hammered along the road I wondered if I should be given charge of the battalion snipers and whether I could persuade the quartermaster to set about getting us telescopic rifles.

I found Rowley in an estaminet with a collection of chits on his table, which he was very busy answering. I thought he looked bleary-eyed and sounded very despondent. He soon explained why.

The battalion, and not only the battalion, but the whole brigade, is in a very bad odour with the divisional command because of what happened, or rather did not happen, in front of Le Transloy. The programme for us there apparently ran something like this: "If fine, capture German trenches: if wet, do intensive work in your own."

Well, it *was* wet, and we did *not* do intensive work. Reason given for this negligence: it was wet.

Personally I see in all this the bitter and disastrous end of failing to acquaint the commanding-officer with the truth about the conditions. But I think I now know the progress of army displeasure.

Corps commander *strafes* divisional commander, divisional-commander *strafes* brigadier, brigadier *strafes* colonel of regiment, colonel *strafes* company commander, captains *strafe* platoon-commanders, and subalterns work it off where and when they can, usually on sergeants and men. It's a game of "Touch-last," or it might be called "Fixing the Responsibility."

The colonel is "going." The brigadier is "going": the colonel to a reduced rank in another of the regiment's battalions: the brigadier home—perhaps to guard the East coast. I should like to be going with the brigadier if half the vials of wrath Rowley predicts are to be emptied. But subalterns do not go home when they belong to regiments that are reputed to have let down their commanding-officers. Their leave is withheld, and they are kept for intensive training, frequent inspections, and permitted to remain on duty all day and a good part of the night, in the hope that by some outstanding exploit in the trenches, next time they go there, they may retrieve the battalion's good name.

So it was for this that we hung on under conditions which no Red Tab will ever know (seeing that not one ever came as far as battalion headquarters), conditions which the colonel himself only surmised, seeing that he never managed (though, to give him his due, I happen to know he tried very hard) to reach the trenches. For this we packed our haversacks with socks, and, more by force of will than by any gift of strength, managed to keep out of hospital, while those who have arrived there are enjoying the comforts of wounded heroes.

Well, well! However much want of forethought there may have been in sending men up to those trenches for practically ten days on end without special precautions against trench-feet, sheer bad luck is the cause of nearly all our troubles. We went into the line just when the weather finally broke down. Those trenches had been getting bad: we happened on them just at the cracking-point; and since provision was not made against that moment, someone must bear the blame.

Fate is grimly ironic in time of war. She speaks through the lips of two-headed Janus, as many a good officer has found to his cost. When we left Hébuterne the battalion was congratulated in divisional orders upon its fine work. We did less than our duty there. Now, after giving all we had, after countless minor heroisms (those stretcher-bearers and cases like Jackson's), after endurance such as I fancy some of us will be physically incapable of repeating, we are—well, to put it succinctly, "in the soup."! The two-headed one looks on us with the sour face. Perhaps with less reason he will turn another face another day. Meantime we must grin and bear it, or just bear it, if the grin sticks. What really gets one's goat is the thought that these men who have "stuck it" should be those marked out for hardships and punishment, while those who "chucked up the sponge" are now safely at home.

Lord preserve us! We shall get through it some day.

And that's that—as the coster said when the apples ran down the sewer.

Ribbons

Needless to say, no recommendations have been forwarded. The brigade being judged to have behaved badly, none will be considered. This is a charity to me; but my logic breaks down before the reasoning which concludes that, because a brigade has been foolishly handled or officers have been negligent, no corporal can have done more than his duty.

Ribbons! Could anything be added to make one more cynical about them? If anything were wanted I have only to recollect how those Australians told me (with what truth I do not know) that when a battalion had done well in the line so many decorations were "dished out," and they decided who should have them by the toss of a coin. I shall never see a man wearing the D.C.M. again without thinking of Jackson and successful brigades, or an M.C. without remembering why Rowley sent my name up.

When I told Jackson this morning I had put his name up, but no recommendations were to be forwarded, he looked bored and unconcerned; rather as if I had betrayed his confidence to fools. I had.

The surprise of the day is that Rowley's leave has gone through, and he starts for England tomorrow. He vows he is not coming back, and I do not expect he will. Poor old Rowley! The war has taken full toll of him. A friendly, generous-natured creature, with the Englishman's finest birthright—a sense of fair play—he can afford a few vices, having that superb quality, and right from the beginning, in spite of everything, there has been friendship between us. If only all the affection of which he was capable had been polarised. . . .

Another surprise is that I am to take over the company. Hardy has always acted as second-in-command, but I hear it is the colonel's wish that I should take over. Rowley says the colonel is very pleased with Hardy and me and only wishes he had more like us. I hate to feel ungenerous, but if we are any good, either we have been hiding our wonderful lights under a bushel, or it has taken the colonel a long while to discover them. In spite of this kindness I am not sorry he is leaving the battalion, and but for the fact that I think Hardy's idea of discipline stupidly mechanical, I would as soon he had the company. It will be a thankless and merely temporary appointment. But the men need more consideration than I shall be able to give them, and for this reason I shall be glad to be in charge. Hardy is a sportsman, and I haven't a doubt that we shall work together perfectly amicably.

THE PITIABLE COMPANY

The whole of the company is billeted in one large house. It is a wretched dilapidated place, full of small rooms. The men are packed in it like sardines. Their clothes and equipment are not yet free from the mud of the trenches, which is unbelievably difficult to remove. A number of them really ought to be in hospital. What they want is a few days' complete rest and change. What they are getting is intensive training. The wind of adversity blows hard.

All officers will attend all parades.

The first parade this morning was at 7.30, and, with the barest intervals for meals, we have been on parade till 7 p.m. Rowley has gone, and Hardy and I curse our luck till we grin. The colonel remains, and this afternoon, "*All officers to the C.O. at 4*" was the preliminary to what will perhaps be his last fulmination. Hardy and I happened to know that we were really exempted from his displeasure, but that made the hearing of it only a little less unpleasant. I do not like his tone. I do not believe the average soldier is the most ungrateful creature in the world. The men are "fed up," and small wonder. Who wouldn't be, on finding himself, after those unspeakable trenches, condemned to ceaseless parades, shut up in this village with no time or scope for any kind of decent recreation or enjoyment? What wonder that they grumble and fill their letters with hopes of leave? It's not discipline, it's change these men need.

If ever I have a company of my own, I know of some essentials to that contentment which is the foundation of all good discipline. A battalion on rest wants a company canteen, a reading- and writing-room with games, inter-platoon and intercompany football matches every free Saturday, musical instruments, a gramophone—anything; and company concerts at least once a week.

Once we get past these eternal inspections—once we get clean and sound again—once we get rid of this colonel, who seems to have a "scunner" on the men, we'll see. Tomorrow evening, at any rate, Hardy and I take the company to a divisional entertainment at Molliens Vidames. It is significant that we do so at our own expense.

COURT-MARTIAL

The battalion is desperately short of officers. It appears that sick officers are kept on the establishment for some time after they have left the regiment, and that there is no such thing as temporary supplies while they are away. At the same time, with idiotic recurrence, orders keep coming to the adjutant to supply officers for the different courses in progress, and though he tears his hair he must find somebody to send. Hardy is the latest requirement. He goes for a Lewis-gun course in a day or two, and that will leave me with the company to myself. In for a penny—in for a pound. What with parades all day and chits from the orderly-room arriving all night, we nearly work the clock round as it is, and we cannot do more. That silver lining hymned in the music-halls at home is about due.

Today I have had a new experience. Only this morning I discovered that one of the men of Hill's platoon was due for a court-martial at Molliens Vidames today. Rowley had offered to speak for the man, and had taken the particulars, but going suddenly on leave, I suppose he had forgotten to hand them on.

I was horrified to find the man was to be on trial for his life, and actually at 8.45 a.m. of the same day nothing had been done to prepare his defence. Moreover things looked very black. He had slipped away when the battalion was leaving Caours, taken off his shoulder-straps and escaped to Paris, where he was arrested ten days later; and that, after having been "crimed" for absence without leave twice previously, made a bad case.

I heard what he had to say: handed the company over to Hardy, and trudged the couple of miles in the rain to Molliens Vidames.

We assembled in the town-hall, which has been temporarily converted into a music-hall for the divisional entertainers. The *pierrot* drapery still adorned the stage where the court sat. In the middle of the stage were the judges, consisting of three senior officers. On the right was our assistant adjutant, prosecuting. In the centre the prisoner between an armed escort, and on the left myself in the capacity of "prisoner's friend." A sergeant of the police as doorkeeper made up the entire assembly. In such surroundings it seemed impossible to believe that this man's life hung in the balance.

The evidence was not disputed, and there were no witnesses for the defence. I put the man on oath and gave him leading questions. I wanted to show that, despite appearances, the man had not deserted, but, after getting drunk, had wandered off like a fool, and then, putting off the day when he would have to face the music, had not troubled to seek out the battalion.

According to his own story he had been a miner in civil life. In this occupation he had always earned plenty of money, and drunken bouts between spells of work had become a habit with him which he could not break. When he had finished his confessions I gave evidence on his behalf, saying I knew he was a brave man who had often volunteered for patrols in the trenches.

The prisoner was marched off. I saluted the presiding officer and made my way back here while the court deliberated. I wonder what the result will be? I do hope he will get off, for the man is sound enough when he is sober; but I fancy the decision will turn on whether he actually missed duty in the trenches or not.

The stark crude simplicity of the whole proceedings continues to amaze me. It helps to bring home the fact that life is cheap today.

THE LOST PAL

I have the melancholy task of writing to the near relatives of the four men in my platoon who were killed. There is no doubt now that Connor, the only Irishman I had, was killed by one of those whiz-bangs that dropped among us while we were standing outside headquarters. One of the three stretcher-bearers, who was only slightly wounded, has returned. He is certain that the shell which badly wounded Spencer killed Connor. I wonder whether it is any comfort to his wife to know that he was killed after working heroically for three days at a job voluntarily undertaken? I miss Connor. He was characteristic of the most lovable race in the world. Every day now his pal Matthison asks me if I've any news of Connor, and when I say no, he shakes his head and adds, "No, sir, I'm sure he's killed. I said so when he didn't come in."

But every day he repeats the question.

December

"*A horse, of course*"

I am coming to the conclusion that the only man in the British Army who is paid "piecework" is the Deviser of Courses in this brigade. I, who have never learnt riding, am just detailed to accompany the transport-officer to Molliens Vidames for a lecture by the A.D.V.S. on "The Care of Horses and Stable Management." Truly one's education is never complete. The care of men must make shift. Enter horses.

There are two: the transport-officer's and that unfortunate beast of the doctor's which recently came within an ace of drowning in the mud. It now looks a bag of bones; but Oliver misinterprets my reluctance to mount by assuring me it is getting better and the exercise will do it good. I explain that I have not been in a saddle since the days when my nurse and the pony-boy led an equally unfortunate-looking animal between two breakwaters on the sands at Worthing. But Oliver is very encouraging and we both hope for the best.

Sickness and confinement seem to have given the doctor's nag an undue affection for his companion's tail. He seems determined to reach it, though I draw the reins to my chest and speak to him ever so kindly. I really must persuade him to walk, for neither he nor I can stand this bumping. Merciful Heavens! I shall break the end of my spine. *Bump, bump, bump!* I swear, I sweat, I shove my knees together till I wonder they don't meet; I ride with a tight rein and then with a slack one; I rise to it, I fall to it, I lean back, I lean forward; I press in the stirrups, I pretend I have none. It is no good. Do what I may, the ears of this dejected bag of bones prick back towards me like railway-signals and his eye becomes a red lamp.

Leaning along his neck, I suggest to Oliver that perhaps we needn't hurry, and Oliver, being a kindly disposed person, walks his magnetic horse, with most comforting results—for about a dozen yards. But good riders do not, I believe, like walking their horses permanently; so Oliver discovers it is getting late and suggests we might push on. Sticking on is my concern, and whether I shall succeed in this feat grows more and more doubtful as a trot breaks into a canter. Shades of John Gilpin! I wish this beast would keep his eyes and ears to the front. And what are we doing now? Galloping, I do believe. Heavens preserve us!

They do. I do not break my neck. I do not even fall off; but full of gratefulness to God and the horse, enter the cobbled streets of the town looking as if I had been boiled in oil.

With as much swagger as possible I dismount and we attend the lecture. What the gentleman is saying I really cannot now consider, for I live in fearful anticipation of things to come. I have just about cooled down when the lecture is over.

Oliver must have heard my prayer during the lecture, for as we come out he asks me whether we shall ride back together or whether I would rather come along on my own. With the air of one preferring a saddle in the Grand National to one in the Derby, I reply that I think perhaps I might as well come along on my own.

Fair and softly now! We shall arrive all in good time. There is no bewitching tail for you to follow, and if we are patient with one another, my poor, dear, kind, terrible bag of bones, we may come to some understanding of each other's limitations before we reach the nose-bag. Look! we are gaining confidence already; and now, as you lightly foot it forward, I declare I should not fear if home were another half-mile out of sight. However, here we are. Let us be content. I am sure we both give thanks at having come to the end of this perilous journey with our lives.

But oh! I wonder, as I get to the ground, what will happen to my legs on parade tomorrow? They are stiff as boards, and semicircular.

THE NEW BRIGADIER

The old brigadier has gone. I have met him two or three times lately, and my hope is that he may live long in the circle of his family, riding to hounds and engaging in those other pursuits for whose performance he was richly endowed by Nature. And may the legend of "the old army" die happy.

Such a fussation last night! Battalion to be inspected by new brigadier today. Every scrap of leather to be taken to bits, every speck of mud removed, every man to be rigged out somehow, gas-bags to be worn just so, every round of ammunition to be taken out and cleaned ready for two parades (one at 7.30 and another at 9) to make sure we are all correct.

Then off to the parade-ground this morning, and, once arrived, breathing hardly allowed to spoil our immobility. General salute, march past, and off we go, having learnt from the general that our motto henceforth will be "Keep Smiling." A little trite, perhaps, but highly seasonable, seeing that we haven't been smiled upon for a goodish time.

Is the victim-hunt coming to an end? Devoutly we hope so; for when the heavens are full of thunder and the gods quarrel the lives of men are precarious.

I hear my "deserter" is not to be shot. He is sentenced to two years' hard labour. No one believes he will do it. "Meritorious conduct" in the trenches might wipe out the whole sentence.

Away to Daours

Another triumph on the part of the Deviser of Courses! A junior subaltern is wanted for a general course at Daours, seven miles east of Amiens. Mallow, the late bombing officer, is at a loose end, there being three other officers to his company; so my company is handed over to him (he being a full lieutenant), and I am detailed for the course. The adjutant explains that he is very satisfied with my work, but simply has no one else available and a place must be found for Mallow. What does it matter that I passed through a senior-officer's course in England nine months ago? This will be a change for me.

I begin to feel like Caesar's dust, except that whereas that immortal clay could stop but one bung-hole, I can fit any. I am very sorry to be relinquishing the company to Mallow, because, although of course he knows the work, and is efficient enough, I dislike the thought of my men being under him.

Apart from that, I am only sorry to be going because it puts leave this year out of sight, and I am fast coming to that stage when the thought of leave becomes an obsession. I still hope to "do my bit in the Great War," and am fully conscious it won't have been done till certain yards of French territory have been regained by efforts wherein I am concerned; but these last few weeks have taken bellyfuls of wind out of my sails. So it seems. Perhaps I should feel differently if I could only get well again.

The colonel goes tonight. Who can be sorry?

I have great satisfaction in the thought that one of my last actions as company-commander is to comply with a request for a "smart N.C.O." for a month's course at Divisional School by sending Jackson. At least he will have a decent billet, good rations and interesting training for a while, and probably receive another stripe when he returns.

I seem to have developed a perfectly fiendish passion for justice. I wonder why?

On dignity of living

In this railway-carriage on the way to Amiens there are a number of French civilians, middleclass people, probably on their way to business. They please me intensely, especially the women.

The woman in the corner might be anything—a typist, an aristocrat, a mother; perhaps she is all three. It has taken generations of culture to produce the dignity of living, the pride of personality and the perfect *savoir faire* she shows. She is beautifully but inexpensively dressed in black, her features are small and refined, and her voice has musical variety, betokening vivacity that is thoroughly enjoyed and at the same time under control. Though I hardly understand a word of her conversation, I should be delighted to listen to her and watch her dignified movements for the rest of the day. Dignity: that is the quality possessed by nearly all these people, and above all others I esteem it. It can only come to those who know the art of living and who, in learning that art, have suffered deeply. Now I reflect that only those who have the sensitiveness common to these people are capable of deep suffering. The boorishness of army life makes one susceptible to this charm, and I am pleased to think that a refined Frenchwoman is possessed of sufficient telepathy to be conscious of my admiration and of sufficient pride to enjoy it.

Treasure in a sack

The school is at a large house standing in its own grounds, about ten minutes' walk from Daours station. The rooms are now bare and rather dilapidated, but the wallpaper and the mirrors suffice to show there has been good living here. I share a small bedroom with three other subalterns. There is not room to swing a cat; but then "room" is a comparative term, as we learn out here, and the rough canvas beds are quite adequate.

Castlereagh having fallen sick, I have been obliged to find another servant. This one, Cox, is a man of forty-three: he has a large family in England, so I thought practice might have enabled him to help me take care of myself. And his heart is good, if his head is never on very active service.

Now, in this small bedroom, he kneels unpacking my valise. Not all my tackle is in it. The tendency of letters and rubbish to accumulate has crowded three pairs of boots into that sack, which I gave into his keeping when he got into the train at Amiens. I can't quite understand it, because the sack felt very light when I carried it upstairs just now. However, Cox assures me it's all right. He cuts the string and fishes for the boots. Slowly his hand emerges, producing—a large Spanish onion!

We shout with laughter; but though this is a rich joke, it is also a serious matter, as any soldier with three pairs of broken-in marching-boots to his name well knows. Cox goes haring off to the railway-station, but I am afraid he will not secure the boots. I remember a Breton peasant sat opposite him in the carriage, and unless that peasant has very large feet, or is super-honest, I think he will appreciate the exchange. His uncooked onions are not much good to me. Not a subaltern, not even an orderly, will buy them. I can't even change them for a gross of green spectacles.

JERKS AND DRINKS

There are about five-and-twenty officers at this school, and a similar number of N.C.O.s. The course lasts three weeks. I haven't the energy to pump up enthusiasm over the work, but we are a merry band and, perhaps because we are free from regimental responsibilities, there is more good humour about than is common, at any rate to my battalion. Without a wholesome tendency to rag on any pretext, we should be having a deadly-dull time since there is nothing essentially entertaining about getting up before it is light, having a scrambled breakfast and doing physical jerks on the frozen lawn outside, especially if you feel rheumaticky.

Similarly, drill, 9-10: bayonet-fighting, 10.15-11.15: lecture on pay and mess book, 11.30-12.30: and a similar air with variations from 2 till 6.30, really isn't exciting when you have many times repeated these stages of instruction since you entered upon them two years ago. But here, for the first time in France, I am meeting men on whom a literary allusion is not lost, and men who can take a rise out of a sergeant-instructor without impairing his authority or spoiling good feeling.

In the evenings we are woefully at a loss for amusement, being restricted to a piano in the common-room and a French billiard-table in the small room adjoining. Almost the only practicable method of showing sociability is to order drinks and get up to some variety of horseplay. We do both increasingly as we get to know one another and the common stock of goodwill grows, so that our evenings tend rather in the direction of drunken carousals. When throats become hoarse with roaring out songs, and a man of "Pongo's" elephantine weight begins dancing, we are lucky if we get to bed before a couple of chairs are broken and anybody needs assistance up the winding stairs.

The Staff-Captain's Lecture

At the Town-hall we attend a lecture by a divisional staff-captain in a room which is used in the daytime as a school. The staff-captain is a tall fair man of aristocratic bearing, keen eyes and a genial manner. He is talking about the necessity for keeping the initiative, and pointing out the many ways in which troops holding the line may show themselves masters of the situation, even though the time for an advance over the German lines be delayed till the Spring. Our one object should be to prevent the enemy from ever feeling comfortable, and to this end we should keep patrols going and raid the enemy trenches whenever there is a chance. *Morale* is the great factor, and by keeping the initiative we shall help to destroy the German *morale* and so make the work of advance ten times easier than it would be if, through slackness, we allowed the other side to feel themselves "top-dog."

He is tremendously keen, not in the least omniscient, and adding to his keenness humour, and being himself obviously fearless, his words catch on. One sees the force of his argument, and the incitement to hold the advantage only seems like the encouragement of a good trainer who wants rugger forwards to use all their weight in the scrum and is able to show them how to do it.

It is not until the lecture is over that one reflects on his advice in terms of actuality. Then one sees a raid as a foul, mean, bloody, murderous orgy which no human being who retains a grain of moral sense can take part in without the atrophy of every human instinct.

I've a desire to go back and tell this gallant gentleman that unless he can infuse into my blood hatred such as I seem psychologically incapable of feeling towards an unknown enemy, much as I should like to be able to help keep the initiative, and quite ready as I am to sacrifice my life for this end, I honestly don't see how it's to be done.

A Man of Quality

I have been getting to know one of the fellows who shares my room, and now I realise that it is his society that is making this course the pleasantest event I have experienced out here. Superficially he is a very odd mixture. He has been a divinity student, but before the war he had discarded the idea of going into the Church. The experience has left him with a deep reflective streak which lies under the most turbulent high spirits. Dales is the centre of every rag, and he rags with wild zest and absolutely imperturbable good temper; yet ten minutes after pitching himself against impossible odds and being utterly scragged and flattened out, he will lie on his bed ready to talk about classical and modern poetry or the relationship of politics to religion.

He has a laugh. It is uproariously loud, sometimes almost hysterical; but if it were only for his laugh I should choose his company. When he is not amused, his long face is the most serious at the table, and he slips from solemnity to his uproarious mirth at a step. Beer he espouses, quoting Calverley and Belloc in support of his taste, and he assures me there is a mixer of cocktails in Amiens who almost makes the war worth while.

Underneath this boisterous exterior there is one of the gentlest souls I have ever met. He has real feeling for poetry, and the other day confessed to the constant attempt to write it. He will show me nothing of his own, but the other night he wrote out this, which he says he read in the *Saturday Westminster Gazette*:

> *I was a sailor sailing on sweet seas,*
> *Trading in singing birds and humming bees,*
> *But now I sail no more before the breeze.*
>
> *You were a pirate, met me on the sea;*
> *You came with power behind you, suddenly:*
> *You stepped on to my ship and spoke to me,*
> *And while you took my hand and kissed my lips*
> *You sank my ships! You sank my sailing ships!*

He wrote from memory and I copy what he wrote. I believe the little poem epitomises his feeling about the war.

"*Leaping upon the spears*" is one of his favourite phrases, and he quotes it in connection with the advice about "*maintaining the initiative.*" Certainly I would prefer that exercise in his company to it in any other out here. The man has innate nobility. I learnt slowly how he came to be at the school; for that he should be is surprising, as he has already seen several months' active service in the trenches as a subaltern.

He was wounded in the foot early on July 1st, and, going home, enjoyed himself in hospital and on leave as only Dales could. But some vile pang of conscience made him feel he was too happy for the times; so although he was marked for "home service" he told the doctor he felt fit enough to come out again. His wound has not yet healed and occasionally troubles him, but he makes very light of it. The adjutant of his regiment sent him on to the school really to give the wound a chance to heal.

THE CANKER OF WAR

Dales and I, together with two or three others, have come into Amiens for the weekend, as is the cheering custom of the school. Any vehicle out here serves to give a man a lift, and we all boarded an empty French ambulance which brought us in. We have booked our rooms at the hotel and had a bath, wandered round the town, lined up in a long queue for a hair-cut, and now sit in a large well-lit restaurant having dinner.

There must be a hundred and fifty officers dining here, fellows from every imaginable regiment, and we are all doing ourselves very well. Oysters, salmon mayonnaise, chicken, wine, and again wine and liqueurs; we neither stint ourselves nor are stinted. And of all people in the world just now I suppose we are best able to enjoy a good dinner. It will cost forty *francs*, but money has lost its value, and what man with a good appetite would not have an expensive dinner if he knew it might be his last? Let us eat, drink and be merry, for in a few days we go up the line.

The imminence of fate begets a happy-go-lucky attitude to life that must breed strange consequences if ever the war is over. The lives of this company are cheap; and men must wrest some compensation from the prospect of short life. No doubt most of these young fellows have come from sober, English, middle-class homes, but war has come to give them one crowded hour of inglorious life and then an age without a name.

The most feverish among us appear to be in the Royal Flying Corps. Members of the "Suicide Club" have more opportunities for this kind of thing than most of us, and they seem to be making the best of it. The American Bar was full of them, and here they are, dining as lavishly as the rest of us, though after a day over the enemy lines tomorrow they will again be free to repeat the gaiety, if they are not killed.

The war has cheapened life till it is of little or no value. Life, no doubt, is sweet to all, but no one will persuade me half of these fellows have any real sense of its value. It has become a mere plaything, "merry and bright" while you can keep it, a burst squib if you can't. There is no need to sentimentalise over it and fancy yours is of more value than that of the last man who lost his. Fate plays pitch-and-toss with us: the lighter the coin the more it rings. There's nothing serious left, and if there were, what has it to do with us, except in so far as we retain the regard of men and women as being "the thing"? If this war is a drama, well, let it be musical comedy. "Up we go and the best of luck."

Religion, philosophy, the arts: what have they to do with us? Words, words. Are you a good sportsman? That is our test; and a good sportsman rates his life at the value of thistledown, and the lives of the enemy at the price of rats' tails. Cheerio! Let's have another drink. Moreover there are women in Amiens.

So it all appears.

Angle of vision

We are nearing the end of this course. Today the corps-commander came and gave us a lecture on Self-help. He is a man of great reputation, having won fame at Ypres in 1914, and we were duly impressed to see him in the flesh walking and talking like any ordinary mortal. There were no signs of amazing intellect, but all the characteristics of a well-bred English gentleman—self-confidence, friendliness, honesty and power of resistance.

He made no attempt to disguise his obvious enjoyment of the war, and, for my part, I should have despised him if he had. It stands to reason that anyone in his position, so long as he is not overwhelmed by his responsibility, must be having the time of his life. For the higher command the war is the great adventure. Into it they can and do put tremendous zeal and endless thought. At the same time they have all the excitement of a bigger game than any other. They are working a great business, fascinating to manage, with prizes of enormous kudos for success. Defeat would be the certain portion of armies commanded by men who did not enjoy their job.

Our lecturer was full of sympathy with the man in the trenches and of appreciation for his miseries. He was dead keen that not a single Tommy should have a worse time than is unavoidable, and suggested a variety of useful ways in which we could mitigate the evils of our lot. But alas, when he came to our greatest evil—mud—he made a real *faux pas*, which shows how distance lends enchantment. To get rid of the mud he suggested we should use biscuit-tins. I am sorry I could not get up and move as an amendment that we should use toothpicks. They would be as serviceable.

The Christmas Party

It is Christmas Day. We have spent the morning in bed and the afternoon in slippered idleness round the fire. Now we are gathered round the festive board. Other than wine we have no guests; so we make the best of wine: the toasts are many and the whiskies double. Rider, a dark-eyed, genial soul, sits on my right, and the fiery red-haired Dales on my left. There's a fierce pang as we drink to Absent Friends, but even that gives way to merriment. 'Tis mine to propose the commandant's health, and who'd have believed I could have found so easily-wagging a tongue? There are many bottles on the table. I arrange them in a row to illustrate how a great tactician like our host will use his men. The moves are met with cheers, and with a fluency I have never found before, the speech goes on. I see their laughing faces . . .

> *Peer through the smoke, the laughter and the wine,*
> *Twelve months beyond, and where are these that met*
> *In cordial friendship, singing Auld Lang Syne,*
> *Pledging each other never to forget?*
> *Ghosts! Ghosts! they flit about the vacant rooms*
> *Where Memory wanders, like an ancient crone,*
> *Telling the beads of many different dooms*
> *In dreary wastes within Death's hungry zone.*
> *The best are dead; and we, who were the rest,*
> *Walk a strange world that is without the best.*

New Year's Eve at Corbie

It is New Year's Eve, and we are at Corbie, on the way back to our battalions. Dales and I stroll out to the church of this low-lying town that stands at the meeting of the Somme and the Ancre. In the moonlight we see the big square tower, rising above flat, marshy ground, and it brings to mind the associations of peace and stability, of solid life and spiritual aspiration. Looking in, we see they are preparing for a midnight service. How gladly we would wait and spend the night in here! But not this year. We have appointments with Fate to keep and must be some miles nearer the place of his choice before the bells begin to ring. We hurry back to catch the train.

Rail-head has been moved forward since last I was in these parts, and shortly before midnight the wheezy engine drags us noisily up the hill to Carnoy. The flashes in the sky and the everlasting boom of guns tell us the war is also seeing another New Year in. Of how many more will it take toll?

We call at a signaller's cabin to ask which huts our regiments occupy, and there, with strangers, drink to the coming year while the clock strikes twelve. Another minute and we have all dispersed in the darkness and mud.

January 1917

THE NEW BROOM

The battalion has just come out of the trenches where they have been for two days. Times have changed since our debacle at Lesboeufs in November. Two days in, two days out, back for two days and then out for a week, is now the order of the times—times which have begotten not only short spells in the trenches, but the most rigorous care and preparation before going up to prevent trench-feet, including the general issue of rubber boots which are given to the men at Ginchy and returned there when they come out of the line.

Not only the times have altered. The battalion seems hardly recognisable with its new colonel, new officers and fresh drafts. Hardy is full of the spirit of the new broom, and all that was gets contrasted very disparagingly with all that now is. Hardy was never anywhere near the front line at Lesboeufs, so perhaps he has some excuse for minimising the iniquities of that place and speaking slightingly of his old captain.

But Mallow, who "went sick" after two days of that experience, has less excuse, and betrays himself for what he is by never losing an opportunity of reviling the man who came nearest to being his sworn companion (at any rate over the bottle) while he was still here. I do not like men who only grow great by the infirmities of others. But I can forgive Hardy because he is young and keen, and something of the chameleon is natural to young things.

I see that I have missed the tide by being away from the regiment when the new colonel arrived. Whether I belong automatically to the bad old order or not, I don't know; but in the spring-cleaning, the old and new furniture found its place a fortnight ago, and when they celebrated the occasion I think they omitted the toast of Absent Friends. No matter. The trenches are fine places for testing bubble reputations, and I for one am prepared to accept their judgment.

The colonel appears to be an excellent fellow. A professional man in civil life, he started in the army as a subaltern, and now wears the D.S.O. If his manner is conceited, that is a minor weakness. He is keen and takes an intelligent interest in the battalion. He has instituted weekly roundtable talks with officers at which the old indiscriminate cursing is omitted. He has wit and good humour, and at present is the object of much hero-worship.

I shall catch the tide when it turns again. Meantime humble-pie has its merits. It is unenvied.

Uncongenial society

Hardy has gone on a month's course to Paris. For the first time I am so companionless I wish myself in any other battalion. Just now the hut contains two of the new officers posted to D Company. They are loud, swaggering, insensitive hulks, very proud of their belts after their apprenticeship as commercial travellers. Preferring the company of gentlefolk, I should be happier living with the men.

I met Dales today and went over to his mess. It was a delicious relief. "An officer and a gentleman." It's a matter of character. Without character there can be neither. Men of mean spirit, bearable at other times, become unbearable in the trenches; for in the trenches, want of spirit stinks.

I also ran across "Pongo." He flattered me with the very cream of flattery by begging me to come to dinner at his mess because he wanted me to make an after-dinner speech. I had the greatest difficulty in declining; but success that is due to the length of the bottle might be dismal failure if repeated.

Tonight I go up the duck-boards with a 'fatigue-party carrying barbed wire. Last night I had the whole company out, loading up empty shell-cases on the railway-line over the hill.

Never has the desire for leave been such an obsession. I am almost due for it. Another fortnight and it should come at last.

The Medici prints

My dear in England has sent me half a dozen small Medici prints, and I cannot describe the joy they are to me in this stricken waste. "Beauty is truth—truth, beauty." Here the soul feeds. Here is life's purpose—the creation of beauty. Rubens' babies will never be too fat again: they express the wealth of physical life. Botticelli's women I shall never quarrel with again: they are incarnations of spiritual loveliness. And this girl playing the 'cello to her companion's accompaniment on the harpsichord, what breathing melody the silent picture speaks! Here is the soul of harmony.

Art lives by all that war destroys. Art celebrates or prophesies the perfection of life. War shatters its very fabric and breeds this desolation that now surrounds me to the horizon with a blasting ugliness that has made what is our haven for the moment a hideous corrugated-iron Armstrong hut.

Dignity and impudence

This afternoon we marched to Guillemont, where we are spending the night (those who are not "on fatigue") in shelters that are half dugouts. Shells dropped in Trônes Wood as we came by, but otherwise the march was uneventful.

At dusk on the road outside I saw an incident that gave me a certain malicious pleasure. Major Smythe was coming along with his orderly. A very tired-looking Australian, returning from the line, passed them on the road. He failed to salute. He was a small, tired man; I doubt if he even saw more than the boots of our tall major. The major called to him, but the man merely looked round and walked on.

Whereupon the orderly was sent with a message. He returned, and the irate major stood looking furiously after the delinquent, who turned once more, this time merely to extend his fingers to his nose after the vulgar manner. There was not a military policeman in sight, so the incident closed pleasantly. A most ill-disciplined gesture: still, vulgarity has its uses.

Lying in a rough bunk, I've been reading Conrad's *Victory*. The coming and going all round, and the tremor made by a big gun that has its emplacement very near, made it difficult to get into the book, but I hung on, determined to see if an imaginative experience wasn't possible out here. Although I succeeded, I was disappointed. It's not a real romance but only a pumped-up literary effort: effective, strained, and finally, of course, melodramatic. No doubt it would pass muster in a drawing-room: here it seems a thin, "drawn," hot-house plant; the laboured psychology is merely poverty-stricken analytics.

Literary veneer does not change the nature of the shilling shocker.

In a Flers dugout

As a battalion we tramped the old duck-boards again yesterday afternoon, and now we've two companies in the front line (this time to the right of Lesboeufs) and one in the second, where there is a big new dugout. C Company is back in reserve, doing fatigues at night, salving during the daytime and occupying a large dugout, with officers at one end and men at the other, at a spot near Flers called Bull Dump.

Outside it is snowing gently. There is wrath and recrimination within; for, after carrying a rum-jar right up here, somebody set it down on a stone and the earth has drunk most of the rum. I think the men would forget the tragedy, only the strong odour pervades the place and they are not philosophic enough to be content with smell instead of taste.

Now they have begun to talk about the *Kaiser's* peace proposals. It is pathetic to hear their comments. I wonder how much of their present desire for peace is due to want of rum.

Dull work

The cold turned to rain, and after two days of duck-board tramping, carrying wire, stakes, rations, bombs and duck-boards up to the front line, we came out in the rain and just had time to get clean and look round the town of hutments that is now Carnoy, before we were ready to go back to the line.

Last night I had to take a party up and now we're going up again. I am tired: physically and mentally tired. Leave deferred maketh the heart sick. I am sick of the energy of those belching guns firing over our heads as we tramp the never-ending duck-boards. I am utterly tired of the mechanical routine of this existence.

We are for the front line. Mallow is in command and I am the only other officer.

Shell-hole trenches

There are no regular trenches here: what we hold is really a rough line of converted shell-holes. Last night I explored the place, stodging through the mud from one post to the next. I ran into the colonel, armed with a pole, ploughing his way along. He was willing to talk of leave and very nice about it, saying I should get my chance all right in a few days.

Mallow has a small dugout here, which he occupied yesterday evening; but during the night he withdrew the right half-company and himself to the second-line dugout (we can only move here under cover of dark), for there is to be a bombardment this morning of a German sap that has been advanced towards our line on the right. I am in charge of the left half-company till Mallow comes back tonight.

The end of the journey

Noon. The "show" has begun. Our artillery is making rare good shooting. Boards go up in the air and there's a regular strafe on our right. But the usual retaliation has also begun, and heavy shells are beginning to drop about. We have a tiny corrugated-iron shelter here, made for the signallers. There are two of them and three other men beside myself in the shelter. I think we had better move out of this. *Crack!* Hullo! What's that? Looking up we see a hole in the iron just over the place where I had been sitting. Something must have come through there. Going back I find a hole in the clay seat on which I had been sitting ten seconds before, and putting my arm a foot into the wet clay draw out the great jagged rim of a shell. It is still warm.

"Get out of this, you fellows, and spread yourselves down the trench.—That's it!—Get some distance between you. Look there, Burt, you've water-boots on. You can go through the water down to . . ."

★★★★★

What's happened? I am lying on a duck-board looking up at the sky. Dusk is falling. There's a young lance-corporal looking down at me as if I were a curiosity. I ask him what has happened.

"You bin knocked out," he replies smiling. "We thought you was dead."

Something has happened, but I can't remember what. There's been a great nothingness, and I cannot remember what happened before it. I seem to have been dead, and death apparently is nothingness. Why can't that fool stop grinning and tell me just what's happened?

He says I've got the company. I don't know what the devil he means. I never had a company in the line. Oh! I know. This is Hébuterne. 'Fall': 'Fame': 'Fate.'

"Where's Mr. Hill?"

The boy grins.

"Gone back home long since."

"Where's Mr. Smalley?"

He grins again.

"Gone back to Blighty, sir. He went weeks ago."

This is maddening. I tell him to go to blazes and find somebody who can tell me what has happened.

My head is like a furnace: yet it feels as if it were made of jelly, and hullo! my ears are bleeding. Gradually I begin to remember.

I get up and find there are three wounded men here. They say a shell came over and dropped right in the parapet in front of me, wounding those in either side and flattening me out against the back of the trench. There's a great hole just over there, so I suppose that's what happened. The shelter has clean gone.

Darkness begins to come on. The wounded men go back; luckily they can all walk. I am all right now, except that I can't keep awake. What I wonder is, whether the colonel will let me have leave right away, as soon as we come out.

Mallow returns, and I tell him I shall be all right after I have had a sleep. I follow him back to his dugout, slowly because something's happened to my right leg and I am frightfully stiff. He gives me a drink of cocoa and I fall asleep.

Now he wants me to go back to the dugout in the second line. Why should I? I only want a good sleep. No, I will sleep. He wakes me again, saying I'd better see the doctor. Reluctantly I try to get out of the dugout; but it's dark outside and I can't see the way. I come back and, telling him I'll go when the moon gets up, fall asleep again. Again he wakes me and this time I go in company with a runner. Jog, jog, jog. My head aches; but I should have been quite all right. I could have waited till tomorrow.

Here's the second-line dugout. I crawl down the steps, and some ministering angel gives me another drink. Now I can go to sleep.

No. The colonel passes overhead and sends down word to me to go back to the doctor.

Trudge, trudge, trudge: every step is one less to be taken. And here at last is the old dugout. The doctor's asleep. Then let him sleep; only give me somewhere to lie down. The M.O.'s orderly comes worrying. The doctor wants to see me now. I pick myself up again. He plasters up my ears and then tells me I had better go to the dressing-station. They will probably put me into hospital to rest for a few days.

Rest? I want no rest in hospital. I want to go home on leave. Damn it! They can't cut out my leave for hospital.

The medical-officer at the dressing-station wants to know what has happened. I tell him all I know and then beg him to let me have just a week's home-leave. He is very sympathetic, but says he can only send me on to the base hospital at Bray.

Now in an ambulance, rattling along. This is comparative comfort. Now a large marquee with beds, and there's a nurse. She tells me to get into that one. God! The comfort and ease! I sleep at last for twenty-four hours straight off.

ROUEN

I am in bed at Rouen No. 4 General Hospital feeling rather a fraud, for I've every limb intact and only a dull headache and a thick ear. I slept for two days at Bray. Then I was so stiff they carted me out and brought me here on a stretcher. There's a colonel of the Gordon's opposite. He is sick. We are a mixed crowd of sick and wounded.

The doctor comes round and I tell him all I know.

"People who lose their memories go home," he replies, as if he were uttering a threat. Home! My God! I am going home!

Le Havre

We are on the ambulance-train travelling to le Havre. A whole week I have been at Rouen eating my heart out for this hour. Now the train crawls on, stopping continually. We shall get there if we've patience.

Yes. This is le Havre. It is nearing midnight. We have just missed a boat. That is the *Glenesk Castle*, and we are now going on board. Down below, everybody! Here are cots, packed tight together so that there is only just room for the nurse to move between them. I can get into my own cot without help, thanks very much. That dark fellow, looking so ill, is a German officer.

I am asleep before the boat moves.

The cliffs

Breakfast in the saloon—a very nice breakfast, beautifully served. We are well on the way. Now up on deck. The sea is like a mill-pond. It is cold and there is no sun. Some officers are playing cards in that little cabin. I watch them like a ghost, and then turn away to come out on deck again.

There, through the grey mists, I see the cliffs. My whole body trembles.

I wonder where the battalion is. It is going to snow. I believe they are going to Sailly-Saillisel. I wonder if Jackson has been made a sergeant.

The Adventures of an Ensign

Contents

The Adventures 139

To
My Wife.

The Adventures

Chapter 1

Fair sets the wind for France!"

This story, like so many others in England's military history, opens at Waterloo Station. We shall abridge the formalities of introducing its central figure, for he can only claim attention in connection with certain military events in which he played a diminutive role. Indeed, save for the fact that he is wearing the service uniform of one of the Guards' regiments, there is nothing to distinguish him from the thousands of other second lieutenants, insignificant even as he, whose share in shaping the destinies of the world on the battlefields of France and Belgium has likewise begun at one or other of the great London termini.

Here, then, is our Ensign—a colloquial phrase for referring to a second lieutenant of the Guards, for the title was dropped many years ago—in company with a brother ensign, his fellow traveller, known to the ante-room at home as "The Lad," and, like the other, for the first time "proceeding on active service." They are going out alone—that is to say, not as part of a draft—and beyond the known fact that they are bound for the Guards' Base Depot in France, what military writers call "the fog of war" envelops their future.

"Thank goodness, we're not conducting a draft!"

Thus our Ensign, as he stood on the platform at Waterloo, to his fellow-traveller, indicating with a jerk of his head a flushed and heated youth, heavily laden with pack and equipment, who was chivvying a party of men to the train.

"Probably we should get up to the Front quicker if we were!" replied his companion gloomily. Waking and sleeping, The Lad was haunted by the fear that the war would be over before he could get into the firing line.

"We shall get there quick enough, don't you worry!" replied the other; "there's something happening in France. I was at Broadstairs yesterday, and we heard the guns all day!"

For this was in those summer days of 1916, when even in Kent the air throbbed to the unending tremulo of the guns playing the overture to the Battle of the Somme.

It was a beautiful morning—a Saturday—and the train was very crowded. The two officers started their journey under the most favourable auspices. On returning to their compartment of the train, after purchasing papers at the bookstall, our Ensign found a bearded cleric seated upon his Wolseley valise on the floor of the carriage, for every seat was taken. The Lad and our young friend made room for the ecclesiastic upon the seat between them, and in the conversation which ensued The Lad identified the stranger as a bishop travelling down to Winchester to see a school cricket match.

"In this heat," said The Lad to our Ensign, after taking leave of the bishop at Winchester, "he must have mentally blessed us for coming to his rescue, so I think we've made a pretty good start!"

At the port of embarkation, which the censor will hardly let me name, a timely hint recurred to them as they drove down to the docks in an ancient fly. The advice had been offered by a veteran of Mons and Ypres.

"Don't go on board the transport too early," this authority had said, "or the M.L.O. or one of those fellows will rope you in for the job of O.C. troops going across. They generally pick on somebody who is not conducting a draft!" So the two young officers, having ascertained that the transport would not sail till the late afternoon, dumped their kits on the quayside and fled back to the town for lunch. Cold beef and pickles and very stale bread and tired butter laid out on a stained tablecloth, in a depressing atmosphere of faded victuals, amid red wallpaper, whisky advertisements, and dyed grasses—truly we English love to soften the pangs of parting from our native shores! Nevertheless the travelling companions made an excellent luncheon, and even professed to recognise feminine allurements in the dingy slattern who served them.

The transport which was to take them to France was not a prison hulk such as bore young Colonel Wesley to his first taste of active service on the West Indies expedition, nor was she verminous like the coffin ships that conveyed the Guards to Malta in '54; but when it is noted that she was clean, nothing remains to be said. There were a few bunks for officers below; but these were appropriated by the early comers. Everybody else, officers and men, sprawled about on the decks and in the bare open spaces made by clearing out the first and second class saloons—for, in her youth, the transport had been a passenger steamer. The ship was very crowded. On board were big drafts of the King's Royal Rifles, with their black cross badges, of London Territorials, and of Irish Rifles and Irish Fusiliers, a fine rowdy lot of Irishmen these two last, as well as some yeomanry and various oddments coming back from leave.

Our Ensign, who possessed to some extent the faculty of observation, noticed that the leave men did not seem to return to the prospect before them with that blitheness of heart of which the lady war writers tell us. On the other hand, the men were by no means gloomy. They just sat about on their packs and smoked their fags and chatted about the good time they had had in Blighty, and cracked a little joke or two about the life to which they were going back.

Our two young Guardsmen walked the upper deck until the transport was well out in the open sea. Then the prostration became so general that progress was a sort of egg-dance. So they turned their steps towards the stairs leading to the lower deck, where they ran into a grenadier subaltern. They stopped and chatted. He was going back from leave. They told him they were going to the base.

"Do you think they'll keep us there long?" asked The Lad hastily.

"Can't say," answered the other; "things are pretty quiet up Ypres way."

Then they talked about the amenities of life in the Salient, and about mutual acquaintances out in France with the Guards' Division and in the brigade at home.

"I believe there's some kind of restaurant place on board for officers," suddenly remarked the grenadier; "suppose we go and have something to eat!"

They found a tiny place, literally crammed to the narrow door with officers, packed as tight as herrings in a barrel, round several small tables, the napery of which showed signs of the tossing of the vessel and the rough-and-scramble of the accommodation. Fortunately someone there espied a submarine through the port-hole, and in the ensuing rush for the deck the three officers managed to wedge themselves in at a table. Here, in the course of time, they received successively from the hands of the perspiring stewards a piece of cold beef, a sardine in a saucer, a loaf of bread, considerably damaged, a knife, a spoon, a teapot full of very hot and very strong tea, and a plate. With these ingredients they contrived to make a very fair supper on the co-operative system.

After that the trio parted company, and our Ensign and The Lad, after much scrambling over prostrate forms, found an empty boat into which they clambered, and slept comfortably till daylight.

Our Ensign awoke to find The Lad shaking him. The rising sun was daubing the wide stretch of sky with a grand splash of colour. The transport was lying alongside a quay where lines of khaki figures were forming up on the greasy planking among cranes, gangways, and stacks of packing-cases.

"Listen!" said The Lad in a reverent voice.

But our Ensign had already heard it—that steady throb of distant cannon, an incessant pounding, as it seemed, upon the roof of the sky.

The guns of the Somme!

An officer, the snout of a megaphone to his face, was bawling orders.

"All leave men to come ashore at once. The remainder stay on board!" he boomed from the quayside.

"H—l!" exclaimed The Lad in a tone which suggested that peace might be declared before they could disembark.

"H—l!" echoed his companion.

Then they went and searched the vessel for breakfast. A Coldstream sergeant, whom The Lad had met on a bombing course somewhere at home, meeting them, volunteered the information that hot cocoa was going in the cook's galley. There, sure enough, our heroes found two grimy-looking privates in their shirt sleeves presiding over dixies of some dark and scalding liquid. The procedure was simple. You grabbed a mug from somebody who had finished—officers and men were all mixed up together in that little place—and had as many dips as you could contrive in the scrum. Hot cocoa in the chilly dawn is nectar.

Soon after the travelling companions landed, and a very friendly M.L.O. abbreviated formalities for them and indicated an hotel where breakfast and a bath might be obtained before they went on to the Guards' Base Depot, the intermediate stage on their journey towards the Front.

The air still vibrated to the throb of distant gun fire. The whole town was throbbing in sympathy. The morning *communiqué* was full of the story of the British successes on the Somme, with a long tale of prisoners and guns captured. People stood about the docks and at street corners in the bright sunshine discussing the great news. At the barber's where they were shaved, at the hotel where they bathed and breakfasted, the newcomers heard little else save enthusiastic comments on the British advance.

Later in the day our Ensign and The Lad found themselves staring wide-eyed at a broad stretch of hillside, covered, as far as the eye could see, with a vast and mighty camp—a sea of tents and huts and sheds all astir with life.

Here, presently, they reported at an office in company with a throng of officers from every arm of the service, and were directed to proceed to the portion of the camp set apart for the Guards' Division. A long, well-kept road, fringed on either side with tents and huts of all descriptions, led them through a series of camps, past orderly-rooms and guard-rooms and cinema sheds and Y.M.C.A. huts and church tents, with little gardens and regimental crests worked in white and black stones, to a low slope, dotted with huts and sheds and bell-tents in orderly rows, with a well known flag floating from a flagstaff on the roof of a long low building.

A white star on a red and blue ground—it was the brigade flag.

Chapter 2

And look . . . a thousand Blossoms with the Day
Woke . . . and a thousand scattered into clay.—Omar Khayyam.

Within the confines of that camp within a camp, the young officers found themselves at once at home.

In the long pavilion over which floated the Brigade flag, our Ensign and The Lad found the Officers' Mess—a long dining-room and an anteroom, with bright curtains and basket-chairs, and a bridge-table or two, and the latest papers—rather like a golf pavilion. On the white distemper of the wall some one with an artist's hand had executed a few hasty sketches of the Guards in their uniforms of peace time—an officer in overalls, a private in white fatigue jacket.

In the mess the newcomers found assembled officers from every regiment in the brigade—youngsters who had just come out from home, veterans returning to the Front for the second or third time, officers passed for light duty acting as instructors at the great training ground where drafts of all arms waiting at the depot underwent a further period of training before being sent up to the firing line. Here our Ensign was joyously hailed by officers of his own regiment, who gave him the latest news from the Front. Here, too, he experienced that first unforgettable shock—he learnt of the death of a brother officer, one who had been his friend, killed in the trenches that very morning.

Along one corner of the little "square," white bell-tents were pitched in neat array. In these were quartered men from every regiment in the brigade of Guards, waiting their turn to be drafted into the firing line. The long stretch of canvas on the hillside, surrounded on every side by similar lines of tents stretching far away into the distance, reminded our Ensign of an old photograph he had seen somewhere of the Guards' camp at Scutari in '54, then, as now, hemmed in all round by the camps of other brigades.

The camp was the picture of neatness. The well-metalled road traversing it was kept scrupulously clean. The officers were quartered in a little colony of square Armstrong huts, with canvas sides and timber flooring, set up in mathematically precise rows across from the Mess at the foot of a delightful little garden, laid out behind rustic fencing enclosing a Badminton court. The officers' huts were gay with coloured prints cut out of *La Vie Parisienne* and *The Sketch*, the little gardens bright with flowers, the natty paths carefully swept. In short, the whole place was the perfection of order.

Life at the Guards' Depot in France differed from life with the Guards at home to this extent, that, instead of having their drills on the "square," the men were marched up daily to the common training-ground, situated on a plateau overlooking the camp. Each day one or two officers per regiment were detailed for the uncongenial duty of marching the men of their regiment up the dusty winding hill to the training ground, one of the pipers of the Scots Guards at their head. The other officers, save the piquet (or orderly) officer who had his round of duties at the camp to attend to, took a short cut to the ground, involving a brief but precipitous climb up a steep hillside.

Our Ensign still carries in his memory a picture of the training-ground as he saw it on that first hot morning. It was a spectacle so overwhelming that it drove from his mind for the moment all the impressions he had been absorbing during his months of training with the Guards. As he gazed at the vast panorama of the plateau, he felt his heart throb in answer to the patriotic appeal of that picture of Britain in arms. For, from all sides and by every road, he saw dense columns of men converging on a great central parade-ground. With brass band, with drums and fifes, or with pipes and drums at their head, the thick brown columns poured in by every approach, the men in full marching order, their rifles slung, the sweat trickling down their sunburnt faces from their climb up the steep ascent. Cockneys, men of Kent, men of the Midlands, and men of the West country, "Geordies," Lowlanders and Highlanders, Catholics and Orangemen, Australians, New Zealanders, Canadians . . . all were there. You could almost hear the pulse of Empire beat as they swarmed in their thousands on to the parade-ground.

Undulating ripples ran here and there along the close ranks of that vast host as company after company ordered arms and stood at ease. Commands were shouted: instructors, with yellow arm bands on their sleeves, ran hither and thither in the press. Still that endless stream of khaki deluged forth on to the parade ground: still the blare of brass, the squeal of fifes, or the skirl of pipes proclaimed the coming of fresh legions along the roads of the camp.

"Take a good look at that picture!" said a captain of the Coldstream at our Ensign's elbow, "for you've never seen so many British soldiers together before!"

Our Ensign nodded. Truly that place of assembly was an unforgettable sight, a picture that he knew would never fade from his mind.

The Guards' officers, our Ensign learnt, were to accompany the men of their regiments to the different courses of instruction given at the training ground—bayonet-fighting, wiring, bombing, and so forth—under instructors trained in the firing line. Thus he and The Lad presently found themselves listening to a sun browned sergeant of the H.L.I., whose bonnet looked somewhat incongruous worn with "shorts," expounding in the accents of "Glasgie" the whole art of laying out barbed wire entanglements. While his men were busy with the prickly rolls of wire, stakes, pickets, and mallet, our Ensign heard French being spoken behind him.

He turned and saw a detachment of Canadians, thick set, sturdy, and rather swarthy for the most part, drawn up in front of another "wire lecturer" a dozen yards away. By the instructor's side stood a Canadian soldier, a corporal, who, as the lecturer proceeded, translated his remarks rapidly into French.

It was rather an extraordinary performance. The lecturer was a Cockney.

"You tike the stike, . . ." said the lecturer, suiting the action to the word.

"*Alors, vous prenez la broche . . . comme ça*," fluently translated the

interpreter, adding shrilly—
"*Mais faites done attention, nom de Dieu, vous, Le Sage!*"
"... you measure orf five yards, like this 'ere...."
"*Et puis, vous mesurez cinq aunes ... au pas n'est-ce pas?*"
Listening with wondering ears, our Ensign realised the strength of the Empire tie that had sent these French Canadians, who could not speak our language, across the seas to war.

It was a scene of amazing activity, that training ground. The brisk breeze that blew joyfully across the sun-bathed plateau brought with it the sounds and smells of a great fair, fitful bursts of music, bugle-calls, shouts and cries, the pungent odour of horses, the acrid taste of dust, the faint scent of burning wood.

One day a long train of German prisoners wound its melancholy way through the camp en route for England. Our Ensign stood by the roadside as they passed and noted how the indifference faded from the faces of the officers at the head of the *cortège*, how the weary and mud-stained figures behind them shook themselves free from their apathy at the scene of busy movement enacted all around them. The columns marching along the roads, the charging lines of bayonet-fighters, the endless lines of practice trenches, the bustle, the orderly confusion, the noise.... all this must have made them realise the giant strength piling up behind the fierce onslaught before which they had laid down their arms on the Somme. The sad procession passed our Ensign by with the dawn of a great enlightenment in the eyes of the prisoners.

The forcefulness of the training at the camp was amazing. Men who had got a little stale in long months of training at some pleasant centre at home were shaken up into life by the galvanising vigour of the instructors' addresses. There was one sergeant in particular, an instructor in bayonet-fighting, to whom our young man never tired of listening.

That sergeant was magnificently built, with the finely developed physique of the army gymnastic instructor. He was simply attired in a vest, khaki trousers and gym. shoes, his short-sleeved jumper leaving open to view a brawny and sunburnt pair of arms that wielded rifle and bayonet as easily as though they were a swagger-cane.

He was a fine picture of British manhood, that sergeant, as he stood bareheaded in the sunshine on the parapet of a trench. Behind him dangled from a long gibbet the sacks of straw upon which presently the budding warrior would test his skill with the bayonet; before him, a sea of sunburnt faces, a wide horseshoe of capless, jacketless men, sleeves rolled up, rifle and bayonet in their hand. In fluent direct English he would harangue his audience somewhat after this style—

"Now then, lads, just you listen to me for a bit. You all know what you joined the army for. You didn't join just to learn a bit of arm-drill, nor yet to polish your buttons and look pretty, nor yet to go out walking with a pack o' gals . . . yes, I can see a lot of you know all about that too. No! you joined the army *to fight!* That's what they've brought you out here for! *To fight, to kill Germans,* . . . that's your job out here. You've left the gals and the pictures and the pubs behind in England. This here is *war!* D'you know what *war* means? I'll tell you. War means that if you don't kill the other feller first, he'll blooming well kill You! Now you just get that into your thick heads.

"Listen here again! This little friend here" (patting the bayonet), "this little friend o' mine on my arm . . . some of you lads have had plenty of little friends on your arms in your time; I can see that with half an eye. . . . this little sticker here is going to help you to get back home alive to the gals and the pictures and all the rest of it. Shells are all right, the rifle's all right, but it's what's on the end of the rifle that's going to save your life when it's man to man in a stand-up fight.

"When a great hulking Hun sees one of you chaps coming for him close in with the bayonet, what does he do? Does he send a messenger with his compliments to Fritz at the battery behind him and ask him, please, for a barrage? Does he lower his sights and take careful aim with his rifle? Not on your life. For why? Because there isn't time. The old Hun blooming well knows that if he don't stick You, you'll stick *him!*

"Now you've learnt your bayonet practice, and I could teach you here by the book, so that you'd do it all so pretty you'd make a Guardsman blush. But I can't teach you quickness: I can't put the ginger into you so as you'll go hell for leather for the Huns first time you see them, and through them and their blooming trench before they can say '*Potsdam.*' You don't want to use your brains, you don't want to reason it all out nicely; *you've all, every one of you, got to be the man that sticks first!*

"There's lots of fellers been out here who thought they'd take it easy, and trot up to Fritz and give him a gentle prod and watch him surrender. Do you know where most of those fellers are, lads? Under the ground, that's where they are, with a nice little wooden cross, and a bit of writing atop to say what fine chaps they were. Ah! a dead man's always a hero. But you don't want to be dead, lads! A wooden cross is not the sort of cross you've come out here after. You want to live, and go home to the gals and tell 'em all what a hero you are.

"Now we'll try a little bit of assaulting . . ."

Thus he would run on, the very incarnation of the soldier spirit, erect and manly, the sunshine playing round his light-brown hair and the polished steel of his "little friend."

Despite the manifold interests of the training-ground, time hung rather heavy on the hands of our young man. Every day the very firmament quivered to the distant thunder of the guns; sometimes in the night, particularly towards dawn, the throbbing of the air was so marked as to awaken the officers in their airy huts. There is something uncontrollably unsettling about gun fire. It upset our young man sadly, and he chafed at his detention at the base. As for The Lad, he positively raged.

Sometimes our Ensign marched the party for the training-ground up the hill behind the piper with his kilt of Royal Stuart tartan. Notwithstanding the dusty climb, our Ensign rather liked these marches up the hill and back. The weather was beautifully fine, and the men were always in excellent fettle, so laughter and chaff flew from mouth to mouth. Nothing sharpens wits so well as throwing a few battalions of different regiments together. The humour was generally pointed, but often decidedly witty, and the jokes were always taken in good part. One morning the young officer, plodding along in the dust at the head of the training ground party, heard a voice behind him exclaim—

"Eyes right to the Welsh Guards, lads!" The officer instinctively glanced to the right, and saw a gentle nanny-goat gazing sad-eyed from behind the hedge at the column as it passed. This sally at the expense of the regimental pet of the Welsh Guards elicited roars of laughter, in which—in justice, be it said—the Welshmen of the party also joined.

Thus the summer days rolled on, and with every day our Ensign grew browner and fitter for the fray. One evening at the bridge-table the Adjutant of the Guards' Base Depot, after opening a message brought in by an orderly, said to our Ensign who was his partner—

"You're for the Guards' Division tomorrow evening, and," turning round to The Lad who was writing a letter at the window behind him, "you too!"

That night the two young officers went to bed with a joyful heart. Tomorrow they were going to the Front.

★★★★★★

The guns of the Somme are throbbing more frantically than ever. Time flies: time presses sorely when the blood runs hotly in the veins. Let us hasten, then, over the ceremony of departure, and pause but for a moment to watch the group at the door of the Mess waving a last farewell to the two figures, girt on with all the panoply of war, stalking into the mellow dusk of a perfect summer evening down the road to the camp *commandant's* office, where a motor-lorry is waiting to take them to the train.

"Now we shan't be long!" murmured The Lad as the lorry whirled them away through the white dust. He spoke true. Ere three months had run their course that eager spirit was swallowed up and lost in the mirk and reek of those very guns to whose summons he had so impatiently listened.

★★★★★★

It was The Lad who did the trick that secured our young friends a compartment to themselves through both stages of their long journey up to the Front. In the gloomy yard in which their train—of prodigious length, it seemed to be—was drawn up The Lad produced a piece of chalk from his pocket.

"Watch me!" he said with his merry smile.

On the door of the first-class *coupé* which they had selected for themselves he wrote in chalk—

"O.C. Troops."

"Infallible!" replied The Lad to his sceptical companion. "A fellow I met at the machine-gun course at Chelsea put me up to the dodge. It scares 'em all away. You see? We shan't be disturbed!"

Nor were they, though at various times before the train started heavily laden young officers approached the carriage. At the sight of that forbidding inscription, however, they bolted precipitately. And so our young friends journeyed through the night in much comfort to the old French town where they were to change trains and spend the day.

After a shave, a bath, and breakfast, they set out together on a pious pilgrimage to the grave of a friend who for a twelvemonth had lain buried in the British Military Cemetery beyond the racecourse on the outskirts of the city. Without difficulty they found the simple grave at the foot of its big white cross, with many newer and whiter crosses all around. After consultation with the Corporal Gardener, a first-gravedigger kind of person with lugubrious mien and Yorkshire accent, they purchased from a genial Frenchwoman at the lodge of the cemetery a number of plants to be put on the grave.

"A'll tell 'er A'll put un in!" said the Corporal Gardener, and, raising his voice to a shout, he bawled at the woman—

"*Moa . . . fleurs . . . tombo . . . arpray!*"

"*Vous allez les planter vous-même?*" replied the woman with perfect comprehension—"*bon, bon.*"

And thus, our Ensign reflected, a British graveyard forms a tiny link in the chain of the *Entente* to bring Normandy and the East Riding together.

After that came an interminable railway journey lasting from after luncheon that day until far into the next afternoon. But for a tiny break *en route* it would have passed altogether out of our Ensign's mind, that snail-like progress from Normandy to Belgium. Somewhere about the hour of 7 in the morning the long train halted in what seemed to be a tract of flat and barren country. Alighting, our heroes found themselves opposite a long low shed with open doors, giving a glimpse of gleaming urns and piles of bread-and-butter, towards which everybody in the train seemed to be flocking.

Behind this wayside canteen our travellers found a small and cheery room, with a bright red-tiled floor, natty curtains, and old-fashioned furniture, where two or three ladies were dispensing breakfast to the officers. In comparison with the boon of breakfast in that barren place, after a long, cold night journey, the charges were outrageously low. But better than the steaming tea, the delicious sandwiches, the tempting fruit, was that little glimpse of England—the pretty English room, the warm welcome of those devoted Englishwomen in their pleasant English voices.

Nothing more happened to break the tedium of their journey until actually they had set foot to the ground on alighting at their destination.

At that moment, the ears of our heroes were affrighted by a sound, the like of which neither had ever heard before.

Chapter 3

Whee . . . ee . . . ee . . . oo . . . oo . . . Plunk!

A rushing noise as of great wings beating the air, a reverberating crash, like the slamming of an iron door, blended with the sound of jangling glass, of splintering wood; then an unfamiliar, high-pitched cry, "A . . a . . ah!" followed by a mechanical chant on a rising key, as it passed from mouth to mouth—

"Stretcher-*bearer!*"

The platform of the station was deserted. A very familiar name stared down upon our heroes from the lamps. Their fellow-travellers by the train ... a handful of all sorts, officers, Australian privates, some R.A.M.C. orderlies, a couple of Belgian interpreters ... had long since vanished into safety.

The sky seemed full of odd noises. Every minute or so the new arrivals heard the long-drawn-out whistle of a shell, cut short on its rising note by the crash of the explosion. The first shell they had heard had seemed to strike very close at hand: the succeeding crashes, though equally loud, appeared to be farther away.

Everybody knows the sound of a shell, even when he hears it for the first time. Concerned mainly with the fear lest the other should notice that he "had the wind up," our two young Guardsmen hastily pulled their kits out of the train, and leaving them where they fell on the platform, made for the station-hall.

There they saw two men on their knees beside a stretcher. To the right of them a notice painted in white on a blackboard announced the office of the R.T.O. or Railway Transport Officer, where our young men had to report.

In the R.T.O.'s office, installed in what had probably been a lamp-room or something of the sort, they found most of their fellow-passengers assembled. Under the influence of their original welcome, everybody was conversing in whispers.

The R.T.O. was shortish in his manner. (It is not easy to be polite under shell fire.)

"Report at Headquarters of Guards' Division!" he said curtly to our Ensign and his companion when they had given in their names and regiment.

"Where is that?" said our Ensign promptly.

Resignedly the officer explained. Yes, it was a goodish way; no, there was no conveyance of any kind; yes, they would have to go through the town; no, it was not safe; the town was being shelled. Had they not heard the shell fall outside the station a minute ago?

"Next! Australian Light Horse?"

The R.T.O. turned to the next man.

"We'll just have to foot it," said our hero to The Lad as they made their way outside, "unless we can get a lift of some kind. We'd better leave our kits here in charge of someone!"

Outside in the station-hall our Ensign heard a stamp and a click beside him, a familiar sound, the sound of a Guardsman saluting. Our Ensign turned and saw a private in breeches and spurs, a well-known crest in his cap, an old sleeveless raincoat flying out behind him like a pair of wings.

"I have a horse for you, sir," he said, "to take you up to the transport. I couldn't get here before on account of the shelling."

Our Ensign and The Lad were going to different battalions. The moment of parting had come.

"Your mess-cart has come for you, sir," said the groom to The Lad, "but the driver waited outside until the shelling had stopped. If you will come along with my officer, I can show you where I left him."

On a long country road lined by tall poplars our Ensign found a couple of horses and a little Maltese cart. He and The Lad shook hands; the latter climbed into the cart, while our Ensign mounted a small brown mare. Then the cart rattled off towards the centre of the town, while our Ensign trotted down the road, the groom behind him.

Presently our young man drew rein to allow the groom to come up level. The Ensign began to talk to the soldier.

"They," said the groom, with a jerk of his head in the direction which the mess-cart had taken, "are in rest, sir. Our battalion is in the line. The transport officer thought you would dine with the Transport, and then go up along of him and the rations after dark tonight."

The groom was a veteran of the original Expeditionary Force. So was the little mare which our Ensign was riding, the man told him.

"Many's the fine officer that little mare's carried, sir," he said, scanning her affectionately: "there was Captain X., him as was killed back at Soupeers, and Captain Y.—it was on the Zillebeke Ridge where he got it, sir—and Captain Z., him as was shot by a sniper in the trenches at Givenchy. Ah! I've seen some grand gentlemen go, sir!"

He shook his head mournfully.

"Maybe you'll want this little switch of mine, sir," the groom added, handing our Ensign a small ash plant; "one or two draws o' this won't be after hurting that little mare, she's that idle!"

Our Ensign welcomed this change in the conversation. The groom's train of thought made him slightly uncomfortable in the circumstances.

For a mile or so along the road out of the town the noises still resounded from the sky. The shells came "*whooshing*" over so loudly above their heads that our Ensign felt an irrepressible titillation in the neck—a strong inclination to duck. To distract his thoughts, he looked about him.

It was a flat and uninteresting country, but well wooded and very green. Every house they passed was wrecked by shell fire, more or less completely; but he noticed that there were still some civilians about. Practically all the soldiers they met, he observed, were Guardsmen, and, though their cap-stars and buttons were dull and unpolished, their uniforms stained and often badly worn, the men were all well shaved and well brushed, with puttees neatly tied and boots well greased. They were taking their ease in the cool of the evening, standing gossiping in the streets of the villages through which our; Ensign passed, or sitting on the benches outside the *estaminets*.

A ride of more than an hour brought our hero and the groom to a muddy sidetrack which led into a pleasant green field. Here a number of tents were pitched. From a field in rear a prodigious squealing of fifes and beating of drums resounded in a hopeless cacophony. "The Drums" (by which generic term, in the Guards, the fife and drum band is understood) of two battalions were practising in separate groups under the trees.

The transport officer and the quartermaster made our Ensign welcome in the mess-tent, gave him a drink and a cigarette, informed him that he was to dine with them, and eventually showed him into the Interpreter's tent, where our hero was much astonished to find his kit lying. It had apparently been wafted there by some supernatural means from the platform at the railway station. This was, of course, the quartermaster's doing, but our Ensign was as yet too ignorant of usages in the field to appreciate that heaven-sent boon, a good quartermaster. So he accepted it all as a matter of course, and proceeded to change his clothes and don warmer things in anticipation of his first night in the trenches.

The Belgian interpreter was sitting on the bed in his tent, warbling a little air to himself. After our Ensign had disabused him of his first impression—namely, that the newcomer proposed to take forcible occupation of his sleeping apartment—he became extremely affable, and produced water and soap and a towel. He was a sunny-natured person with remarkable fluency in English, and made the young officer free of his every possession with unbounded hospitality.

Then our Ensign dined in the mess-tent off an enamel plate, and drank innocuous Belgian beer out of a tin mug. A captain of the Coldstream, who turned out to be the transport officer of his battalion, dined with the party. Outside the daylight was failing and a few pale stars had begun to twinkle. The drums had ceased their practice, but the crickets and the frogs supplied the table-music in their place.

"I hope you can ride," said the transport officer to our Ensign, with a note of warning in his voice.

Our Ensign pleaded guilty to a slight familiarity with that gentlemanly accomplishment.

"... because," the transport officer went on, "we have a good eight miles to go, and the limbers with the rations started an hour ago. So we shall have to ride fairly hard for the first part of the way to catch 'em up."

Our Ensign smiled in a superior fashion, as much as to say the other could not ride hard enough for him. "*Unconscious of his doom, the little victim plays!*" Our young man was to have a rude awakening.

By the time the groom had announced that the horses were waiting, our Ensign was ready for the road. He had to carry on his person his whole panoply of war—revolver, glasses, compass, gas-helmet, ammunition pouch, and lamp—all slung on his belt, which he was wearing outside his raincoat. He felt like a trussed fowl, and it required a helping hand from the groom to get him into the saddle. When he was up, the quartermaster handed him a steel helmet, which the groom slung on the saddle for him. Then the transport officer led the way out along the muddy sidetrack on to a better road, and immediately spurred his powerful horse into a fast trot.

Several thoughts passed through our Ensign's mind in rapid succession. The first was that, if he did not shake "The Fat Lady" (for such was the mare's name) out of her contented amble, he would be left behind in the dark, and irretrievably lost. The second was that, if he went any faster, he must certainly part company with one or other article of his equipment, which was dancing a merry jig round his waist. The third was that he would take an early opportunity of verifying a suspicion which had crossed his mind at dinner, from certain allusions in the conversation—namely, that the transport officer man had acquired his familiarity with horses in the hunting-field in Ireland!

Our young man had retained the ash plant, and, under the influence of half a dozen "dhraws" applied to her flanks at regular intervals, the mare bestirred itself, albeit protesting.

Thus our Ensign rode forth unto battle, in the Ethiopian blackness of a close muggy night, sorely shaken, jingling like a jester, drenched with perspiration, with a feverish eye on the dim figure of the rider jogging briskly through the darkness ahead of him.

Far away in the distance, vivid white lights spouted continually into the sky. Of gun fire there was little. It seemed a quiet night. By the roadside, from time to time, the jagged silhouette of a broken wall, a tottering chimney, a devastated church tower, stood out against a patch of lighter cloud. Figures took shape suddenly out of the gloom, marching in silence through the night, filling the empty road with the acrid smell of hot and dirty men, filling the air with the crunch-crunch of their feet. Guns jingled past them at the trot, with cursing drivers plucking at their horses' heads to keep their teams to the road.

Presently, a continuous rumbling echoed out of the patch of blackness enveloping the road ahead. Low voices came back with snatches of conversation. The dark outline of a long string of tossing limbers loomed out of the gloom. The transport officer galloped off up to the head of the column. A whistle sounded. The rumbling ceased. The limbers stopped. The transport officer's voice spoke out of the darkness; our Ensign could not see the speaker.

"We send our horses back here,"—our Ensign heard him spring to the ground,—"better put your helmet on now! We are going to walk, and we generally get shelled to blazes over this next bit that's coming!"

Stiffly, our Ensign slipped his foot out of the stirrup and precipitated himself from the saddle. He was wondering to himself whether all wars were as uncomfortable as this one. He had only thought of death on active service as a quick finish in the midst of an exhilarating charge at the head of an excited band—not of a death that came screaming suddenly at you out of the dark, when you were clammy and stiff and tired, and generally uncomfortable!

The young man doffed his cap, and carried it in his hand. He put on his helmet. It was heavy, and hideously unwieldy. He felt it would topple over on his nose with very little provocation.

They plodded on in silence at the head of the rumbling limbers. After an hour's walk through the blackness (our Ensign had not the remotest idea where they were), the blur of many figures sitting about the grass of the roadside bulked out in the gloom. The transport officer switched on his light. The familiar features of the drill sergeant who had initiated our hero into the intricacies of squad drill at home stood revealed in the bright beam. About him, in silent groups, were the ration parties, who, without delay or confusion, set about the work of unloading the limbers.

The night was singularly quiet. Not a gun spoke. Never a shell came to justify the transport officer's gloomy forebodings. Only from the higher ground ahead, the never ceasing fountain of white lights showed that the opposing lines of trenches were unremitting in their vigilance.

Darkness not only obscures the eyes,—it also clouds the memory. The next thing our Ensign remembers was coming to what looked like a row of ancient *tumuli* in a field and a gap in a hedge which seemed to be shaken by a violent wind, though the night was perfectly still. There was a loud "*swish . . . swish . . .*" in the air and a quick "*patter . . . patt*er . . ." all around. Then a voice said very distinctly out of the darkness—

"Blast that machine-gun!"

The swishing sounds ceased, our Ensign turned on his lamp and saw an officer in a Burberry with a revolver hung on his belt worn outside. The new arrival instantly recognised him as one of the most joyous spirits of the ante room at home. He was known to all and sundry as "Peter."

"Hullo!" said the other, switching on his light, "there you are! I didn't know if you'd be up tonight or not. I believe you're coming to our company. I suppose you are going to see the commanding officer now. He's in the dug out. I'm out with a carrying party. See you later. Where the devil's that orderly gone?"

He turned off his light and was swallowed up in the dark amid a shuffling throng of men. Our Ensign found the commanding officer in a small dugout with a very low entrance. Candles in white metal candlesticks threw a yellow light over a roughly carpentered table, where maps were spread out amid the remains of a meal. In the corner an officer was bending over a telephone.

"This is the adjutant speaking," he was saying, ". . . oh, that is Mr Barnard . . . right . . . Minnies were they . . . yes, it sounded like them . . . not in the trench . . . good . . . right . . . we'll get retaliation!"

"Four Minnies into No. 1 Company, sir," he said, putting down the receiver and addressing the commanding officer; "Barnard thinks he'd like some retaliation. Shall I ask for it?"

The commanding officer nodded and offered the transport officer and our Ensign a drink. Then he told our Ensign that he would be attached to No. 2—Peter's company,—the latter was commanding in the absence of the regular company commander who was on leave. The company was at present in support in trenches close at hand. The battalion was coming out of the line the next night. Then they talked of the general situation, the advance on the Somme, the situation in the Salient, what the Russians were doing, whether the Rumanians would come in. Finally, our Ensign took his leave, and the transport officer escorted him along the trench to a small and extremely evil-smelling dugout, where they found a grenadier subaltern working out chess-problems on a travelling chess-board, by the light of a candle stuck in its own grease on the table. He explained to the transport officer that he was in command of two platoons left behind to help with the carrying work at night.

That night our Ensign slept in a low narrow hole, scraped out of the parados of the trench. On turning in, he found that his servant, whom he had brought up with him from the Base, had spread the dug out with nice clean sandbags. With his haversack for a pillow, and his raincoat spread over him as a wrap, the newcomer, who had never spent a night out of bed in his life before, slept solidly for eight hours. When he awoke the trenches were flooded with sunshine, and a most comfortable smell of hot bacon stole across the clear morning air.

★★★★★★

The company was not in the firing line, so that the men could move pretty freely in and about the trenches. The weather was very fine and warm, and the existence was not strenuous. The following evening Peter marched half the company away into reserve, on relief by another battalion, leaving our Ensign behind, with two platoons to help with the carrying. In two days' time our hero would rejoin his battalion in reserve.

The new arrivals in the company mess in the dirty little dug-out were genial souls. Our Ensign took his meals and played chess with them, and discussed the papers which came up with the utmost regularity in company with the letters every afternoon. After dark our young man slung his lamp and his revolver on his belt and went round the trenches and the outposts, his orderly at his heels, a Celtic type of youth, MacFinnigan by name.

The two days passed pleasantly enough. There was a little sporadic shelling, generally after the passage of a Hun aeroplane, glittering aloft, with black crosses on the under-surface of its planes, amid little puffs of shrapnel and the *"peugh . . . peugh . . . peugh"* of the anti-aircraft guns. The first afternoon—it was at tea—two sharp salvoes of whizz-bangs rang out from farther up the trench. Our Ensign sallied forth to review the situation. Up the trench he found a big grenadier lying on his face motionless in a great welter of blood, while round the traverse an Irish Guardsman was flat on his back on the trench-boards, a little rosary between his fingers, with a stretcher-bearer ripping up one of his *puttees*, which was soaked with blood.

The wounded man lifted a pallid face to the officer as he came up. The stretcher-bearer was soothing him gently as he worked.

"Be asy now," he was saying, "a little skelp like that won't kill yez. I'll put yez in the dugout beyond ... ye'll be grand and snug there till it's dark, and then we'll take yez down."

"The others is all right, sir," the stretcher-bearer added to our Ensign; "him round the traverse was killed on the spot, but there's nobody else touched barrin' this chap here!"

The wounded man said nothing, but his breath came heavily. His face was very pale. The officer saw him tucked away into the dugout, and went back to tea with a heavy heart. It was his first casualty. . . .

The next night our Ensign led his two platoons out of the trenches in the wake of a guide sent up to meet them. He was a little disappointed to find how lightly his responsibility as an officer rested upon him. He had not the least idea of where they were going as they followed the guide out into the darkness.

Their journey came to its finish on a timbered walk, leading past a long array of shelters dug out of a bank and protected by layers of neatly built-up sandbags. Everybody had gone to bed, for it was after 2 a.m.—that is, everybody save our Ensign's servant, who, after our hero had seen his men safely into their quarters, led the officer into a fine roomy dugout with a wooden door and wooden flooring. There, on a bed made of sacking stretched over a framework, he found his sleeping-sack spread, with his pyjamas on top; his canvas washing-bucket, full of hot water, smoked on a primitive-looking washstand; while a complete change of clothes was laid out on a soap-box beside the bed.

"And what time will I call you in the morning, sir?" said Johnson—such was the name of our Ensign's servant—at the door.

"What time is parade?" asked the officer.

"There's no parade for you, sir,—only rifle inspection at eleven. Perhaps you'd care for a bath in the morning, sir!"

Our Ensign jumped at the suggestion and ordered a hot bath for half-past nine. He crept gratefully into his sleeping-bag, his mind bewildered by the sudden contrasts in his new and remarkable life. . . .

Chapter 4

The period in reserve had brought the whole battalion together once more. The companies were no longer separated as they had been in the trenches. Our Ensign found the officers established in regular messes in the sand-bagged shelters of this pleasantly rural retreat, and the whole routine of the Guards running smoothly on very similar lines to the life in barracks at home.

Life was not at all strenuous in reserve—at any rate not in the day-time. In the trenches the men get short commons in the way of sleep, so during the period in reserve they are not worked very hard. At night, however, fatigue parties were generally sent up to the support or front lines on various digging undertakings. Otherwise, a rifle inspection in the morning, and sometimes, additionally, an inspection of feet (an army may fight on its stomach, but it marches on its feet) or of gas helmets, was the only parade of the day.

Each company took it in turn to be "in waiting"—that is to say, to be in readiness for any emergency. The company in waiting furnished the guards and fatigue parties for any special jobs about the camp. During the period in waiting, which lasted twenty-four hours, from one afternoon to the afternoon of the following day, the officers of the company in waiting were not supposed to leave the precincts of the camp, and, the company commander excepted, they took it in turns, during the period "in waiting," to act as piquet officer, whose functions in reserve were practically confined to stamping the letters with the battalion censor stamp in the Orderly Room (a sand bagged shelter), before the post corporal collected the mail in the afternoons.

Our Ensign slipped very easily, almost imperceptibly, into his place as a tiny cog in the great wheelwork of the army in France. He came out prepared to have a roughish time in very congenial company—and in neither respect was he disappointed. The mess in which he found himself had all the attraction of a cosmopolitan club in miniature. His fellow officers in the company to which he had been posted—No. 2—had what was known as a double-company mess with the officers of No. 1 Company.

At the quarters in reserve the mess was located in an ambitious sort of sand bagged shelter, with stain-glass windows, timber floor and walls, a white deal sideboard (home made), and a long table and chairs. Here our Ensign met his company commander, a serene and placid person, with a somewhat judicial manner, who, for that reason, answered to the name of "The Beak." Most of the other officers our Ensign had known at home, so that he did not feel so much an intruder as he had feared he would.

The double company mess was a very happy family. In every stratum of society type balances type. It is this easy counterpoise that makes the world revolve. That great leveller, the *war*, has thrown together in officers' messes for a spell of intimate association a number of men whose pursuits in other circumstances would all have radiated in different directions. In that mess there were, amongst others, a brace of budding diplomats, two Balliol undergraduates, a rancher, a "literary gent.," and an engineer. Some of the officers had decided to adopt the army as their profession, and to remain on in the regiment after the war, but others would simply return to their pursuits and professions on the proclamation of peace.

The pleasant *camaraderie* which reigned in the double-company mess must be based, our Ensign decided, on the equilibrium of all these different temperaments and mental outlooks balanced one against the other. So far as regimental duties were concerned, every type was tempered down to the average consistency given by the identical training which every Guards' officer receives on the square at home.

Therefore, though many and furious were the arguments on every conceivable topic with which the young lions of the double-company mess whiled away their leisure hours, there was perfect accord in the general realisation by each of his duties and responsibilities as an officer. In the privacy of the mess there might be heated wrangles regarding the respective merits of No. 1 and No. 2 Companies; but the whole mess presented a solid front in backing the two companies against the rest of the battalion, the battalion against the rest of the brigade, and the regiment against every other regiment in the brigade of Guards.

Our Ensign had two or three spells in reserve at this peaceful spot, and always looked forward to returning to it after the battalion's turn of duty in the trenches. There was practically no shelling; any German shells that came over mostly fell in a more exposed position several hundred yards away. All around them lay spread out the fair garb in which summer dresses the Belgian countryside, and not even the ruined farms or the shell scored roads could detract from the beauty of the poppies and cornflowers running wild among the neglected fields, or the roses and the hollyhocks and the snapdragon that bloomed in the little gardens of the ravaged farms.

The men revelled in the snatch of quiet, in the pleasant surroundings, in the beautiful summer weather. When their clay's work was done they sat about in the shade, writing letters home, reading the newspapers, or idly watching the afternoon spectacle of German *v.* British aeroplanes. Some spent every moment of their leisure in dragging one of the canals in which Belgium abounds for fish. The drag net was a marvel of ingenuity, constructed as it was out of rabbit netting, barbed wire, bits of string, sandbags, and branches, towed along by eager hands on either bank. Incredible as it may seem, the fishermen made quite respectable catches of pike and eels, which they cooked for supper over wood-fires, and consumed with relish,—all heedless of dark allusions by their less enterprising comrades to the fabled discovery of portions of a German helmet in the maw of one of these aquarian monsters.

The officers went for walks in the neighbourhood, extending their rambles, with the perversity of youth, to the ruined city of Ypres, still the shell-trap *par excellence* of the countryside for miles around. One afternoon, a subaltern in our Ensign's mess who went by the name of Apollo, from his statuesque appearance, and who was a perfect Baedeker of information about the local attractions wherever the battalion went, took Peter and our Ensign and one of the Balliol men, known as The Don, to a certain field where, among various shell-holes and felled apple-trees, a few rows of depressed currant bushes yet lingered.

The currants were red and scanty and abominably sour, and an unusually large number of "dud" shells were falling in dangerous proximity to the party from an "Archie" or anti-aircraft gun that was vigorously shelling a German raider. There was plenty of fresh fruit in the mess where the young men could have sat in the cool of the shelter and eaten their fill, but they preferred to stand in the hot afternoon sun and munch unripe currants at imminent risk of their necks. Truly youth is a wonderful thing!

Another day a band of them strolled out over the fields to a certain billet, where previously the battalion and other Guards' battalions had been quartered for some time. There they visited the pretty garden which the Guards had laid out with wonderful centre pieces, representing the different regimental crests of the Guards in coloured stones. But, while the Guards had been away, the heathen had raged. There were shell-holes in the garden, and the rains had begun to gnaw at the centre-pieces. . . . In the Salient everything, living and dead, seems vowed to destruction.

The night fatigues were dull, dangerous, and depressing. Night after night parties sallied forth with pick and spade, often in gum-boots, if there was work to be done on a wet trench, and plodded through the darkness to a more or less apocryphal rendezvous.

All the open ground close up to the Front in the Salient is sprayed by machine-gun fire at night, and a brisk burst of shell fire in addition was no uncommon experience for the nightly fatigue parties. Sometimes the sapper folk would be late at the trysting-place, and the men would stand huddled up together like a flock of sheep on a moor, while the officers would fret and fume and mutter dire menaces about "reporting the fellow to the brigade." Then the sapper would arrive, and the officer, about to deliver himself of a few weighty and well-considered remarks on punctuality, which is the politeness of soldiers as well as of kings, would find himself confronted by an obsequious R.E. corporal protesting that the "orficer" was "jest over there."

Translated into the plain language of fact, this indication might mean anything from 300 yards to a mile; but at length the sapper officer would appear, silencing with honeyed words and profuse apology the torrent of reproach bubbling at the Guardsman's lips. After that the sapper officer would take charge, and the Guards' officer would find his role restricted to walking up and down for anything up to three or four hours, bored to tears, unable even to smoke, because smoking on these night fatigues is forbidden to the men. He had not even the mental occupation of keeping the men to their task. They knew that they could not go home to bed until the job was finished, whatever it was, and therefore every man worked with a will, jackets discarded, sleeves rolled up.

Everybody who has been up in the Salient knows what the "trenches" there are like. The Hun holds the high ground everywhere: he has the dry soil, the observation. In the British lines the ground is so wet that a foot below the surface you strike water ... and probably a dead man as well, so thick do they lie in this blood-drenched region. Therefore the parapets are for the most part built up, and indeed the whole defences—parapet, traverses, and parados—have to be built up with sandbags, which, under the influence of shell fire and the weather, have to be continually renewed and repaired.

A parapet that will shelter a platoon of the line will not do for a platoon of Guardsmen. It is a question of inches. When the Gurkhas relieved the Guards in the trenches in the Bethune region early in the war, the Guards had to put a double tier of sandbags along the fire-step so that the little hillmen could look over the top of the parapet. Therefore, in the Salient, it often happened that the Guards found themselves sheltering in the open behind a thin parapet in bad repair, behind which they had to kneel in order to protect themselves against the enemy snipers.

Work, with a capital "W," loomed large in the orders of every company commander of the Guards in the Salient. In truth, there was much to be done. In places, the trench lines were not connected, parapets were low and by no means bullet proof, parados were distinguished mainly by their absence. Thus, when one battalion of Guards relieved another in the Salient, it took over not only the trench but a vast programme of "improvements," as the house builders say.

The first night our Ensign went up to the front line with the company, the Guards' battalion which they were relieving had a big scheme of work to hand over. As junior officer, our Ensign was given charge of the men in the front line, for the first half of their turn "in," whilst The Beak and Peter remained, according to usage, in the company headquarters in the support line. For the second half, Peter was to relieve our Ensign.

While the relief was being effected, an ensign of the outgoing company took our young man round the trench, and, with the air of a commissioner of the Office of Works, showed the new comer the work which had been begun, which the incoming company was to finish. The barbed wire was probably defective and would have to be inspected and possibly repaired; here they had put in three new traverses; here they had repaired the parapet that had been blown in by an enemy trench mortar; there they had started to build a parados; this part of the parapet was not bullet-proof . . . they had had a man wounded passing there the previous day; and so on, and so forth. The officer explained everything with admirable lucidity, and then, his men having all filed out, trotted away, leaving our Ensign, rather bewildered, standing on a precarious trench-board, half immersed in yellow water, with an overpowering odour of death in his nostrils.

Both The Beak and Peter presently came up to help him over his difficulties at his first taste of trench warfare, and together they mapped out a scheme to spread the work remaining to be done over the time they were to spend in the front line. The platoon sergeants were called into consultation: they had already got the sentries posted in the fire-bays, and the rest of the men they set at the task of filling sandbags. It was agreed that our Ensign should go out and have a look at the wire, and also the outside of the parapet, to see how it could best be made bullet-proof.

A little later the officer, in company with his orderly, his rifle slung at his back, a handsome and self-possessed young man, who was introduced as the wiring corporal, and a rugged Irish sergeant called Kinole, slung his leg over the parapet and dropped out into the open on the other side.

It was a dark windy night. In front of them the German star-shells were soaring aloft, and the night was alive with noises reverberating in the darkness. Machineguns on both sides coughed their harsh "*tack-tack . . . tack-tack-tack.*" Rifle shots rang out here and there; and every now and then, with a bang and a whizz, a Verey light whirred up into the dark sky from the trenches behind the little party. Somewhere on the right a mighty British *strafe* was in progress: our Ensign could hear the steady racket of the shells and see their orange flicker in the sky as they burst against the surrounding blackness.

The chinking of tools resounded very faintly out of the dark in front of them.

"'Tis Fritz out workin'," muttered Sergeant Kinole hoarsely. "Iv'ry night 'tis the same, sir. . . . He works like anny ould mole."

The party crossed a very wet ditch and came to the wire. Here the wiring corporal took the lead and they all crawled along behind him, bending their heads low, as he did, to examine the strands of wire against the sky. In places the wire was broken and would have to be replaced.

Then our Ensign took a look at the parapet from the outside. There was no room to strengthen it from within, and outside the trench the ground sloped away into a morass. The only thing would be to lay an earth foundation and build it up on that. The sergeant hopped back into the trench, and presently returned with a horde of bulky figures with pick and shovel who scrambled over the parapet, and, dropping on the other side, started shovelling dry earth on to the wet ground at the foot of the parapet.

All night they worked and shovelled and built, inside and outside the trench, while the star-shells spouted and the machineguns rapped loudly. With the first flicker of dawn they trooped in, and then, while the dawn was breaking sullenly, the men stood to on the fire-step all along the trench, while our Ensign, empty and cold and dreadfully sleepy, wondered why the trench smells were so overpoweringly accentuated in the early morning.

With the coming of dawn the men stood down, our Ensign inspected rifles, the commanding officer, on his daily round of the trenches, appeared and asked him a question or two, and after that, amid a general sizzling of bacon all along the trench, the officer made for the earthen cave which had been pointed out to him as his quarters. There was the faithful Johnson with a mug of hot cocoa; there was our Ensign's blanket and his air-pillow arranged on a carpet of clean sandbags.

Our young man slept until ten o'clock, and then rose to find his washing things spread out in the sunshine, Johnson close by boiling his shaving water in a mess tin. He made a leisurely toilet, then sauntered down the communication trench to the company headquarters, where he breakfasted joyously with The Beak and Peter off eggs and bacon and tea and bread-and-butter and strawberry jam. Of course the double-company mess was broken up when the battalion was in the line, so, by mutual arrangement, No. 1 Company took the mess cook, and No. 2 the mess waiter. It was the latter, rather more dishevelled than his wont, who served the three officers at breakfast in a tiny dugout four feet square.

One turn in the trenches is very much like another. Sometimes they got shelled, and on the first occasion, our Ensign, emerging rather hastily from his cubbyhole to find out what the noise was about, was shamed into complete nonchalance by the unshakable phlegm of the men. He soon learned to adopt the prescribed air of indifference to such attentions from the enemy, but, like most people, he never got used to shelling. Once or twice he went out patrolling with his orderly, a completely fearless, wholly unsqueamish, and eminently practical young man. It was a messy business, crawling through the wet grass in the dark, and rather trying to the nerves. But, as a sage friend of our Ensign's used to say, "If you can't see the Hun, he can't see you," and our young man more than once drew comfort from this practical maxim as he and MacFinnigan crawled through No Man's Land with eyes and ears strained for sight or sound of the enemy.

Letters and newspapers arrived with unfailing regularity in the front line every afternoon at tea-time. So they knew all about the great events that were happening on the Somme, especially as the latest bulletins came up daily from the army headquarters, and were stuck up (by means of a cartridge driven into the sandbag walls) outside the company headquarters. Everybody speculated endlessly as to the moment when the Guards would be hurled into that boiling cauldron in the south. Rumours of all kinds were rife: everybody had his own theories and "information," especially the men. Our Ensign used to hear them gossiping round their breakfast fires in the trenches, where every cookhouse rumour was thoroughly examined.

At last one day, when the Battalion was expecting to go out of the trenches altogether for several weeks' rest, it was reported that the Somme was its next destination. This time rumour spoke true. About one o'clock a.m., on a mellow summer night, the Battalion marched quietly by companies across the market-place of an old Belgian town, where it would in a day or two entrain for the Unknown.

Chapter 5

And now the scene changes. The stage is set afresh for another act of the great drama in which our hero plays the leading part or the tiniest of roles, according as we take his conception or history's of the great events amongst which his life is running its course. For, by analysis, war is found to be made up of millions of little dramas in which the "lead" is played by every single combatant, in which the greatest actors may have but the shadowiest of roles, in which the most portentous moments of history are but "noises of." It is only the historian, coldly surveying the stage through the lorgnette of posterity, who can disentangle the myriad threads of these subsidiary incidents and weave them into the mighty drama, in which the great actors are seen in their proper roles, where such pygmies as our Ensign are but blurred figures in a vast stage crowd, a moving background, as it were,—after the Meiningen school of the drama,—against which the events of history are enacted.

The scene shifts, then, from Belgium to France. Gone are the flat plains, the ugly red-brick houses, uglier than ever now that war has stripped them from roof to cellar; gone the dull, straight roads with their strip of uneven, red-hot *pavé* in the centre; gone that everlasting ragged silhouette of Ypres' ravaged towers, seen from every angle of the salient; gone the stagnant canals, the dirty estaminets. Slow and protesting, with many halts, the train bearing the Battalion southward, through the heat and dust of a blazing summer day, leaves the Belgian scene of war behind. It carries them deep into the fair land of France, among the green hills and undulating valleys, the long white roads, the pretty and prosperous villages, the old-world *châteaux* with their seigniorial dove-cots and weather-stained towers peering forth from the summer foliage, the natty *auberges* with their white curtained windows and little tables before the door.

This is all but the "front cloth," however, behind which the stage is being set for the drama in which the Battalion is yet to play its part. This fair picture of France, spread out in the warm afternoon sunshine, is only the foreground. Behind it somewhere, where the guns are growling dully, lies the Unknown, the Land of Adventure for which they are ultimately bound.

Motor-lorries met them at the railhead where their train journey ended, and whirled them, in a long procession of white dust-clouds, to a large and comfortable village where already other Guards' battalions were lodged. As the men, white as masons with the dust, descended from the lorries, our Ensign looked about him. There was the Billeting Officer, perspiring and protesting (as is the way of the Billeting Officer), the quartermaster-sergeants, his accomplices, beside him. On every door stood the traces of their handiwork. "2 Platoons, No. 1 Coy.," "1 Platoon, No. 4 Coy.," "Pioneers," "2 officers,"—these were some of the inscriptions our Ensign saw scrawled in chalk on the doors of houses and sheds and on the posts of the farmyard gates.

Three platoons of his company, our young man discovered, were billeted in the buildings of a big yard behind an *estaminet*, a number of large sheds and outhouses, some of red brick, others with merely wattle walls, running round three sides of the yard. Our Ensign ardently desired a wash and also a drink, but he found that all the officers were busy looking after the comfort of their men, seeing that their quarters were reasonably clean, and inquiring from the dispassionate French peasants as to facilities for water. That is the rule of the army,—the men first, the officers afterwards.

So our young man lost no time in following the example of The Beak and Peter, and visited his platoon in their billet. They were very well off", for their lodging was in a large, dry, clean loft, with a cement floor, above the stables. He and his brother officers between them were successful in begging some straw off the lady of the *estaminet*, whose sole concern appeared to be for her fowls. . . . *Ah, Monsieur, il y avait des Anglais chez nous qui ont volé mes poules. . . . Oh, la, la, qu'ils ont volé! . . .*

But our Ensign soothed her fears by clinching on the spot a contract for eggs for the double-company mess, as long as the battalion should be there, and by paying down five *francs* on account. Quite mollified, the lady showed them a horse-pond near by where the men might wash, and the village well, where (after due analysis of the water by the doctor, in accordance with the brigade order) the men might draw drinking water.

Leaving the men, stripped to the waist, carrying in their hands little ends of soap and rather dingy towels, swarming about the horsepond, our Ensign and his brother officers fared forth to locate their own quarters. In the village street they found the billeting officer the centre of an indignant group. In the whole of B——, he announced, wiping his damp brow, there were but four beds for officers—the company commanders were to have these,—the rest must forage for themselves. The double-company mess was quartered in the *estaminet* behind which the greater part of our Ensign's company was billeted. There might be some tents for officers later....

There was a chorus of obloquy. What slackness on the part of the billeting officer! Had one ever heard the like? Why, the place was full of comfortable-looking houses where, for a *franc* or two, one might get a clean and comfortable bed! One wouldn't mind paying...

The discussion lasted whilst the young lions of the double-company mess lapped up white wine and soda in the dark and filthy backroom of the *estaminet* where the mess was situated. Poultry walked between their legs: there were millions of flies: a dishevelled wench stirred a saucepan over a red hot stove, and ancient, gnarled peasants, murmuring "*Bien le bon jour, m'sieurs!*" entered and sat down with them at the table. Apparently the backroom was a kind of village club. In the front room of the *estaminet*, judging by the trampling of feet and the frantic cries of "Doo beer, Ma!" the greater part of the battalion was refreshing itself after the heat of the day.

Peter had a servant, a prodigy among men, and a pearl among servants, which his name was Cardwell. Even our Ensign lowered before the Admirable Cardwell the banner he bore so proudly aloft on behalf of the faithful Johnson. For Cardwell spoke French: Cardwell knew the ways of the peasants: Cardwell had been known to extract a meal and a bed out of the dourest old harridan who ever bolted her door with the cry—"*Je ne veux pas des soldats chez moi!*"

So Peter drew our Ensign aside, and whispered—

"Cardwell will find us something: leave it to Cardwell!"

But even Cardwell drew a blank in B——; he returned to the *estaminet*, where his "master," as the soldier servants say, was sitting hopefully among the flies and the poultry and the peasants, and ruefully announced his failure. The village was overflowing with refugees from the occupied territory (under the French Government relief scheme): the billeting officer had spoken true,—there was not a bed in the place. But then the faithful Johnson came to the rescue. In the courtyard of the *estaminet* he had laid out soap and water and a towel for our Ensign to have that much-needed wash; and he informed his "master" that tents were to be had, and if our Ensign would furnish the men to draw the tent from the quartermaster, and indicate a spot where it should be pitched, he would attend to it at once. There was a clean garden behind the *estaminet* which might do, the man added.

Peter and our Ensign inspected the spot, and decided that it would do: the needful authority was obtained from The Beak, the tent was pitched behind the *estaminet*, and the two officers had their kits deposited therein, thereby inaugurating a tent partnership which lasted through the summer.

That evening a select party consisting of our Ensign, Peter, Apollo, The Don, and a tall and serious minded subaltern of their Mess, whom everybody called Roderick, dined in state at a hotel in a neighbouring town, to which they were conveyed through the kindly offices of a motor-ambulance driver. There, among all kinds of big-wigs of the Guards' division, they ate a thoroughly bad dinner, at an extortionate price, washed down by utterly spurious *Château Laffitte*, and professed themselves hugely delighted with their evening. It was a glorious summer night, and when they got back to their billet Peter and our Ensign pulled their valises out of the tent and slept beneath the stars.

As the result of an argument on the art of foraging on active service, springing from severe strictures on the paucity of the fare at the double-company Mess, Peter and our Ensign were bidden to dinner the next night with a brother officer, who professed, after experience of active service in half a dozen wars, to be able to get an epicurean meal in any village, no matter how short local supplies were—and B—— was very short.

The troops going through on their way to the Somme had seen to that!

The veteran acted as his own cook, and the four—for one of the company commanders made up the *parti carré*—dined under an apple-tree, beneath the stars, off three young ducks and two young chickens, with delicious fresh peas and new potatoes. The guests contributed, as their share of the repast, two bottles of *Roederer* purchased in the neighbouring town.

As a dinner it was a *tour de force*, for heaven alone knows what blandishments these succulent dishes represented: as a meal, it was a frankly gluttonous performance. Our Ensign, who was piquet officer that day, felt that he could scarcely walk, so gorged was he with food, when he rose from the table under the apple-tree to go and turn out the guards. But in war you learn to be thankful for what you can get today, for the morrow is ever uncertain.

The battalion arrived at B—— on a Sunday, and at six o'clock on the following Tuesday morning it was on the road again. It rendezvoused with the rest of the brigade at a given point *en route*, from which the whole brigade marched to its destination at V——, some seventeen or eighteen miles distant.

The day was a regular "scorcher." Even at the early hour of their departure there was a touch of fiery heat in the sun's rays. There was not a cloud in the sky, and already the heat was shimmering among the corn-stooks in the stubble. The road was deep in dust, and every wayside leaf was powdered white.

The country was terribly hilly, and the men—who were in marching order, their steel helmets strapped on the back of their packs—were sweating freely even at the end of the first mile of the march. Trench warfare gives the men scant opportunity for exercise, and a long march in the summer heat over hilly roads with a heavy load is a strain on the fittest of troops.

But the men made light of the heat and the dust as they trudged along, marching at ease with their rifles slung, with the drums crashing out in front of them. When soldiers are standing a march well, there is a constant ripple of conversation, of chaff, and little snatches of song running up and down the ranks. The men were frankly delighted with the pretty French countryside, the cows in the fields, the sheep on the uplands, the geese and ducks and cocks and hens in the villages—all these were reminders of their country homes, reminders such as they had seldom seen in the mournful land of death from which they had come. A donkey braying behind a hedge, a drove of pigs on the road, set them all a-laughing. Like children, they commented in a running vein of criticism upon everything they saw.

"Och!" said a voice behind our Ensign, "'tis kilt I am wid the heat intoirely. Did ye ever see the like o' thim lads in front? Sure, they're runnin' us off our legs!"

"'Tis the same old game," declaimed disdainfully Sergeant Kinole, plodding along at the head of the platoon; "I know them lads in front of the company! One, two—left, right—keepin' the step with the Company Commander's horse. I declare to God we'll all be goin' on our hands and knees be the time we get in!"

This flight of fancy elicited a general laugh. Then the running commentary broke out afresh. A venerable-looking old peasant was digging in a field.

"*Bon jour,* Daddy!" cried a voice.

"Is ut diggin' spuds ye are?" asked another.

"Arrah, let him be," said a deep voice. "Tis diggin' his own grave he is, th' ould rascal!"

The "ould rascal" looked up from his digging with a sheepish, toothless grin, and the battalion tramped by in a cloud of dust and a ripple of jests and laughter.

They joined up with the brigade and marched on, drums beating gaily in front, baggage limbers and carts and cookers trailing out to the rear, through the torrid heat. The passing of the brigade was an event in the little town where our Ensign and his friends had dined. The streets were crowded, every window had its frieze of faces, every shop-door its knot of gossips, to see the column go by. It was the first time for a century that the Guards had been in those parts.

The heat was truly terrific. The sun beat down fiercely out of a brazen sky. The dust was choking: the hills merciless. The chatter and the chaff gradually died away, and when the whistles sounded for the regulation halt at the end of each hour of marching, the men fell out, dragged off their packs and dropped heavily on the grass.

At last, when the sun was high in the sky, they reached their destination. V—— was a straggling little village built on either side of the slope of the white highroad, smothered in dust, shaken to its very foundations by the incessant rumbling of motor lorries passing through, with a soporific and neglected looking *château*, where ducks promenaded solemnly in the courtyard, a wisp of river and a camp of huts.

The men were lodged in the huts,—regular cauldrons of heat they were, too, infested by flies,—pitched on an unprotected slope of sun-baked earth from which every blade of grass had been trodden. Huts had been set apart for the officers, but they would have none of them. Someone, with a taste for epigram, said the place looked like a dismantled poultry show. The officers, one and all, voted for quarters in the open air, as the weather was so beautifully fine.

After various negotiations, in which Apollo, who had the gift of tongues, played a leading role, permission was obtained from the local *châtelain*, who was henceforth known and is referred to in this narrative as The Baron, to pitch tents on the grass in a pleasant old apple orchard across the road from the huts. In this picturesque old-world *verger* the officers of the battalion were lodged. Headquarters' tents were ranged at one end of the orchard, the officers' tents pitched all round its edge, and the different company messes installed in the open air.

For ten delightful days the battalion spent a peaceful routine existence. The order went forth that cap-stars and buttons would be polished, and once more, at the morning inspection, our Ensign found himself, as in bygone days in barracks at home, scrutinising the men of his platoon for any signs that might betray a hasty or indifferent toilet. The division or the brigade—anyhow, the authority that governs these things—decided that the village streets were unduly dirty, and the supervision of a daily scavenging party was added to the duties of the Piquet Officer. Rubbish and dirt lying about the camp were collected and burnt, the village streets were picked clear of empty Woodbine cases and sardine tins and matches and bits of newspaper, and swept and garnished, so that when the brigade marched out of V—— it left a clean village behind.

Three times within a hundred years had the high tide of war swept across the village and the little *château* where The Baron and three generations of his family before him had been born. On a windowpane of his house was still to be seen the name "Julie," scratched with a diamond on the glass by the wife of a Cossack officer quartered at the *château* in 1812, while Europe was breathing again after the departure of The Ogre to Elba.

In 1870 The Baron, while yet a lad, had seen the Prussians, most insolent of conquerors, lodging at the *château*; forty four years after, in the heyday of their victorious advance, he had watched their cavalry passing through the village before the Battle of the Marne had sent them to the right-about and shattered all their hopes. Since those black August days of 1914 The Baron had seen all manner of fighting men in and about his ancient home, *poilus* and *cuirassiers* and *spahis* and *goumiers*, at first, and then, after a little time, the British,—English and Scots and Welsh and Irish, and Indians and Australians and Canadians and South Africans.

From the windows of his *château* he had seen the whole flood of battle flowing down to the Somme—and he was a little shy of soldiers. For in war, he told our Ensign over a glass of home-brewed cider, poultry goes a-missing from the farmyards, and the game vanishes from the woods, and the orchards are bereft of fruit, and young trees unaccountably hacked down. . . . "One does not grudge it, . . . *enfin, c'est la guerre!"*

But when The Baron found that the newcomers did not loot his chickens or poach his rabbits or break down his trees, his heart warmed to his guests in the orchard. He sent the officers, as a present, a hamper of his delicious home brewed cider; he plundered his kitchen garden to supply them with vegetables at a very moderate price—*les affaires sont les affaires, nest-ce pas?*—(and vegetables are hard to come by where the locust hosts of the Somme have passed), and he sold them his ducklings. One night he dined with the double-company mess beneath the apple-trees in the orchard, and made himself as charming as a well-bred Frenchman can. Of the Guards he said: "*On voit bien ce sont des gens qui savent se conduire!*"

It was The Baron who told the double-company mess of the little river in which they enjoyed many bathes in the hot summer afternoons. It was a few miles distant, an ice cold, crystal clear stream with a chalky bottom, that emptied itself into a deep and surging mill-pond at the foot of a ruined mill. Our Ensign and his brother officers used to ride over after tea, and, passing by the mill-pond, where the men of the Coldstream and grenadiers quartered in the neighbourhood used to disport themselves, would ascend the stream a little and plunge in off the grassy banks.

They often had a silent spectator of these bathes—a grey-haired man who sat for hours, a dog beside him, fishing in the stream. One day they spoke to him, and discovered that he was a citizen of Lille, a *réfugié*, waiting in a quiet spot for the day of victory. Patting his dog, he used to say in his mournful way, "*Lui, aussi, est Lillois: c'est tout ce qu'il me reste de ma famille!*"

Thus the summer days went by very pleasantly. Routine duties filled in their mornings, short route-marches to keep the men fit, parades, company drill, and, of course, daily "orders"; in the afternoons there was bathing or rides out to other Guards' battalions quartered about the place, or a concert by the Irish Guards' band, which had come out in its turn from London to spend a few weeks with the Guards' division. One afternoon The Lad, whom our Ensign had not seen again since their rather hasty parting under shell fire, came over with one or two others from his battalion and stayed to dinner in the orchard. Our Ensign and some of the others returned this visit, and dined with the other battalion in a camp of huts in a wood, and, after a very merry dinner, wobbled perilously home on bicycles in the dark, over an execrable road.

The weather remained magnificent. Every night the majority of the officers slept outside their tents in the orchard, under a velvety sky spangled with a vast array of stars, sometimes with the moon hung like a great lamp among the trees. The awakening in the freshness of dawn was a sheer delight, with the birds chirruping in the apple-trees, the sky benign and blue in the gentle light of the newly-risen sun, the grass which formed their *descente du lit* glittering with the morning dews. The men also, in their camp, dragged forth their packs at nightfall from the huts and lay down to sleep *à la belle etoile*.

On Sundays there was Brigade Divine Service in an orchard behind the *château*. On one or two occasions the band was in attendance and accompanied the old English hymns with fine effect. It was an unforgettable scene—the lines of tall, well-knit figures in khaki, bare-headed, standing on the grass in the sunshine or in the shade of the fruit trees, the brigade chaplain in his white surplice in the centre, close to him the little group of officers, a few patients with bandaged heads or arms from a local casualty clearing station, a knot of wide-eyed French youngsters, and the deep tones of the men's voices blending with the solemn strains of the band.

No less impressive was the Irish Guards' Mass held on the same spot every Sunday at an earlier hour, the R.C. Chaplain to the battalion, his leggings protruding unexpectedly below his sacerdotal vestments, celebrating at a portable altar surrounded by the kneeling figures of the big Irishmen—a wonderful and deeply impressive sight. Mass invariably concluded with an Irish hymn—

"*O glorious Saint Patrick,
Dear Saint of our Isle!*"

which the Irishmen used to sing with immense religious feeling and with a volume of sound that must have made the *château* windows tremble.

Every day came news of further successes on the Somme: every day our Ensign and his friends discussed the battalion's chances of an early share in the great push: every day there were fresh rumours of great tasks supposedly awaiting the Guards on the Somme; but nothing ever came of them.

On the last day of their stay, the king, who was visiting the army in France, came to see the brigade, and walked into the orchard where the officers of our Ensign's battalion were quartered and where they were waiting to be presented. The double-company mess had ransacked the village for flowers to put on the mess-table in honour of the occasion, and had procured some beautiful La France roses which, placed in soda-water bottles, lent a nice touch of colour to the table. It was at the mess-table under the trees where they were presented to the king, so they felt that their labours had not been in vain.

The battalion left V—— with many regrets on a dull steamy day, and marched to a dirty fly-ridden camp in the woods of M——, where it rained mercilessly and life was squalid and drear. There they stayed for two days and a half, a wonderful night bombardment of the Hun lines by the British artillery the only diversion, and then received unexpected orders to leave. Everybody believed that the battalion was going straight into the fight, and some of the young officers summoned the battalion barber to their tents and got their hair cut on the strength of the rumour.

But their hour had not yet struck. The village of L—— was their next destination.

Here they spent two days, and were then informed that they were going into the trenches again for a short spell. This rumour was at first received with incredulity. Nevertheless it was true.

By the following evening the battalion was once more in the front line.

Chapter 6

Inscrutable appear the ways of the staff to the young lions of our army in France. For a month the battalion had been fondly nursing the idea of going into action, yet here they were back again in the old routine of trench warfare. True, they were on the battlefield of the Somme, though that singularly diminutive stream was away to the southward of them; but there was no sign of immediate action in their neighbourhood—the traces were all of the fighting which had been.

A modern battle is run very much on the lines of a railway time-table. The attack is entrusted to certain armies, and the corps of which these armies are composed send their divisions and brigades "over the top" in due course and duly take them out of the line, whereupon fresh troops take their places. Each corps has its own billeting area, towns and villages and camps, where its troops are billeted on the way to or from battle. As one division or brigade moves out of one billet, the successor moves in by schedule, just as, on the railway, one train follows another on the same set of metals. This disposition of troops in a vast battle, over widely devastated country, is a very important feature of the operations; for nothing must be left to chance, and, with the tide of battle ebbing and flowing, success or failure may depend on the accessibility of the reserves.

But the hot blood of our young officers does not always comprehend these strategical considerations, and our Ensign's battalion groused mightily at the way the Guards were being "shunted about," while the rest of the British Army were busily collecting laurels on the Somme.

The battalion took over from some very cheery "Kitchener chaps," and the officers of the company which our Ensign's company relieved in the support position—a bowl shaped chalk quarry with some excellent dugouts—provided our Ensign and his brother officers with a very good luncheon. As No. 2 Company had been in the front line on the last occasion, it was now their turn to be in support, where their only duties were fetching rations and water for themselves and the companies in the front line. During their wanderings the double-company mess had received some fresh members, including one Bryan, who went to our Ensign's company, and one Duke, who went to No. 1,—our Ensign had been friends with both men in barracks at home, and their coming in no wise disturbed but only increased the *camaraderie* of the double-company mess.

The principal duty of the Guards in these trenches, as far as the front line companies were concerned, was to "clean up." This part of the line had been the scene of a holding attack in the earlier stages of the Somme battle. The troops concerned had done their work, but had not been able to hold the ground gained, and had fallen back to their front line, which had had a regular pounding from the German artillery. The trenches were badly battered and required a lot of repair, the dead bodies were scattered thickly about, and the atmosphere, especially in the warm showery weather then prevalent, was very bad.

So every night parties sallied forth, some to wire, others to repair the parapet, others again to bury the dead and salve the equipment lying about, both British and German. The burial parties had the worst time: you wanted strong nerves to stomach the sights about those trenches. Our Ensign used to see the fruits of these midnight salvage enterprises laid out afterwards in the trench—pay-books and identity discs and rifles and boxes of ammunition and helmets—ready to be sent down to the brigade. Altogether, during the few days they were in that part of the line, the battalion buried several hundred bodies and brought in a very large amount of salvage, for which good service they subsequently received the thanks of their brigadier.

Life was pretty quiet in those trenches. The Hun was having such a desperate struggle to keep his line together where the sledge-hammer blows were being dealt, that in the quieter spots he was only too glad to live and let live. The daily Intelligence Summary showed clearly, on the plain testimony of German Army orders, letters found on the dead, and the less reliable statements of prisoners, that not only was the invincibility of the German Army exploded amongst the very men who had most sedulously spread the myth, but that the German Higher Commands were seriously concerned at the growing demoralisation of the troops, as shown by such significant symptoms as desertions, slackness in patrolling, and the like.

As a scrupulous chronicler of the adventures of our Ensign, I must not overlook a curious experience that befell him one morning in these trenches. Lured by the promise of a perfect dawn, he ventured forth before breakfast to visit the officers in the front line, foolishly omitting to take his Burberry with him. As he was walking down to have breakfast with The Beak and Bryan in the chalk quarry, he was surprised by a drenching downpour of rain. The approach to the front line was very simple—any one of four communication trenches would take you there—but, in his haste to get home out of the wet, our Ensign took a wrong turn and presently found himself in a part of the front line which seemed unfamiliar to him.

Now, out in France, one trench looks very much like another. It was daylight, and the sentries had stood down, and in that downpour every man who was not on duty would naturally take shelter in the dug outs. So our Ensign was not surprised to find the trench deserted, thinking that presently he would come to a sentry who would tell him where he was. He noticed rifles leaning against the firesteps, and boxes of bombs in shelves cut in the parados, and here and there a pack or a mess-tin left outside a dugout. In fact, the trench looked very much as most trenches do in the early morning, after the men have had their breakfast and are snatching a few hours' sleep.

In places the trench was very battered: at one point a huge gap had been blown clean away, so that he found himself in full view of the German lines. Presently, as he hurried along, with his head down before the driving rain, he began to notice that the trench showed signs of most unusual untidiness. Picks and shovels were lying about all over the place: here a greatcoat had been trodden down into the mud, there a box of small-arms ammunition lay gaping on the ground. Then, even as he realised that the broken fire-bays were void of sentries, and that the trench was deserted, he came to a dead stop. For there, in the bottom of the trench, half a dozen yards from him, a khaki clad figure lay face downwards in the mud.

An eerie sensation crept over our young man. He felt like the hero of that stirring tale of old Clark Russell's when he boards *The Frozen Pirate* and finds himself in the midst of an arrested life. For, after stepping gingerly over the prone figure in the mud, he came to a dugout before which stretcher stood. On the stretcher lay a man with head swathed in bandages, and he was dead. So was the stretcher-bearer on the ground beside him, amid a litter of field-dressings. And there were many other dead bodies, besides these two, in that abandoned trench.

Our Ensign faced round and retraced his steps the way he had come, for he was fearful lest he should walk into the German lines if he went any farther. On his return he noticed many little signs that had escaped him in his previous haste,—remains of food spread out on tables in the silent dugouts, old books and newspapers, sodden and mud-stained, some gum-boots lying in a pile behind the trench, a woollen waistcoat hanging on a nail in a ruined shelter; it was a desolate, uncanny place, and our Ensign was glad when he heard the sizzle of bacon and walked into a bombing-post of the Welsh Guards, who were holding the right of his battalion, and was put on his road for home.

The battalion came out of the line on a chilly Sunday afternoon—the approach trenches were so good that reliefs could be effected by daylight—and marched to a camp in a forest, charmingly situated on high ground outside a large village. The forest had not been touched by shell fire; only the trees had been thinned a little to make room for the huts and tents. The ground was clean, not fouled like their last sylvan camping ground in the wood of M——, and the green moss made a soft carpet under their feet. There was a series of camps where the whole brigade was lodged, and the black-roofed huts and the white bell tents made a pretty picture spread out among the trees, the blue smoke from the wood fires curling up between, and *vistas* of forest glades on every hand.

The brigade spent a very agreeable two days in the forest. The weather completely reformed itself. A fine warm burst set in, bringing out all the healthy, resinous odours of the woods. The men exulted in their surroundings—a wholesome change, in truth, from their long nights burying the dead in the rain. When their day's work was done, they sat about in groups on the mossy ground under the trees and smoked and yarned. And (tell it not in Gath!) they sometimes contrived to have rabbit for supper.

There were a lot of Guards in and about the forest. Our Ensign, route marching with the company, used to meet them on the road. Such encounters generally started the men on anecdotes and reminiscences of the old 4th (Guards') Brigade, extending back to the days of the Retreat from Mons. In conversation with each other the men always referred to the Guards by their different nicknames, most Guards' battalions having a sobriquet of some sort. Thus the Coldstream are "the Coalies," the Scots Guards, "the Jocks," and the Irish Guards, "the Micks."

Every morning the drums of the different Guards' battalions in the camps roused the echoes of the forest (and everybody generally) with the stirring strains of the *Grand Réveille*: every evening at Retreat, in the dying sunshine, they made the woods resound to their music until that pause came, bringing every man instinctively and by anticipation to his feet, after which the fifes squealed and the drums rolled out the National Anthem.

The company messes, which were all lodged in one long hut, had a great dinner to celebrate their coming out of the line. Ah! those first dinners when the battalion comes out of the trenches! Will the future—that dim "After the War," which is the great European query-mark today—ever see their like? I doubt it.

How mind and body exult when you have had a hot bath, and there is the cool caress of fresh linen next your skin, and you have cast off your soiled uniform and heavy boots and changed into another jacket and comfortable trousers and shoes, and the port has come from Christopher's, and the mess-sergeant has procured a melon! The past is shoved behind you, with its blood and mud and evil odours; the present is all high spirits and grateful relaxation; and as for the future, you give it not a thought. Yet the future was there, though the Guards in their forest camp did not realise it—somewhere out there beneath that patch of starry sky framed in the low mess door, somewhere in the Unknown where the guns throbbed faintly in the night.

★★★★★★

Their next halting-place in their wanderings was no less pleasant—a large comfortable village which had almost escaped the flow of humanity towards the Somme. The barns where the men were billeted were spacious and clean and dry; milk and butter and eggs and vegetables were obtainable in plenty; and there were beds for all the officers. The whole brigade was billeted in the village, and made its entry down a long slope leading to the main street, with drums beating at the head of each long column of dusty, sun-browned men—a brave show.

Peter and our Ensign had a knotty point of military law to settle with respect to their billet. Is an *estaminet consigné à la troupe*—that is to say, put out of bounds for troops by the assistant provost-marshal for some contravention of the regulations—likewise out of bounds as a billet for officers? For they were not using the *estaminet* part of the establishment—they were merely to sleep in a bedroom above it.

Madame and a mild-mannered old gentleman, who turned out to be her husband, together with three or four peasants, seized upon this tortuous point of law, when *Madame* very frankly stated her case to the two officers and debated it ardently.

"*Ce sont les artilleurs*" Madame sighed, "*qui sont venus comme ça boire de la bière a la porte du derrière . . . on est seule, n'est-ce pas? On ne fait pas attention, n'est-ce pas? Et puis voilà, le Prévôt-Maréchal qui vous consigne pour quinze jours! Mon Dieu, c'est dur!*"

The husband echoed—

"*Sapristi, cest dur!*"

And the peasants, removing their pipes to spit, chanted in chorus—

"*Bien stir que cest dur!*"

The upshot of it was that Peter and our Ensign, deciding that the bedroom was not the *estaminet* within the meaning of the Act, passed a very comfortable night on good beds in *Madame's* exceptionally clean room. They likewise purchased for a five-*franc* note two very plump white and grey lop-eared rabbits, which the *patron* carried grimly into a backyard and brought back neatly and expeditiously slain. The mess waiter fetched them across to the mess, and they formed the *pièce de résistance* at dinner that evening.

When troops arrive in a village out at the Front they swamp it: they make it their own. Within an hour or two of the Guards' arrival in this comfortable French hamlet, neat little boards or flags hung outside the different billets clearly indicating who lodged there, the Headquarters and billet guards were mounted, and, with their clothes brushed and their faces shining with the recent vigorous application of yellow soap and water, the men strolled out in groups to see what refreshment local establishments could offer, and also to buy those sentimental picture post cards in which all soldiers delight.

The main street simply overflowed with troops, big and brown and tranquil; and for an officer to pass along was to run the gauntlet of a never-ceasing fire of salutes. That evening Operation Orders announced that on the following morning the battalion would march on. And our Ensign found himself entrusted with the duties of billeting officer

Chapter 7

Just contemplate the billeting officers parlous position. The briefest period of grace is conceded to him, in which he and his accomplices cycle furiously ahead of the battalion to distribute the billets in the area allotted to them. Even as the billeting officer, dusty and damp-browed, receives, on arriving at his destination, from the staff captain of the brigade, the list of billets set apart for his battalion, he can hear, with the ears of his mind, the battalion marching towards him with the leaden feet of inexorable destiny. Every minute brings them nearer; every minute shortens that brief breathing space in which he must complete all his arrangements and present himself, calm and unruffled, with a complete map of the locality in his mind, at the entrance of the village, to lead the incoming troops to their quarters.

The billeting officer must combine the organising genius of a William Whiteley with the quickness of decision of a Napoleon. He must be gentle as the dove, cunning as the serpent. He must be all things to all men—firm with recalcitrant peasants, persuasive with fussy *beldames*, glib with weary and fractious officers who look for beds when there are no beds.

The billeting officer must be an optimist, unfailing and uncompromising. He must survey the world through the rosy spectacles of the house agent. As in the house advertisements in the newspapers, so to him all residences must be "stately" or "well-appointed," all villas "pretty" or "charming," all rooms "lofty," all barns "spacious."

He and every man of his billeting party are cold and calculating egoists. The four quartermaster-sergeants of the battalion who accompany him are, each and individually, solely concerned with securing the best billet for their own companies. The pioneer sergeant has come forth to seek the largest and roomiest barn in sight for the housing of the quartermaster's stores; the drill-sergeant is heart and soul devoted to the interests of the Orderly Room, the Guard Room, the Medical Inspection Room, and quarters for the signallers and the drums; as for the poor billeting officer, tossed to and fro like a shuttlecock between all these conflicting currents, his dominant idea is to find some kind of decent billet for the commanding officer and headquarters. Nor must he ever lose sight of the fact that, if he gives the officers of his own company anything like good quarters, he will unload upon his own devoted head all the lightnings of the other company messes.

The billeting party, headed by our Ensign, set off on bicycles on a delicious summer morning for the village of F——, the next half of the brigade, on what someone called its "one night stands" about the country. The faithful Johnson had procured for his "master" from the signalling sergeant a bicycle, which, in consideration of a little cleaning and oiling, ran somewhat better than army machines generally do. On the road they fell in with billeting parties from the other battalions of the brigade, and on the face of each billeting officer dull care had graven a deep furrow.

Outside the church of F——, an ugly bogus Gothic structure, red and staring, like the picture on a child's box of bricks, the staff captain met them by appointment, and handed each billeting officer a list setting forth the numbers of the different billets at the disposal of the battalion. Every house in the war zone in France bears a number stencilled on the door, and underneath, an entirely fabulous computation of the numbers of "*Hommes*" or "*Chevaux*" that can be lodged there.

Billeting at F—— was unusually easy. The barns were large and in good repair, and the local inhabitants, while somewhat resigned, were friendly. The four companies were allotted billets without difficulty, and even the drill-sergeant found quarters for all his different charges. But accommodation for the officers was a different matter. Our Ensign found lodgings for the four company commanders, *tant bien que mal*; the interpreter, who was of the party, arranged with the local cure to put up the chaplain; and our Ensign kept in his mind's eye a certain *coquet* little red-brick villa, marked down on his list as affording accommodation for five officers, for the headquarters billet.

But at the very door of the villa disaster was lurking. Two dragoon officers met them in the garden.

"Is this billet free?" asked our Ensign with fear in his heart.

"No," said one of the dragoons promptly; "there are five of us in here—Corps cavalry—been here for weeks."

"But it's down on my list as our billet," objected our Ensign.

"I know," was the calm reply; "we've had about six fellows before you after it—I've told the mayor to scratch it off!"

Our Ensign looked at the list again. Then he saw a tiny smudge, which on closer investigation proved to be an asterisk. "Probably occupied" was the note he read at the foot of the page.

The list was exhausted—none of the rooms they had seen would do for headquarters; so our Ensign, with the optimism of the billeting officer nascent in his breast, started to look for a clean bivouac where Headquarters might be accommodated in tents. They presently found a large grassy orchard which seemed suitable for the purpose. It lay behind a farm, where our Ensign duly demanded the requisite permission.

An extremely dirty, red-eyed old woman was the *propriétaire*. She had a large, bare, and very dilapidated room, swarming with flies, which she offered; but she resolutely set her face against letting the orchard be used.

She wagged her old head stubbornly.

"*Non, non, non!*" she croaked, "*j'n'veux pas! La dernière fois les soldats ont joué au ballon dans le verger . . . ils ont tout abîmé . . . j'n'veux pas!*"

Our Ensign explained with much persuasiveness, but with a horrid fear in his mind that the battalion would arrive any instant, that only officers would be lodged there who never played football, and who, by their very presence, would prevent the irruption of *ballon*-kicking soldiery.

Then the interpreter took a hand and drew a superb word-picture of the innate courtliness and good behaviour of every British officer—of these officers in particular—and of the commanding officer most of all.

The old harridan began to yield.

"*Mais, bien sûr,*" she muttered irresolutely, "*ils vont casser mes arbres.*"

The interpreter spoke again. These officers were rich and generous. They would do no damage, but any damage they might do would be paid for: of that she might rest assured. The officers would buy her chickens, her butter, her eggs: the noble young man at his side was even at that moment ready to invest five *francs* in the produce of the farm (this on a whispered suggestion from our Ensign). She would be reasonable; she would not regret it.

Then, at last, the old lady gave way.

"*Je veux bien, alors,*" she said, "*pourvu qu'on ne va pas jouer au ballon!*"

Thus it was settled, the double-company mess was installed in the old lady's room in consideration of a *douceur* of 2 *francs* 50 a day, and our Ensign rushed away to the entrance of the village to await the coming of the brigade.

The brigade arrived with its usual punctuality in a cloud of dust behind the Drums, each battalion being taken charge of by its billeting officer as it marched in, the quartermaster-sergeants leading the different companies into their billets. The men swarmed into the farmyards and dumped their packs and rifles in the barns, then lined up in the yards of their billets for the customary foot inspection—in bare feet, their boots and socks in their hands. The cookers, all smoking, with their begrimed attendants trudging behind, lumbered into the billets, the little billet-boards appeared outside gateways and doors, the guards were mounted, and then the officers, dusty and hot, came streaming into the messes where the mess servants, surrounded by dogs and cats and poultry and small children, were unpacking the mess-boxes and getting lunch.

Our Ensign walked up to the mess to receive congratulations on the success of his arrangements. He was given a chilly reception.

"I suppose we have the worst mess in the place," said Roderick gloomily; "the cobbler's children are always the worst shod, and the billeting officer's mess always gets the rottenest accommodation!"

"I can't imagine," said *El Capitan*, one of the company commanders, "why you put me to sleep next door to X. I have to go through his room to get to mine, and you know how he hates being disturbed!"

"I suppose you've arranged for tents," said somebody else darkly; "of course the simple life is very healthy and all that, but there's the devil of a storm blowing up, and what sleeping out in the open in your beautiful orchard tonight will be like, the Lord only knows!"

Then the mess waiter, entering, informed our Ensign that there were no potatoes: could he get some anywhere? That *Madame* would not allow the cook to make a fire in the courtyard: would he speak to her? That they had sent up word from the medical inspection room to know whether the Heavies were entitled to be in the same billet: would the billeting officer mind stepping across there and seeing about it?

Our Ensign put down his drink untasted, and holding his head in his hands, staggered out into the hot sunshine. In the street he met an ensign of one of the other companies, dusty, doleful, and dejected.

"Got a good mess?" he asked our Ensign.

Our young man assumed an air of Christian resignation.

"Nobody could have a worse mess than we've got," continued the other, and added pointedly, "but, *of course*, you're all right!"

Our Ensign laughed bitterly and went his way. Black is the lot of the billeting officer.

But when he returned to his mess the soothing influence of luncheon had worked wonders. The gramophone was playing, and the mess beamed at its late victim over its coffee and cigarettes. The sun was shining brightly out of the blue sky; the tents were being pitched in the orchard; altogether life had assumed a fairer hue. The gust had passed. And our Ensign, eating his lunch, reflected that campaigning is, after all, but a series of gusts: a gust of pleasant days, a gust of bad ones; a gust of easy times, a gust of unfortunate incidents and "*strafeing*," when everything seems to go wrong; a gust of peaceful wanderings like the present, and then a gust of war, of stern reality, the gust to come.

That afternoon some of them took horses and rode across to visit the adjacent "Grottoes," which, according to the interpreter, were the principal attraction in the way of sight seeing in that part of the country. In the village outside which the Grottoes were situated, our Ensign came across The Lad, whose battalion was billeted in the place. The Lad, with a party of his brother officers, was, to our Ensign's intense delight, engaged in heated controversy with his billeting officer. As few things are harder to bear than the annoyance of a good example, so is nothing more consoling to the victim of injustice than to see his fellow in the same pass.

The Grottoes consisted of a series of high-roofed caves and narrow galleries cut out of the soft chalk, and running far into the bowels of the earth. To the archaeologist or geologist they would doubtless have proved of enthralling interest, for the old gentleman who had made their exploration his life work had filled case upon case with those chipped and dusty fragments of flint in which the scientific mind rejoices. To our Ensign and his companions the main interest of the Grottoes consisted in the fact that they were beautifully cool, and also that the Germans were known to have made good use of similar caves in such fortified villages as Beaumont Hamel and Les Boeufs.

The young French girl who showed them round by the light of a candle informed them, with all the glib fluency of the professional guide, that in feudal times the Grottoes had been quarries in which the serfs quarried the chalk for local lordlings, and that at different periods of history the caves had afforded refuge to various bands of brigands, including some jolly fellows rejoicing in the name of the Flayers of the North. Refugees had found sanctuary there in the French Revolution, and at the time of the Prussian invasion of 1870 the civil population had likewise made the caves their hiding-place.

"The Grottoes extend for two kilometres," wound up the young French lady; "one *franc* is the charge for the whole trip: fifty *centimes* for the shorter journey."

"How far did she say?" asked one of the visitors.

"Two kilometres," replied our Ensign.

"Tell her we'll give her a *franc* and take the short trip," came back the reply . . . and Science hid her head. . . . "I want my tea!"

As they paid the girl at the entrance, before going away, our Ensign asked her if she were the regular guide.

"*Avant la guerre*" she answered, "*c'était mon père qui faisait le guide. Mais lui et mes deux frères sont partis pour l'armée et depuis, il n'y a que moi et ma soeur qui restent!*"

"Are they all right, your father and brothers?" somebody asked.

"*Papa est tombé à Verdun*" she replied; "*un de mes frères est prisonnier en Allemagne: l'autre est encore là-bas, au front!*" And she wiped her eyes.

You can't move far in France today without stepping into the shadow of the people's mourning.

Then they went back into the blinding sunshine, and, mounting their horses, clattered back to F——. At the horse-lines, where they left their horses, they learnt that "Retreat" was to be played in the main street of the village by the massed Drums of the brigade. So they all strolled off to the main street and found retreat in full swing.

It was a good show. The broad street running between the long, low, white farmhouses, with big gateways opening into the square courtyards, was thronged with men from the different battalions of the brigade. Tall and sunburnt and well brushed, with their cap-stars and buttons well burnished, they lined the sides of the street, leaving the centre of the road free for the passage of the Drums.

In F—— was quartered a labour company of Senegalese, extraordinary nightmare objects, loose-limbed, lanky negroes, with coal black faces seamed with tribal cuts, grinning from beneath high yellow tarbooshes, round the edge of which their thick woolly hair was fuzzed out, huge pouting lips, and a highly comic attire consisting of voluminous *jebbahs* of coarse canvas, snowy white, reaching below the knee, baggy white trousers, and heavy marching boots. Parties of these weird-looking creatures were now scattered about among the thick lines of Guardsmen, jolly as only negroes can be at the sound of music, grinning with a white flash of teeth, and chattering volubly in their African lingo. They were an extraordinary company, and their morning parade with picks and shovels, before going out to work on the roads, was the most excruciatingly funny thing a man ever saw.

Down the centre alley, between the lines of men, came the Drums, four drum-majors with their staffs in front. Behind them came the side-drums, the drummers' hands raised high and falling together, the tenor drums, the fifes and the brass drums. On reaching the top or the bottom of the street, as the case might be, the leading files turned and marched through the succeeding files, each rank following suit.

It was a great moment for the Drums. The whole brigade was in the street, from the brigadier downwards: every eye was on the Drums, and the Drums bore themselves right gallantly. They crashed through all the well known inarches, to which the brigade had trudged many a weary mile in France, and then came the crowning moment, the march based on the regimental airs of the brigade of Guards.

One after the other the old familiar tunes rang out, amid a roll of drums that made the very windows rattle,—"*The British Grenadiers*," of the Grenadiers; "*Milanello*," that quaint, jingling march which the Coldstream picked up in Spain, and of which tradition says the original Spanish words are unprintable; the Scots Guards' "*Hieland Laddie*," the frankly joyous "*St Patrick's Day*" of the Irish Guards, and the sonorous "*Men of Harlech*" of the Welsh Guards.

After the fantasia had ended in an abrupt crash, the senior drum-major marched stiffly across the street to the brigadier, and, saluting, asked for permission to dismiss. Then every officer's right hand went to his cap and every man stiffened to attention as the Drums played "*God Save the King*," the tones of which, both on land and sea, announce to the fighting forces the coming of night.

The next day the brigade moved on again.

Chapter 8

Take a large French village, shell it a little and bomb it a little from aeroplanes so that all the windows are broken and most of the roofs damaged, remove the civilian inhabitants, pass several hundred thousand troops through it, plant horse-lines all round it, so that every road approaching it is churned into a morass by the horses' hoofs, make the road running through it one of the main arteries leading into battle, and choke it—day and night—with marching troops and motor ambulances and long strings of lorries, smear it alternately with layers of dust and mud, add several billion flies—horse-, house-, and bluebottle—pop in a hundred thousand rats or so, bring back a few score civilians to take possession of the only whole houses remaining, and serve hot—extremely hot—and stinking. And there you have the village of M———, the brigade's next halting-place, as it presented itself to our Ensign and his billeting party about the hour of noon on a blazing hot day.

Behind them they had a twenty-mile cycle ride, under a fierce sun, against a violent and exhausting headwind. And now, soaked to the skin with perspiration, covered with dust, thirsty, tired, and (to speak for our Ensign only) extremely cross, they pushed their heavy machines up the long slope of the main street amid a dense mass of traffic and clouds of petrol-scented dust.

They were early for their rendezvous with the staff captain: in fact, they had more than half an hour to spare. They stacked their bicycles together outside the town major's office, which was to be their trysting place, and forthwith went their several ways in search of shade and refreshment, to meet again at the appointed time. Our Ensign was carried off by a billeting Coldstream officer to a Y.M.C.A. establishment, where, among more flies than our Ensign had ever seen together before, they quaffed some cold, green liquid, retailed at a penny a glass as lemonade by a bespectacled Hebe (*masculini generis*) behind the cake-laden counter. Our Ensign and his brother officer absorbed several glasses of this refreshing beverage, and then went forth to find the town major.

He was sitting in his office, a large, clean-shaven major of infantry, urbane and charming. He mopped his brow, and sighed when he saw them enter.

"Oh dear!" he groaned, "you keep on coming in, and I haven't the least idea where you are all to go. I do hope you're not expecting anything great in the way of billets: you'll not get 'em here. Half the place is in ruins, and the dirt! and the smells! You never saw anything like it! Oh, damn these flies!"

He whisked his handkerchief round his head.

"Well," he continued, "I think there's some Perrier left: I believe I got the last case in this part of the country: and I expect there will be some whisky, too. Come along into the garden: the rest are there!"

His frankness boded ill: like billeting officers, town majors are generally optimists, and chatter gaily about the "unexceptional advantages" of the billets in their domain. The two officers followed their host in silence into the garden, where they found the other billeting officers of the brigade, in various stages of exhaustion, conversing in gloomy tones over the town major's whisky and Perrier.

The garden was a dirty backyard contrived so as to collect all the sun's rays as in a burning glass. It commanded a view of a flat green field in which the principal object was an abandoned incinerator.

In due time the staff captain appeared and distributed the billeting lists. He, too, was brutally frank about the accommodation: they had best expect nothing, he told them. Our Ensign found allocated to his battalion a short patch of houses in the main street, opposite and on either side of the town major's office. The list looked promising enough: several billets were marked down as furnishing accommodation for as many as a hundred men at a time: one even—as shown on the list—would take two hundred. But as soon trust a company prospectus as a billeting list; the element of truth is about the same in both.

It was a quarter to one when our Ensign started his round of the billets. The billeting parties had come across country on their bicycles; the brigade was going to cover part of the journey by rail and march the rest; they were not expected to arrive before three o'clock at the earliest, so our Ensign felt that he could take things fairly easily.

The peasants were not friendly—and why should they be, poor creatures?—returning, with the French peasant's fatalistic attachment to his native soil, to find their houses wrecked, their gardens ravaged, and their barns and sheds occupied by an ever-changing succession of foreign soldiers. They came to their house doors and pointed silently to the barns and outhouses about the yard, then shut the door in our young man's face.

Things went all right at first. Everything was filthy and swarming with flies, everywhere the ground was befouled, and in many of the once trim gardens, amid the full-blown roses and the straggling and broken lines of peas and scarlet runners, water logged and evil smelling dug outs were crumbling into oblivion—mementoes of the days when the German artillery was close enough up to shell the French troops in their billets. But our Ensign managed to get billets for three out of the four companies, though most of the places had holes both in the roof and in the wattle walls. He intended to put the remaining company in the billet noted as accommodating 200 men.

This was where the billeting list let him down badly—an act of base betrayal. For the farmer came out of his house at the officer's summons and announced, politely enough but with great firmness, that the *granges* were no longer available, for the harvest, which was to be brought in that afternoon, would fill them to the rafters.

Here was a staggering blow indeed. The whole battalion was provided for except the officers; and now, unless the town major could allot them another billet, the whole billeting scheme would have to be rearranged and a quart crammed into a pint pot—that is to say, a thousand men packed into billets for 750.

Back to the town major's office our young man went. It was already half-past two; neither headquarters nor the messes nor the officers had yet been provided for. The town major was out. He had been carried off by the brigade medical officer, who was clamouring for a site for the field ambulance. Sending one of his party to watch the entrance of the village in case the brigade should appear before its time, our Ensign set off feverishly on the track of the town major.

It was three o'clock by the time that our young man had found him. There was no sign of the brigade as yet. Heedless of the clamouring throng of petitioners at the town major's heels, our Ensign resolutely button holed him and poured his pathetic story into his sympathetic ear. Our young man's desperate situation stirred the generous heart of that town major.

"The harvest again!" he groaned, clasping his brow. "I'll go and see what I can do with the fellow, but I fear we are undone!" As they hurried up the street, he explained to our Ensign that, by virtue of some dark arrangement between the British and French authorities, the peasants had the right to claim exemption from billeting to make room for the crops.

The town major's fears were justified: the farmer was in the right; his position was incontestably sound; they would have to forego the billet.

Together, the major and our Ensign inspected two other billets—"emergency billets" the town major called them, the last two in the place. One was occupied by an artillery store, but they contrived to filch from the gunners accommodation for one platoon; the other was a gaunt barn, open all along one side, with shell-holes in the further wall, and the corrugated iron roof abundantly perforated by shrapnel.

Our Ensign shook his head, thanked the town major, and fled. The whole billeting scheme had to be rearranged. He picked up his billeting party once more and started the round again, reshuffling the billets, redistributing the men, cramming in half a platoon here and tucking little packets of men away in there, deaf to expostulation and entreaty, coldly ignoring the dismay in the faces of his quartermaster-sergeants. Half-past three! No brigade yet: now for the officers ...two or three in this empty room, with sacking stretched in front of the paneless windows, and the mess across the entrance hall in a dirty apartment, where fat bluebottles hovered greedily about decaying fragments of bully beef; this silent and forbidding house, to which they obtained access through a window, with three filthy little rooms, would accommodate six or seven officers—say, the members of the double-company mess: some tents could be put up in the garden at the back; another mess here, the company commanders there ... but where, oh where, to put headquarters?

There was nothing suitable under a roof, but our Ensign remembered the field with the incinerator behind the town major's garden. Four o'clock: not a drum to be heard: the brigade was late: back to the office to obtain from the ever-patient major a lien on the field. Done! and three tents promised into the bargain in case it rained that night and the billets leaked.

It had already started to rain when our Ensign, his appointed task over, hastened down the village street to the cross-roads by the river by which the brigade would come in.

There he found his fellow-billeters in the brigade, each with his tale of dirty billets and leaky roofs and swarming flies, each with his story of the treachery of billeting lists, for the harvest surprise, our Ensign found, had been sprung on them all.

They waited patiently in the rain for hours. The traffic never ceased to pour into the village in a double stream, going in both directions to and from the battlefield, troops and guns and transport and ambulances and motorcars. A red-capped sergeant of military police stood on point duty at the crossroads, immutably calm and affable amid the confusion and the din; eternally side-tracking strings of horses, which were not allowed through the village, and which persevering grooms, well knowing the prohibition, hoped yet to be able to get through, patiently answering inquiries from dust powdered lorry drivers who had lost their way.

The shades of evening deepened gently amid a depressing drizzle, but still the brigade did not come, still the traffic flowed past without a moment's break.

"It looks as if the brigade were not going to arrive until after dark!" said one of the billeting officers; "and in this squash there'll be the most holy confusion—the Lord help us!"

A grenadier subaltern, who had discovered a wayside *café* just past the crossroads, led some of them to it. None of them had had anything more substantial than a sandwich since breakfast, and they demanded food. All that *Madame* could produce was a box of wafers, very sweet and sickly, which they ate with some excellent coffee which *Madame* prepared over the stove.

Outside night fell, muggy and wet. Then the brigade transport, which had come by road, arrived, a long train of rumbling limbers, with the transport officers on horseback. They had no news of the brigade, but a little later a staff car, which the billeting officers stopped, reported that it had passed "some Guards or other" on the road about two miles back.

And then at last they came ... at eight o'clock. The dark and the traffic notwithstanding, the Guards made their entry to the tap of drum, and, despite all forebodings, each battalion got safely tucked away in its billets. When he reached the mess our Ensign found that his brother officers had so many remarks to offer on the slowness of the train that had conveyed them, and the general inefficiency of railway transport in particular, that they altogether omitted to comment on the nature of the billets which he offered them.

Though the sleeping quarters were indescribably bad, the actual mess-room proved to be better than might have been expected. It was a room in a small farmhouse occupied by a Frenchwoman, whose husband was in the trenches, and who, after the gifted Apollo had talked to her a little in his most Parisian French, proffered her services as cook. And so, while the traffic rumbled, and the rain splashed down outside, they made a good dinner, and eventually repaired to their squalid lodging in excellent spirits. There they found their sleeping valises spread on the dusty floor, and there they laid them down to sleep, promising to turn every available servant on to swabbing in the morning.

M—— proved itself to be every bit as bad as it had promised. The billets were positively filthy, and for days the battalions of the Brigade swept and garnished and burnt, filling in the rubbish pits which gaped, stinking, in every garden, and leaving a trail of chloride of lime behind them wherever they went. Fly-papers and flyswatters proved illusive against the indomitable breeding energy of the flies, and only days of unremitting hard work contrived at length to abate this very disagreeable and very unhygienic pest.

It rained for days on end. In a few hours the deep dust of the road turned first to a thick morass of mud, and then into a liquid lake of slime which flowed across the gutters to the very gateways of the billets. To avoid wading in mud up to the ankles, the men built little causeways to bridge the gutters, using the bricks from the more dilapidated houses, and laying branches on top. Nearly all the billets leaked, and the yards, filthy as they always are abroad with a vast and sodden midden-heap in the centre, were ankle deep in slush. What was possible to do with tarpaulin to stop the gaps in roofs and walls was done, but while the rain lasted the men had a very thin time, which they bore, as all men do in France, without grousing, reserving their grumbling for superficial and insignificant details, as is the way of the British soldier.

The billets were so bad and the weather continued to be so wet that a rum issue was ordered, though the season of the daily rum issues had not yet arrived. An officer superintended the issue of rum to each company, for the regulation is that each man must drink his tot on the spot where it is issued, in the presence of an officer—this to prevent hoarding and its attendant evils.

Accordingly, our Ensign found himself one wet evening attending the issue of rum to the company. On the floor of the barn stood a lighted candle, the centre of a number of mess tins representing the portions of the different groups in the company. At our Ensign's side was the company sergeant-major with the rum-jars. Silent and expectant, the men stood all around and in the yard without.

The company sergeant-major poured the rum out into the different tins, announcing as he did so the name of the recipients—"No. 5 Platoon," "The Cooks," "The Pioneers," and so on. Then, after much shuffling about in the outer darkness, the men got formed up, mess-tin in hand; but before the first received his noggin, the company sergeant major put to our Ensign that time-honoured question, "Would he try a little drop?"

Rum on an empty stomach before dinner is not to be recommended, but our young man knew what was expected of him, and with suitable gratitude accepted the offer. About a mugful of raw spirit was thereupon poured out for him, greatly to his dismay, but he picked it up, and crying "Here's luck!" drained it. The rum burnt his throat and brought the tears to his eyes, but he finished off the portion and held the mug upside down, as the men do, to show that it was empty—all this amid profound silence, with every man's eye upon him. Then, one by one, the men emerged out of the gloom into the yellow circle of light, with outstretched tin or mug, received their portion, tossed it off, inverted their drinking vessel, and moved away, wiping their mouths on the backs of their hands. When every man had been served, the company sergeant major picked up the last tin, and, tipping it down for the officer to see the contents, said—

"For the sergeants and myself."

This last portion was divided between them and consumed. Then the C.S.M., shaking the rum jar, said—

"There's some left yet, sir."

"Everybody had his tot?" asked our Ensign.

"Yes, sir," was the reply.

"Right," answered the officer; "tip the rest out!"

(For such is the inexorable rule of the army: what is left over from a rum issue must be spilled. Rum does not keep.)

"Sir!" replied the C.S.M., and in obedience to the order he emptied a brown gush of the spirit upon the earthen floor under the sorrowful gaze of the men. Our Ensign would have gladly given them an extra tot all round, for the night was raw and chill, but an order is an order....

And now the Guards found themselves within measurable distance of the ultimate goal of all their wanderings, the Battle of the Somme. Day and night the little village street resounded to the tramp of marching columns, to the thunder of the jarring, quivering trains of ammunition lorries. In that cramped and crowded village the only parade-ground was the dirty courtyards of the different billets, where the most stentorian word of command would often be lost in the roar of traffic from the street.

But while the stream of men and munitions flowed unceasingly eastward towards the Somme, from the battlefield came daily reports of further successes. Every sign pointed to the imminent participation of the Guards in the great offensive. There were frequent conferences, and, day after day, the Guards marched out by platoons, by companies, by battalions, past the little military cemetery, past the vast camps stretching away to the horizon, past the gangs of grubby German prisoners working on the roads, to the training-ground, where the coming attack was rehearsed in every detail. There were field days and night operations and lectures and several false alarms, ... warnings to be in readiness for immediate departure, which were afterwards cancelled.

A few days after the arrival of the brigade at M——, the Guards' Divisional Canteen turned up and installed itself in the main street, and was followed shortly afterwards by the Guards' Divisional Cinema, which was set up in that very barn with shrapnel-riddled roof which our Ensign had rejected as a billet. Tarpaulin supplied the missing wall, a little gas-engine furnished the power, and on the many wet evenings that the Clerk of the Weather bestowed on the Guards at M——, "the pictures" proved a great attraction. There, on one of the rare fine afternoons, our Ensign and a large party of his friends sat in a stifling atmosphere and saw the Somme battle film. Save for a few gunners and sappers, the whole audience consisted of Guardsmen, and their comments on this celebrated series of pictures were instructive—for they made none. They only cheered and laughed every time "Fritz" was seen on the screen.

The Guards' Divisional Baths—a travelling concern this, that plants itself in any empty building that seems adapted to the purpose, or, in default of such a building, erects its own premises—happened along with its array of tubs and heating apparatus and vast supplies of towels and clean shirts, socks, and underwear. Every day parties of men were marched down by an officer under a scheme that ensured to every man one bath a week.

There was much entertaining between the different messes. Everybody was always dining out with one or other of the company messes in the different battalions, with the brigade machine gunners, or with the stokes mortars, who are charming fellows, but whose propinquity in the trenches is unpopular owing to the disagreeable tendency of their murderous weapons to draw fire.

In the double-company mess all went as merry as a wedding bell. *Madame*, in whose house the mess was lodged, proved herself a jewel and cooked them wonderful omelettes and ragouts, and a *Potage Bonne Femme* before which Escoffier himself would have doffed his hat. The mess raged and wrangled and argued, as young men do the world over, but the underlying good fellowship was never disturbed. The past tense is ever a kindlier critic than the present, but our Ensign, looking back on those pleasant summer days, cannot recollect that there was a single discordant element in that little band of men.

But the sand in the hour-glass had all but run out. At last the word for their departure came. And Battalion Orders that evening closed with a significant paragraph. Under the heading Dress, it ran—

"The polishing of buttons and cap-stars is discontinued until further orders."

A bon entendeur, salut!

Chapter 9

From now on, the shadows of the events that stood before began to be more sharply-defined. As the brigade marched out of M—— behind the Drums on a dull grey morning, there were many besides our Ensign there who felt that the moment was close at hand when they would take their places in the battle-line of the Somme. Indeed, hardly had the men got shaken down in their new quarters—a bivouac on a bare and dirty hillside amidst rolling downs covered, as far as the eye could see, with camps and horse lines and abandoned trenches,—than a message arrived—

The battalion is on ten minutes' notice!

Now they were on the very fringe of the fight. The bivouac was within the zone of "the heavies." All that day, with a blinding flash of green flame, a sickly burst of yellow smoke, and a ponderous roar, the big guns gave tongue from their positions among the downs. All that day, down the white road running through the ruined village on the fringe of the bivouac, snorted and rattled and tramped the vast outgoing traffic of the battlefield. Motor ambulances whirred by in a constant stream, slowing up at the end of the village, where in cavernous dugouts white-robed surgeons toiled over the human debris of the fight. Motor-lorries fetching shells, ammunition limbers and water-carts going down to be filled, baggage carts—all through the morning and afternoon our Ensign saw them bumping slowly down the hill in the dust.

Between the gaps in the traffic, marching in a dense white haze, came the remnants of the battalions which had just written Ginchy in letters of blood upon their colours. Our Ensign had seen that splendid Irish Division marching into action less than a week before, with pipes skirling out the old Irish airs and green flags waving, a jaunty, defiant, deathless band. Not a whit less jaunty, not a whit less defiant, though the Reaper had been busy in their ranks, our Ensign saw them again today, slow-footed and mud-stained, dirty and unshaven, yet marching with the gait of victors.

Somewhere down the road the cry rang out—
"'Tis the Dubs.!"

In an instant the road was overflowing with Irish Guardsmen, swarming forward in the dust-clouds raised by the Dublin Fusiliers in their passage.

"Jasus! 'tis the Micks!" rang out a voice in the midst of the column. Cheery salutations were exchanged. Here and there a brown hand stretched out from the roadside grasped a muddy one thrust forward from the ranks of marching men in a warm clasp. Chaff was freely bandied about as the Irishmen trudged past, "Dubs." and Munsters and Connaughts and the rest.

"So they didn't get yez this time, Micky, me boy!" shouted a droll Irish voice from the roadside.

"True for you, Patsy, true for you!" flashed back the answer from the ranks. "I'll be meetin' yez in Ould Dublin yet!"

"Begob! yell have to get a move on yez, the Micks," drawled out a rich brogue from the road, "if ye want to find anny of the Gerboys left! We didn't lave manny of thim for yez! Didn't we an' the Dubs, knock hell's own blazes out of thim?"

There was a roar of laughter and cheers, then brogue and its owner were swallowed up in the dust. . . .

At tea that afternoon somebody announced that the Welsh Guards up in the front line had had a very bad shelling, and were probably coming out that night. Another battalion was to take their places, and two companies of our Ensign's battalion were to go up and replace this battalion in support. After tea our Ensign was sent for by the commanding officer, and told to go on ahead and reconnoitre the route for the two companies as far as the headquarters of another Guards' brigade, so that they should not lose their way in the dark. From brigade headquarters guides would take the two companies up to the line.

It was getting dusk, and there was no time to lose. Our Ensign sent his servant to the signallers to borrow two bicycles; and after beating the bivouac for his orderly, and failing to find him, he selected a bright lad in the company to act as orderly, and a little later the pair might have been seen pushing their bicycles through the dust up the steep road leading towards the Front.

The experiences of that night lingered long in our Ensign's memory. The road was terribly rough; and though, with the coming of evening, the traffic was less, there was still enough about to make riding in the half-light distinctly dangerous. Their way led them past miles of empty trenches, where weather-beaten wooden crosses, hung with withered flowers, remained to tell of the time when the French were holding these positions, then the front line. As they drew nearer to the Front, they passed imperceptibly from the zone of the biggest guns into the region of the lighter pieces. The guns were waking up. Now and then, as they pedalled along, a huge shell travelled over their heads, coming from their rear, "*hooshing*" and wailing as it sped through the air. Now from right and now from left of them ear-splitting reports resounded.

The traffic grew heavier as they approached their destination. At the entrance to a gloomy and shattered village, so wrecked by shell fire that every house was razed, the press of vehicles and of troops going up and coming down was so great that our Ensign and his orderly had to get off and walk their bicycles. Presently all further progress was hindered; so, after waiting for a spell, our Ensign shouldered his heavy machine and struck out among the ruins to try and get round the block in the road. It was very heavy going; but at last, soaked with perspiration and breathless, our Ensign and his orderly emerged upon a fairly clear stretch of road, and pedalled off into the gathering darkness.

Fortunately the way was not difficult to find. At a cross roads, where a mass of blackened poles sticking up against the evening sky denoted the former location of a wood, our travellers branched off to the left into a small country road.

Guns were firing everywhere now. The stench of their fumes lay heavy on the air. It was almost dark, and the green glare of their discharges lit up fitfully the struggling masses that thronged the little road. Long lines of men in single file, stooping beneath the weight of two petrol tins filled with water, slung across their shoulders; similar lines laden with coils of wire, stakes, pickets and shovels; long columns of troops going to relieve battalions in the line; trains of mules, with tossing tails, plodding forward amid a hail of curses; ammunition carts, water-carts, . . . all were jumbled up together in that narrow way. From time to time came the low cry: "Make way! Stretcher-bearers!" and a stretcher would appear carried shoulder-high by four sweating bearers. Now and again, by the flash of the guns of a neighbouring battery, our Ensign caught a glimpse of a form, motionless, under bloodstained bandages. . . .

A few sand bagged steps led into a narrow clearing made in the wood that ran along one side of the road. Over the steps hung the brigade flag. The steps led up to a little kind of entrance way, where a number of officers were standing. Behind them was a heavily sand bagged shelter, where by the guttering light of a couple of candles, the signallers stooped over their telephones.

"*Toot-toot! Toot-toot! Toot-toot!*"

The telephones shrilled their note clearly above the deafening crash of the guns all round. The 18-pounders were firing in salvoes now. The very sandbags shook with the noise. The signallers were shouting down their telephones. Oblivious of everything, an officer sat at the bench beside them and wrote.

They were all Guards' officers in that little place. Our Ensign knew some of them. He spoke to a Coldstreamer whom he had met up in the salient, and asked him what the news was. The Coldstreamer said the Welsh Guards had had a baddish time; the Prince of Wales' Company, in particular, had suffered. He mentioned the names of several men who had been killed. They were all waiting for news of the Grenadiers: they, too, had been having a roughish handling.

An officer with red tabs turned away from a very weary-looking Scots Guards captain, and came towards our Ensign. The young man reported himself, and was told that the guides were ready to take the two companies up to the line.

Then an orderly, covered with mud, emerged from nowhere, as orderlies do, with a message.

"Ah! from the Grenadiers!" said the officer in red tabs, and bolted off towards a deep dugout in the corner.

Our Ensign bade goodnight to the Coldstreamer, and went out again into the road. A regular whirlwind bombardment was in progress. The din was ear-splitting. Every gun for miles around seemed to be firing as fast as it could be loaded.

Our Ensign found his orderly staring open-mouthed at the distant horizon, where a never-ceasing spout of white lights marked the winding line of the front trenches. The lad was very young, and he had not been long in France. As they surveyed the black horizon together and noted the orange spurts of flame where the shells were bursting among the Verey lights, a deep auburn glare suddenly lit up the whole devastation of the landscape, and spread, upwards and outwards, in slow majesty across the night sky.

"Glory be to God, sir!" exclaimed the orderly, "what's that?"

Our Ensign shook his head wisely.

"Looks like an ammunition dump going up!" he said, but he didn't in the least know. It was an extraordinary spectacle, lasting a full minute, during which every single projection on the horizon stood out hard and black against the flaming sky. It reminded our Ensign of the backgrounds of battle scenes in the portraits of the generals at the

"Senior."

Then they started off back to the bivouac in the darkness. When they reached the main road they halted and waited for the two companies of the battalion which were marching up. Presently dark shapes loomed up in the gloom . . . the traffic was much lighter on the road now . . . and the second in command of our Ensign's battalion emerged into the bright glare of the young man's electric torch. Our Ensign indicated to the party the turning off the main road which would bring them to Brigade Headquarters, where the guides awaited them, imparted to his senior officer the news of the casualties in the Welsh Guards, and then set off along that broken road again on his perilous homeward journey.

He crawled into his sleeping-bag at half-past one in the morning, feeling that he had earned a good night's rest.

Chapter 10

"The battalion is moving off in an hour's time, sir!"

Johnson stood over our Ensign, as he lay curled up in his Wolseley valise on the floor of his tent. A canvas bucket of hot water steamed in the servant's hand. Our young man felt as though he had slept but an hour. Still, there was nothing for it, so he staggered in his pyjamas out into the sunshine, where The Beak, in similarly airy costume, was shaving himself at a little mirror propped up against the flap of his tent.

"Is it over the top for us, Beak?" queried our Ensign of his company commander.

"Don't think so yet," mumbled The Beak under the lather; "it's fatigues for today, anyhow, . . . carrying up stuff for the fellows in the front line. Have a good time last night?"

"Ensanguined!" retorted our young man with feeling, as he soaped his face.

Once again he was doomed to travel that dusty road towards the Front, only this time he footed it at the head of his platoon, and he found walking to be a good deal easier than cycling. About the hour of 9 a.m. he led his platoon into the wood, which had been indicated to him as their destination.

Ravaged by shell fire, seamed by trenches, gashed and blood-drenched and blackened, that wood had seen some of the fiercest fighting of the war. Not a tree lived; there was not so much as a green leaf to gladden the eye; not a bird twittered in the branches. The wood and all in it were dead, as dead as the mouldering relics of the fight that were scattered plentifully about in the yawning shell holes, coffined by the crisscross of fallen trunks and torn branches.

The trenches in which the two companies were to live were in places foot-deep in water, so our Ensign and Bryan, by The Beak's directions, got the men to bale them out. By the time they had got the men comfortably settled it was luncheon time. Apollo invited our Ensign to accompany him on a tour of discovery round the wood. Our Ensign shook his head decisively. He thought not, thank you! He had some idea as to what an examination of that wood might reveal. He wouldn't mind going, but he'd have his lunch first. So they agreed to go afterwards, Roderick accompanying them.

Our Ensign felt glad that he had had his lunch when he looked upon the horrors which the deeper recesses of the wood contained. Those who have never seen a modern battlefield can have no idea of its utter and wanton *untidiness* . . . the extraordinary jumble of arms and equipment and clothing, and papers and letters and playing-cards and empty bottles and crumbling remnants of food. The trenches were literally foot-deep in equipment in some places, with here and there a shapeless, inert mass of khaki or field-grey, as lax and limp as a sack of straw, which once had been a man.

One such scene of silent tragedy gave the three an unpleasant shock. It was in a remoter corner of the wood, where the bare and blackened tree-trunks stood closer together, where a line of wrecked dugouts and a profusion of German equipment lying about showed that the enemy had made a stand. As our Ensign and his companions plunged in and out of the fallen tree-trunks and the splintered branches lying athwart the shell-craters, Apollo, who was leading, came to a sudden halt. He stood silent with pointing finger.

At his feet, pinned securely to the ground under a massive elm which had been torn bodily from its roots by a shell, was a skeleton yet clothed in its mud stained and mouldy field-grey. It lay on its face, prone beneath the weight of the tree, its arms outstretched in the form of a cross.

"Poor devil!" said Roderick.

"I expect it broke his back!" observed Apollo, stooping down to get a closer view of the grim figure. But our Ensign, who was fresher than they to these sights of war, said nothing. He was thinking of the shells screaming about those wrecked dug outs, the crash of the falling trees, the reverberating explosions, the reek of sulphur, and that solitary German felled to the earth as he bolted for shelter, and pinned down among the chaos....

******

The Beak met them as they sauntered back to tea.

"Sorry, old boy," he said to our Ensign; "there's a fatigue tonight. It'll be you, as Bryan did the last one!"

"Sir!" quoth the Ensign in his best manner, and proceeded to note his instructions. He was to take a party of seventy men and proceed to a certain R.E. Dump, the map reference of which was given to him, there collect various material, and thence go to a certain brigade headquarters, where he would receive further orders.

It was dark by the time the party started off. It was a black night, without moon or stars, and, as on the previous evening, the air trembled to the ear-splitting crash of the guns. The first thing our Ensign did was to lose his way. There was plenty of traffic on the roads, but everybody was either going up or coming down, and no one seemed to have ever heard of an R.E. Dump in those parts. At last the party met a sapper officer.

"A Dump?" he said, in reply to a question. "I believe they are forming one down there . . . about a mile along this road." And he pointed in the direction from which the party had come.

Our Ensign groaned, then faced about and led his men in the opposite direction. After marching for about a quarter of an hour, they came to a place by the roadside where some dark figures were moving about among large indistinguishable heaps.

"Is that the R.E. Dump?" sung out our Ensign.

"Yes! Is that the Guards' fatigue party?" came back from the darkness.

"Yes!" shouted our Ensign in return, switching on the lamp fastened to his belt.

A staff officer stepped out of the roadside blackness into the circle of light.

"Good evening!" he said genially. "They want you to take some of this stuff up to the Welsh Guards. If you report to them, they'll tell you what to do with it. I've got a guide here. This Dump was only formed this morning, so I don't quite know what there is here; but you just go ahead, and load up the men with anything you think useful. It's all for you fellows when you go over the top . . . you will want plenty of stuff to consolidate with! You'll be all right then, will you? They shell a bit as a rule going up, but the guide will lead you off the road into the open if it gets really dangerous. Goodnight!"

He vanished into the night. A grenadier private loomed up large in the patch of light.

"Guide, sir!" he said, saluting.

Our Ensign called his senior sergeant, and with him inspected the Dump. He then divided his men into as many groups as there were heaps of different material, and got them loaded up with rolls of barbed wire, pickets, stakes, giant coils of French wire, and so forth. When they were ready the men fell in in single file, and with the guide and our Ensign at the head, the party moved off into the darkness.

It was a good two hours' march up to the Battalion Headquarters of the Welsh Guards. The guide led them out on to a narrow track which wound its solitary way across a bare immensity of plain, in and out of shell-holes lying so thick that the lip of one crater touched the lip of the other.

It was a dank, raw night, with occasional gusts of rain. The cold wind blowing down the gentle slope of the plain brought the evil odour of death from the spouting lights on the horizon where the trenches lay.

The plain was a place of death. By the roadside, in every shell-hole, the dead lay thick, British and German—now a solitary corpse, its face a white patch in the gloom, now a little knoll of men stricken down by the one shell.

The going was terrible. Under the effect of the thousands of pounds of high explosive that had worked devastation over the slope the very earth had lost its binding power and crumbled like sand beneath the feet. The darkness was intense. The men kept stumbling under their burdens, and more than one toppled headlong into a shell-hole, often on to the silent form of its uncoffined occupant. Our Ensign had learned already that in night marching the tendency of the head of a column is always to go too fast, yet though he steadied the pace down to a bare two miles an hour, the tail of the party kept on straggling behind. With the sweat running down his face, the officer spent the greater part of the march in stumbling hastily from one end of the long train to the other.

There was a good deal of sporadic shelling . . . principally "whizzbangs," that stank most vilely in the nostrils. Most of the shells seemed to be falling about the road ahead of them, and presently the guide led the party off the track into the open, where everybody had to make the best of his way in and out of the shell-holes. At last the guide pointed to a dim tangle of bare trees on the skyline to the right.

"That's where we shall find the Welsh, sir!" he said.

He brought the party finally up to a white chalky trench, where, in the yellow light of a lantern, a group of officers were standing about the entrance to a deep and cavernous dugout. A regimental aid-post was somewhere in the vicinity, for the sides of the trench were lined with stretchers, and the cry of "Make way for the stretcher-bearers!" kept resounding as fresh cases were brought in. Many of the forms lying on the stretchers on parapet and parados were field-grey. One of these figures, with a livid face, opened his eyes, as our Ensign stepped over him to reach the entrance of the dugout, and murmured: "*Ach! Mutter!*"

Our Ensign reported himself to the adjutant of the Welsh Guards, who was just emerging from the dugout while the men of his fatigue party, their forms looming large against the skyline, sat about and chatted with the orderlies and stretcher-bearers.

"We're just going out of this," said the Welsh Guardsman; "you'd better report to the Scots Guards. The adjutant is about somewhere."

Our young man found the adjutant, and reported himself again.

"R.E. material, eh?" said the latter. "Good. We shall want you to take it up to the left company in the front line. I've got a good guide here. He'll take you along."

Our Ensign felt a trifle dismayed, for he had imagined his night's labours to be over. He glanced at his wrist. It was 11 p.m.

They started off again, past the regimental aid-post, and out on to a sunken road, where the corpses lay thick. As they plodded on, they seemed to come to a village, for crumbling bricks lay about the road. But of houses there was not a sign. Where the tide of battle has passed on the Somme you will not find stone left upon stone.

The guide, who had been leading them very confidently so far, now began to flag. He started to look about him. An awful suspicion seized upon the officer. He knew the symptoms well enough. He guessed what the guide's hesitation portended. There are very few officers who have served in the trenches in this war who have not been led astray by a guide sometime or other.

A shell whizzed noisily overhead, and exploded close by with an appalling crash. Its orange burst revealed for a brief instant the devastation in that village of the dead.

"Mind yourself, sir!" called out the guide suddenly. Two figures came dashing out of the darkness with levelled rifles.

"Hands up!" they yelled.

Our Ensign had pulled out his revolver.

"Stop that infernal noise!" he shouted, and then, heedless of consequences, he switched on his lamp.

Two figures in khaki were facing him.

"Are you British?" cried one, while the other gasped, panting—

"Oh dear! we've just walked into the German lines. Have you seen our officer, sir?" And they mentioned the name of their regiment.

Our Ensign could not help them, and presently they disappeared into the darkness. Then the party went plodding on until, once more, dark shapes loomed out of the night.

A Guards' officer came towards our Ensign. He took off his cap and wiped his damp forehead.

"What a night!" he lamented. "My infernal guide walked us plumb into the Hun lines. All the Huns were yelling, 'Come on! We're waiting for you!' We made a bolt for it. I can't make out why they didn't shoot. I suppose they weren't sure that some of their own fellows weren't out as well!"

Woo-oof!

A shell burst violently behind the group.

"Bad place to gossip in," said our Ensign. "I suppose you don't know where we are, do you?"

"Devil a bit!" was the reply.

"You'll find two of your men down the path a little way," said our Ensign; "they nearly shot us!"

"Right!" answered the other unconcernedly. "Well, cheery-oh! Where the hell's that guide?" . . .

He and his train padded past in the darkness.

Suddenly our Ensign's guide recognised a landmark.

"I know that dead horse, sir," he exclaimed; "it's a little piece along here! I know the way now!"

Indeed, in a little, he brought the party to the mouth of a trench. There our Ensign found a Scots Guards subaltern.

"Here we are again!" observed the latter serenely. "Cheerful spot."

"!!!!!!!!" replied our Ensign. "Where do you want the stuff dumped?"

"What stuff?" returned the other, straining his eyes to peer into the outer blackness.

"R.E. material for the left company," said our Ensign.

"Right company here," answered the officer.

Our Ensign leant back against the parapet and, baring his head to the night, invoked the vengeance of the powers of darkness on the guide. Apparently the guide had likewise discovered his mistake, for from the murky blackness outside the trench our Ensign heard a voice—the voice of one in authority—saying sternly—

"What dead horse?"

"The dead horse wot's lying alongside of two dead Huns!" came the pathetic voice of the guide.

"The dead horse you wanted, me lad," answered back the stern voice, "isn't alongside of any Huns! It's at the dead horse by the pond that you wanted to turn off!"

Our Ensign turned desperately to the officer.

"Look here!" he said firmly, "I've had enough of this nonsense. My men are dead-beat, and we are fed up with being led by a lot of fool guides into every barrage on this front. I'm going to dump the goods here, and you can send word along to the other company to come and fetch 'em!"

"My dear fellow," replied the other, "you can't do that. The other company probably wants your stuff urgently."

"If they want it so badly, they can dam well come and fetch it. I'm going home. It's half-past twelve and we've been footing it since seven!"

"Look here," said the other soothingly, "I've got a sergeant of the left company here with me; he's just brought a message across. You can go back with him!"

Our Ensign wavered.

"How far is it?" he asked sullenly.

"Sixteen hundred yards," replied the other promptly.

Our Ensign reflected that, if this were a prevarication, the other would have said, "Just over there!" or, "A stone's throw!" So he decided he would have to get those additional 1600 yards out of his weary men.

The sergeant appeared—a resolute person; the two officers parted, and once more the fatigue party strung out on its way along the corpse strewn path. The men were very tired, so our Ensign marched in the rear and kept the stragglers together.

A lot of shells were coming over now, exploding noisily in the ruins of the village. But our Ensign hardly noticed them. He was desperately concerned lest, while he prevented the tail of his party from being left behind and lost, the head might be walking straight into the German lines.

The long train sagged, and finally halted. Our Ensign scrambled, fuming, to the head.

"Where's that guide?" he demanded.

"He's just after going to look for the way, sir!" said a soft Irish voice, which added: "Wirra, that's near!" as a shell crashed into the ground close by.

Our Ensign got all the men into shell craters. The sights in those deep holes were enough to make a man sick. Then he told his sergeant he would give the guide five minutes by the watch. If he had not turned up at the end of that period of grace, they would dump their stuff where they were and steer for home by the compass.

Those were the longest five minutes our Ensign had ever spent. He was tormented by the fear lest a shell might fall in the midst of his party, and he should have twenty or thirty casualties to report on returning to the wood. The shells came over fairly thick—about two a minute,—but they all burst beyond the men in their shell holes. The men were magnificently cool. It struck our Ensign that they were more concerned at not having reached their journey's end, tired out as they were, than at the dangers surrounding them.

Then a voice shouted from the darkness—

"Here you are! This way!"

Ten minutes later our Ensign led his party back along the sunken road and across the brown, shell scarred slope. Weary though the men were, they were only too glad to force the pace and leave behind them the sights and sounds of the night.

"They're saying behind, sir," said the senior sergeant to our Ensign, as the party trudged along, "couldn't we go a bit faster?"

"Oh! all right!" replied our Ensign carelessly, and quickened his pace. But he did not tell the sergeant that the same idea had long since occurred to him.

Chapter 11

"The present day has no value for me except as the eve of tomorrow: it is with tomorrow that my spirit wrestles."—Metternich.

The day was already three hours old by the time that our Ensign reached the wood with his weary fatigue party. The trenches were wrapped in slumber, and from Bryan, upon whose recumbent form our Ensign trampled as he groped his way into the company dugout, he learnt that the two companies which had been in the line had already gone back to the bivouac on the downs, and that the two companies in the wood were expecting momentarily to be relieved. There was no news of future movements: none of the officers, Bryan said, knew when the Guards were going to "pop the parapet."

Two hours later, effectively, the relief turned up, and the two companies plodded out into the chilly morning back to their bivouac. It was not until 8 a.m. that the officers got into their sleeping-bags in the tents.

At noon the faithful Johnson aroused our Ensign with the news that a conference of officers had been called by the commanding officer, and that they were waiting for him. He splashed some water over himself, tore into his clothes, crammed his cap on over his tousled hair, and dashed off with a silent prayer that his unshaven chin might escape observation. But everybody was too deep in maps and plans to notice him. He and his brother officers left the conference knowing all there was for them to know about the impending attack, save only the detail that interested them all most keenly—the date!

The battalion was to strike bivouac that evening, and march to a wood on the fringe of that corpse-strewn plain across which our Ensign had led his fatigue party the night before. Two companies were to be quartered in one corner of the wood, the remainder—Nos. 1 and 2 Companies—in a little copse on the eastward edge,—nearest the enemy, as our Ensign, with the shells of the previous evening in his mind, reflected sombrely. It was generally expected that the four companies would not meet again until they assembled for the attack.

There was a little pang of parting in that dirty bivouac among the rolling downs. As a measure of precaution, such experienced officers and non commissioned officers as could be spared were not to accompany the Battalion into action, so as to leave an executive nucleus to carry on with, in the event of heavy casualties. Of our Ensign's mess, Peter and The Don were of this number. Sadder and more dismal faces never were seen than the countenances of these two (and of their comrades in exile also, be it said) as they bade the departing companies God-speed and prepared to join the Transport.

At dusk that evening, in a drenching downpour of cold rain, the battalion moved off into the unknown, our Ensign's company bringing up the rear. Truly it is a dismal thing, this inarching into action! One hears an iron curtain clang down behind one, shutting off the past—and there were fragrant memories in our Ensign's mind of the pleasant *camaraderie* of the vanished summer—while the present glides imperceptibly away before the doubts and uncertainties of the future. The rain splashed dismally down, the road was heavy and slippery with glutinous mud, and all around them the guns crashed out into the night with a roar that seemed to crack the very tympanum. The men hunched their waterproof sheets over their packs, and trudged along in mournful silence; and our Ensign let his mind toy despondently with the difference between his situation and that of men he knew, spick and span and spurred and polished these last, holding decorative positions on the staff at home.

They plodded along the same old highway of the battlefield, as crowded as ever, thronged with the same old mass of tired men, and straining, plunging horses and mules. Plenty of bad language, especially in the blocks of traffic, which were frequent, came back at them from the night, while the rain plopped sadly into the puddles of the roadside; and, with green flash and reek and roar, the shells screamed their way through the night towards the soaring horizon lights. As they drew nearer to the front they heard the whistle and crash of German shells ahead of them in the darkness.

At last they left the road and followed a guide in single file along a muddy footpath, which brought them into the wet tangle of a devastated wood. As the men filed off into some crumbling trenches, our Ensign noticed three forms on the ground covered by waterproof sheets beside the wreck of a Lewis gun hand-cart.

"It was hard luck," somebody was saying; "they caught us coming in . . . shrapnel, it was . . . got these three at the very end of the line."

Then there was much groping and slipping about in the dark, as the officers got the two companies into such accommodation as the broken trenches and gaping shell-holes afforded—a rum issue, at which our Ensign found himself compelled to swallow, according to immemorial usage, nearly a mugful of the spirit, poured out of the stone jars by the dim light of a carefully-shaded candle; and then the men began to contrive for themselves all sorts of wonderful shelters for the night with riddled fragments of corrugated iron sheeting, beams of wood, splintered branches and withered leaves. The officers left them to their task, and made their way to the dugout which the billeting officer had designated to them as their quarters.

It was a great big shelter, as large as a small shed—and a shell hole in the roof, which was the only damage, had been stuffed up with those wicker cases which the German gunners used to carry their live shells in. The place was constructed rather like a log-cabin, dug half a dozen feet deep in the ground, with solid timber sides and a roof of iron girders wattled over. The floor was covered with those wood or paper shavings which, under the influence of the British blockade, the Germans use in preference to straw. These shavings furnish bedding that is fully as clean and comfortable as straw, and certainly far more economical.

There was a very simple military funeral that night under the drenching rain, in the shell ravaged copse. In a shell hole the three victims of the night were laid to rest, and covered in. Two of the men were Catholics, the third Protestant, and both the R.C. and the C. of E. *padres* came up through the rain and mud that night to conduct the obsequies. And the next evening a plain wooden cross, well carpentered and neat, inscribed in black paint with the names and numbers of the fallen Guardsmen, arrived with the rations, and was set up over the little grave, a landmark in that devastated countryside, the place of the unburied dead.

Like the wood which our Ensign had already explored on a former occasion, the copse and the wood beyond had been the scene of one of the Homeric fights of the battle of the Somme. This wood, too, was full of corpses, both British and German, and strewn with rain-soaked and rusting relics of the fray, lying amid battered trenches and wrecked dug outs. During the days they spent in the copse, the men of the two companies spent their whole time in clearing the wood, stacking up the rifles, the bayonets, the equipment, collecting such identity discs as still remained on the dead before burying them, and bringing in to the officers' dugout German shoulder-straps and letters and papers of all kinds. These were in due course sent down to the brigade to be handed over to the Army Intelligence.

In the copse itself a German battery had been posted. There were indications that it had had its home there for many months. The dugouts had been very well made, deep and comfortable, though the British heavy shells had played havoc with them now. In one a provision store was found, with tier upon tier of very mouldy black bread stacked up to the roof, many tins of canned meat (one ingenious ensign introduced a tin of German brawn into the mess and opened it for lunch, professing to find it delicious), and some tins of sardines.

Another was stored with cordite charges. It was beneath the covered entrance leading down to this particular dugout that our Ensign found the mess cook installed over a large fire, with burst bags of cordite lying all around. He was sternly bidden to shift his quarters elsewhere—which he did with an injured air.

Rooting about in the wood with MacFinnigan, our Ensign came upon a dugout which had all but collapsed, a dead German, buried, save for his boots, at the entrance. MacFinnigan, who had no squeamishness about such matters, wormed his way into the dugout, and presently began to hand up newspapers and letters and labels off parcels, brought by the *Feldpost* for the two bombardiers who, as the addresses on the various articles showed, must have lodged there. One was a Jew from Frankfurt-on-Main, who had a large correspondence with innumerable Cohns and Abrahams and Levys, mostly of the feminine persuasion; the other appeared to have been a Bavarian.

Among the latter's letters was one from his wife, which gave a brief but tragic glimpse of the misery of everyday life in Germany in war-time—a side of the question which is rarely illumined in the newspapers. The letter was angry and bitter. After a long complaint about the growing food difficulties and appalling price of everything, the woman, who wrote from a Bavarian village, told of some hitch in the payment of her separation allowance, and narrated how she had been to the mayor to get redress, and had been "flung out" (*hinausgeschmissen*). In a torrent of unpunctuated, ungrammatical German, with many appeals to the "dear husband," she asked if that was the way the wives of brave German "warriors" should be treated, if "they" expected the people to make the enormous sacrifices demanded of them, when "they" unjustly deprived the women of their due.

The husband's answer was there too . . . begun on a field postcard (in the German Army these are issued blank to the men) from the dugout in the wood and never finished . . . interrupted, maybe, by the shell that smashed the dugout and killed the man lying outside—who perhaps was the writer himself. It began in a torrent of abuse—the language of a man of the people defending his woman, setting forth the wife's complaint, asking how men who skulked at home dared so to treat the wife of a German "warrior." . . . And there the scrawling writing broke off short. The guns of the Somme had prevented a Bavarian mayor from getting a postcard which would probably have momentarily soured the taste of his dinner beer.

Our Ensign had been given a definite job in the impending attack. He was told he was not to "go over" with his company? but would act as intelligence officer, and in this capacity accompany the second-in-command with a select party. The duties entrusted to him necessitated a good knowledge of the ground over which the attack was to be made; so one afternoon, whilst they were waiting in the copse, our Ensign got leave from The Beak, and, taking MacFinnigan, carrying a telescope, along with him, he set out to find out some eminence from which he might survey the scene.

Side by side, officer and orderly traversed the long brown slope which our Ensign had hitherto only crossed on a famous occasion at night. Then the darkness had mercifully hidden from their eyes the full horror of the battlefield which now lay in all its ghastliness before them, bare and brutal, in the soft light of a mild autumn day. Our Ensign blessed the name of John Cotton of Edinburgh as he marched along puffing at his briar. Truly tobacco is the sovereign herb in war: not only does it calm the nerves—it also dulls the sense of smell.

As they went up the ridge, our Ensign chatted with his orderly. MacFinnigan had a great thirst for knowledge: a secret was in the air which he would fain penetrate. . . .

"Is it a fact, sir? . . . Some of the men in the company were saying, sir . . . They do tell me, sir . . ."

What was the secret?

Hush, hush!

Wait and see! Whatever it was, it so engrossed our Ensign that it carried him right over the ridge and to the banks of a sunken road that ran transversely to his line of advance, where he was brought up short in his tracks.

Our Ensign had heard of the Germans being mowed down in swathes as they rushed hurrahing in dense formation to the attack of the forts of Liège; he had been told of the bridge at Landrecies piled high with German corpses after the Coldstream had given the Hun a taste of the Guards' rapid fire; he had had described to him how the British naval guns cleaved great furrows in the ranks of Germany's youthful legions on the Yser as they went forward hand in hand, singing their soldier songs, to break through to Calais. He had heard of these things, I say, and had read of them in the papers like everybody else, but he had yet to realise what a shock one can get when the mental picture evoked by a newspaper paragraph comes in contact with the reality.

For he found himself on the high banks of that sunken road looking down upon piles of German dead, two, three, four, and even five layers deep. The road had been put into a rough state of defence, and every embrasure cut out of the bank nearest the British had its ghastly mound of corpses. Their numbers he could not estimate, what their regiment he would not venture close enough to determine; he only knew that these men had died obeying their army order that Ginchy must be held to the last man . . . and the road was full of these gallant dead. By every embrasure one or two dead British soldiers were lying—probably, our Ensign thought, the first men to adventure into the trench of that forlorn German hope: one such khaki-clad figure still had his hands at the throat of the German across whose body he was lying with another German on top of him.

Even the unsqueamish MacFinnigan was overcome at the sight.

"How horrible, sir," he said; and then added, as an afterthought, "but they were brave men!"

Our Ensign lit a cigarette and inhaled deeply. Then he gave one to the orderly, and they passed on up the slope.

Chapter 12

'Twas brillig and the slithy toves
Did gyre and gimble. . . .
—The Slaying of the Jabberwock.

"Did ye hear what that man O'Flanagan was sayin', him I mane as come up with the wather party las' night?"

The speaker was a red-haired Irish Guardsman—what they would call in Ireland a "foxy man"—who was cleaning his rifle and chatting the while with a grizzled comrade, who was composedly scraping the mud off his *puttees* with a piece of stick preparatory to going on parade for rifle inspection. Our Ensign, standing in the open watching a British aeroplane having a thrilling time in and out of Hun shrapnel puffs, overheard the men talking in the trench behind him.

The elder man, busy with his scraping, only grunted contemptuously.

"Didn't he see them with his own eyes," the foxy man continued, tugging at his pull-through, "leppin' the ditch and off across the open the same as they might be a lot of young horses? 'The Lord save us!' sez th' officer, him as was with the wather party, ''tis the cateypillars!' ' Cateypillars?' sez O'Flanagan, the chap as was tellin' us about it— 'cateypillars is ut?' sez he. 'Begob,' sez he, ''tis the first time ever I see cateypillars lep a ditch!'"

The other flung away his piece of stick, rubbed his hands together to get rid of the mud, and cast a leisurely glance over his person.

"Some of you young lads," he said, "do be believin' all you hears!"

"Amn't I after tellin' yez that O'Flanagan see thim himself?" answered the foxy man heatedly, applying his eye to the barrel of his rifle. "Like great crockeydiles they are, sez he, with a crew of thirty men in their inside and machine-guns and bombs and God knows what else, sez he, and little windies to give the lads inside a blasht of fresh air. Is ut tellin' us lies the man was?"

"I wouldn't be sayin' that," the old soldier replied cautiously; "but some of you young lads has no sinse."

And with that he stumped off to rifle inspection.

Now you know what our Ensign and his orderly were talking about so earnestly as they trudged up the ridge in the last chapter. They spoke of the Tanks, or, as they were then called, the Hushhushes, which everybody had heard about and nobody had seen—the mysterious engines which were to lead the Guards into battle on a date not appointed.

Naturally it was Apollo who saw them first in the flesh, or should one say more correctly, in the steel plating? He blew into the officers' dugout after rifle inspection that morning and said in a tone of decision—

"I've seen 'em!"

"Who?" said our Ensign.

"What?" said Roderick more grammatically.

"Where?" said The Beak, whose forensic mind had already divined to what Apollo referred.

"Just off the road, about 300 yards from here, . . . the Tanks . . . a squadron of them . . . charming fellow in charge . . . showed me all round . . . amazing, wonderful . . . come along and I'll take you down there!"

So they all trooped off behind him down the road, and presently in a wayside field came upon those monstrously grotesque and ungainly "ingins," which everybody has seen in the photographs in the papers, and which nobody is allowed to describe. A small and rotund Commodore ... or whatever a Tank squadron commander is called, . . . who confessed to having been out of bed for two nights, did the honours very charmingly, . . . but let us tread softly, for we are on censored ground. Let it suffice to say that a captain, a subaltern, and three ensigns returned to the officers' dugout, and swanked insufferably to their less fortunate comrades-in-arms who had not been among the first to see the Tanks, and that MacFinnigan and another orderly, who had been taken with the party, had the morning of their lives, the centre of an enthralled group of Guardsmen, all panting for information about "the crocodiles."

And for the moment everybody's mind was taken off the future.

But that afternoon—it was September 14th—the commanding officer came up, and the officers were bidden into the dugout for a final conference, at which, among many other equally, but to at least one of them, less important details, they were informed that they would attack at 6.20 a.m. in the morning, and that they would move up into position at 9 o'clock that night.

That afternoon the men sat about in the trenches . . . those of them that were not otherwise employed . . . and talked and smoked and read the curious provincial papers sent out to them from home. Only a bare handful of letters came in to the dug out to be censored that afternoon. The British soldier prefers to do his work first and write about it afterwards. The men seemed bored by the waiting about. They yawned, and cocked an eye at the sky, and discussed the weather prospects for the next day, and argued unendingly about "the crocodiles," and the surprise they would be to "Fritz."

In the course of the afternoon The Don turned up, in full battle array, beaming with delight. After all, he was to "go over" with the company. It had been decided that another officer should remain behind in his place. That officer was one of the party in the dugout in the copse ... a spirit more ardent for battle never breathed in mortal man . . . and he was stricken dumb, beaten to the ground, with the force of his disappointment. Our Ensign, seeing the utter abasement of his grief, reflected on the strange ways that Providence adopts to reveal the pure metal that gleams in men of the British Army.

While it was still light, some of them went out to have a look at the positions which they were to take up that evening, and from which they were to attack in the morning. Night marching across the open, even when you know the ground, is no joke; but when your direction leads you across wide trenches running at every imaginable angle, through tangles of barbed wire and over country that is nothing more or less than an infinite number of holes connected together by a little loose earth, why then, much forethought and preparation are required if you wish to avoid disaster. So the officers who went out reconnoitring took with them one man per platoon to mark the way and act as guides when they should go up that evening. To mark the route the guides stuck a few landmarks about in the shape of rusty rifles, picked up off the battlefield, inserted in the earth by the bayonet and decorated with a German helmet or a haversack—anything to catch the eye at night when seen against the skyline.

The officers dined together in the dugout at 7.30 that evening, a very friendly and very business-like party of men. The table-talk was pure unadulterated shop, the discussion of small details of company organisation with occasional desultory snatches of debate upon that fertile theme—the Tanks. But the greater issues of the morrow were avoided by tacit consent, and a stranger suddenly bidden to that dinner table could hardly have supposed (our Ensign says) that his hosts were preparing for anything more serious than a field-day on a large scale.

Our Ensign has often since looked back upon that last dinner of Nos. 1 and 2 Company Mess—the last supper of the Girondins somebody called it,—the long table (cunningly contrived out of trench-boards) covered with the famous white American cloth cover, the candles stuck in bottles, the white enamel mess crockery, the familiar faces all round the board, the background of raincoats and glasses and revolvers and belts hung on nails hammered into the tree-trunks forming the walls of the dugout; and in the *chiaroscuro* of the upper part of the room the dimly seen features of the mess servants as they passed to and fro.

Someone had stored up a bottle of champagne for this special occasion; needless to say it had been forgotten, and the Girondins raved at the thought that their comrades back at the Transport were in all probability even now toasting them in the goblet that should have foamed at *their* lips. So the double-company mess had to fall back upon a very moderate supply of a somewhat anaemic claret. They would have undoubtedly pledged one another in this rare old wine (vintage, Félix Potin, Amiens), only this formality was unfortunately overlooked in a furious discussion which arose in the matter of fixing the responsibilities in the affair of the forgotten bottle of champagne.

All through dinner messages kept arriving, company sergeant-majors or orderlies bulking large in the low entrance to the dugout. Here an officer scribbled a note or an acknowledgment in his notebook laid flat beside his plate: there a couple of ensigns, amid the stewed pears in soup-plates, the glasses, the candles in their bottles, and the white mugs of steaming coffee, pored over their maps for the hundredth time to fix in their memories a mental picture of the morrow's line of advance. Servants crept in with flasks or water bottles filled, or with sandwiches wrapped in paper. Many were the beverages recommended as sovereign for battle by the veterans. One urged rum-and-water, another neat whisky, a third cold tea, a fourth tea mixed with brandy. The last recipe appeared to command most suffrages, and our Ensign accordingly decided for it.

As the hour of departure drew near, one by one, gradually, the officers rose from the sandbag divan on which they had sat at meat and started to array themselves for battle, girding on their belts hung with a manifold collection of apparatus. One by one they clapped their helmets on their heads and stumped up the little stair into the night.

Thus, imperceptibly, the double company mess broke up, and the partnership of the summer months was dissolved for ever.

It was a cold, clear, starlit night, but still darkish, for the moon had not yet risen. Once outside the dugout, our Ensign heard the low murmur of voices, the clatter of accoutrements from the open space in front of the trenches where the company was assembling. On the road in front he could see dim figures slowly advancing up the ridge: he guessed these to be the other two companies, who had bivouacked in the other part of the wood, moving up to their positions for the attack.

No smoking or talking was allowed; and it was in the most complete silence that at length the two companies moved away, a platoon at a time, each behind its guide. The air was dry and cold, with a touch of frost: it would be cold sleeping out in the open, but anything was better than rain.

The guides picked up their landmarks and led the men without trouble into the segment of trench allotted to them. The trench was crumbling from the autumn rains that had eaten into its shell-scored sides. In parts it had a foot of water. There were many corpses in it. There was no shelling. The night was very still. Only on the horizon, beyond the ridge which on the morrow the Guards would cross, the star-shells soared into a brief span of brilliant life, flickered, and died. Quietly the men slipped into their places in the trench, or, where it was water-logged, into shell-holes behind.

Now the moon, waning from full, began to rise and to shed its silver radiance on the muffled forms asleep in shell-hole and in trench amid the unburied dead. In the cold white light the ruined farm behind the sleeping figures looked like a bleached skeleton, and the devastation surrounding them stood out hard and clear. In the distance the star-shells less brilliant than their wont in the effulgence of the moon, seemed to beckon....

Chapter 13

One Moment in Annihilation's Waste,
One Moment, of the Well of Life to taste—
The Stars are setting, and the Caravan
Starts for the Dawn of Nothing—make haste!
                              —Omar Khayyám.

Our Ensign awoke with a start. His limbs were stiff and cold. He felt frozen to the very marrow. The earth of his shell-hole was firm to the touch under the night's frost. The sky was tinted like a thrush's egg, and in the wide expanse of bluey green the stars were paling to the rising of the sun.

The air was all astir with movement. It was still the twilight of dawn, and here and there about the broken trenches and yawning shell holes, where the battalion had passed the night, patches of white mist hung, like the ghosts of the uncoffined dead that lay so thick upon the barren slope. The atmosphere was cold and deliciously clear, but the earth, warming to the sluggish approach of day, exhaled the sweet and clammy odour of death blended with the scent of freshly-turned clay,—the smell of the battlefield of the Somme.

As our Ensign struggled to his feet and surveyed the scene from his shell-hole, he saw all around him men hoisting on their equipment, talking in low murmurs the while. To restore the circulation to his frozen limbs he walked briskly over to the left, where the trenches of his company lay. He was surprised to find how cool and business-like the men were, as they strapped up their haversacks and struggled into their equipment. They talked in low tones. They groused about the cold, about the discomfort of the night; but on every face was seen a look of relief that the period of waiting was almost over, rather than of apprehension at the trial that was to come.

The old soldiers were, with their ingrained fatalism, very deliberate and quite chatty. The young men were quieter and some a little fretful. But, as our Ensign walked along the trench and exchanged a word or two with the men of his own platoon, he found that, under all the superficial calm, something was smouldering into flame that he had never noticed in them before.

The guns were still barking away steadily. Listening, our Ensign could distinguish the characteristic notes—the sharp salvoes of the field-guns, flinging their projectiles, six at a time, into the enemy wire on the other side of the ridge, the deeper rush of the 6-inch guns, and the swooping flight, starting far away in the rear, of the heavy howitzer shells. Here he ran across the officers of his company. The Beak was as serenely magisterial as ever.

"I wish you were coming with the company, old boy!" he said to our Ensign, who cordially echoed the wish.

"You fellows will go romping gaily through the demoralised Hun," dolefully observed our young man, "and do prodigies of valour, while I shall get the whole of the German barrage coming over the ridge, and probably get done in before I have had a chance of displaying those feats of intelligence which are expected of me!"

"Don't you worry," remarked Bryan darkly; "you'll probably be commanding the company by breakfast-time!"

Then they wished one another good luck and went their ways, for the men were forming up, while over the still morning air a most remarkable sound came floating.

That steady, low throbbing was indescribably exhilarating. The men pricked up their ears and began pointing excitedly to the crest of the ridge ahead, where strange, amorphous masses seemed to be crawling inch by inch through the mists of morning. In a moment the pangs of waiting, which always increase as the fatal hand casts its shadow upon the appointed hour, had fled. Every eye was following the snail like progress of those strange, humming monsters: every mind was rehearsing the effect they would produce when they blundered out of the clinging haze into the enemy's front line. Thus the Tanks made their debut in the history of warfare, and whatever importance posterity may allot to their share in the victory of September 15, to their inventors be given the thanks of the Guards' division, for that His Majesty's Landships whiled away a *mauvais quart d'heure* when the Guards were waiting to attack.

Our Ensign found headquarters in a shell-hole, the commanding officer talking over some final point with the adjutant and the drill sergeant. The sky had changed from pale green to lemon, and the delicate yellow, where it touched the brown line of the ridge, was burnished to a deeper gold by the flood of light from the rising sun. The mists were all but melted. Another day had begun.

So few objects had the tide of battle, sweeping across the undulating plain, left standing, that their outlines, isolated, bare in the clear morning light, left their impress for ever on our Ensign's memory, . . . the blackened tree trunks dotting the ruined site of the village on the right of the ridge, with a forest of bare poles marking the wood behind, the barren ridge between, the confused mass of broken trees to the left denoting that famous D—— Wood in which the horrors of the Somme battlefield reached their climax.

6.15. Everyone is on his feet now—the officers with their helmets well strapped on under their chins, stick in one hand, map in the other, revolver at their belt, their orderly at their elbow; the men with bayonets fixed, gleaming here and there in the sun, armed *cap-à-pie*, their big frames leaning on their rifles in such poses of unconscious grace as would have thrilled the heart of Meissonier or Détaille.

The throbbing of the Tanks has ceased. Still, the guns pound steadily on with their appointed task. There is the low humming of an aeroplane engine somewhere in the sky, but the light is too dazzling for one to see it.

It is an eerie thing to stand on the threshold of history. Before them stretched the ridge, blank as the unwritten page. Would victory or defeat, success or failure, stand inscribed thereon before the sun, that even now was bathing the shell scarred earth with light, had sunk to rest? What hazards awaited them over that low and corrugated crest? What triumphs, what agony, what tears would the next hours bring?

Then the whistles sounded, and with a roar like the breaking of a tropical squall, the hurricane was let loose. Amid the most appalling roar of guns the Guards moved steadily off up the long brown slope, while from the German lines in the distance rose great spouts of red and green and white rockets clamouring for a barrage. Those cascades of coloured lights were frantic in their appeal, bursting high in the air above the exploding shells and dense pillars of white and black and yellow smoke, silent amid the furious din of battle, but emphatic in their cry ... "Help us quickly ... we are being attacked!" ... the S.O.S. of the battlefield.

The whole line moved forward in a dense irresistible impact, wave upon wave. The din was indescribable. The rising shriek of the shells, simultaneous, successive, incessant, formed a vast diapason accompaniment to the snap and whinny and whistle of the bullets whirling through the air.

Our Ensign, plodding along with a select party, led by the second-in-command, in the centre of the attack, felt his blood boiling to the thrill of that mighty roar of noise. The sense of power which the guns gave was overwhelmingly exhilarating. He looked about him, and saw that the men all around were bubbling with high spirits as they trudged forward in and about and around the shell holes. There was no rush about this attack. It was a slow, steady advance, relentless, irresistible. It carried every man onward with it in its stride. It carried our Ensign, new as he was to war, with indifference, as it seemed to him at the time, past white and flaccid figures lying in curiously bent positions in or on the edges of the shell-holes, past men moaning and running with blood, past others shivering with ghastly wounds. In and out of the line trotted the stretcher-bearers, big stolid men,—they are chosen for their inches in the Guards, for they have heavy burdens to carry,—perspiring and blowing and brave, with an utter indifference to danger that was good to see.

As he went forward up the ridge, glancing continually at the map folded open in his hand, for there was a tricky turn to make at the top, our Ensign suddenly came upon a white and silent figure, a young ensign of the Coldstream, lying dead upon one outflung arm, his face towards the advancing line, his feet towards the crest of the slope. He was very young, and our Ensign had known him, as one knows men in the army, from different occasions that had brought them together in the field. He remembered him as a pleasant, handsome boy, and our Ensign noticed, as he glanced at him in passing, that he had not changed in death.

Now they had reached the top of the ridge. The German barrage was in full blast. From the crest the ridge ran down a little and then mounted again to the flat horizon. From crest to skyline the whole intervening space seemed to be flecked with shell-bursts, and in and out of the white and black smoke-drifts went the long steady lines.

About the crest of the ridge and on either slope the German shells crashed heavily, with a thud that made the air tremble, with a reek of sulphur that caught the breath, with sickening clouds of heavy black smoke. Still, the British guns maintained their ceaseless roar, still their shell-bursts dotted the horizon, still the air hummed and whirred with the flying bullets.

The advance had stopped for an instant. The lines of Guardsmen before, around, and behind our Ensign halted erect upon the skyline. Men wiped their brows, for the going had been heavy, and passed the time of day with their friends.

Our Ensign caught a glimpse of many of his friends—The Don, with his best Balliol manner, the strap of his helmet under the point of his chin, his eyeglass in his eye; Bruce, one of the company commanders, was there too, sitting in the shell-hole into which he had been blown, taking a careful compass bearing; also Apollo, tying up a sergeant who had been hit.

Then the advance went forward again—steady, slow, relentless as before, and presently once more it came to a halt. Something stirring was happening on the lower slope of the ridge. There the lines were rushing forward. Between the drifts of the smoke there was a glimpse of charging figures, a glint of the sun on naked bayonets....

As our Ensign stood gazing through the haze of the shell-bursts the lines enclosing him seemed to go wild. A mad yell—not a cheer, but the deep-throated battle-cry of an ancient fighting race—rang out all about him. He glanced around to find himself in the midst of the Irish Guards, "whorooing" like a thousand souls in torment, laughing, shouting, yelling. In the centre of the picture was a striking group. Three Irish Guardsmen stood together, magnificent men all, built as massive as oaks, their eyes dancing with excitement. One leaned upon his rifle, his head thrust forward as he gazed enraptured upon that charge down in the valley; the centre figure was bareheaded, and across his chest, blown flat by the breeze, was the green flag of Erin with its golden harp; while the third Guardsman, holding his rifle with its shining bayonet in his left hand, rested his right upon his comrade's shoulder. And the man with the flag was bellowing like a bull—

"Go it, the Coalies! We're behind yez, me boys! The Micks is on your heels!"

Below, at the foot of the slope, a sturdy figure, a little silver hunting-horn to its lips, plodded serenely forward, ... the commanding officer of the Coldstream Guards in his familiar French shrapnel helmet, with the ridged crown under its khaki cover, in the midst of the shouting, charging line of the remnants of his battalion who had rallied to the horn of the Tanatside Harriers.

Then amid a fierce crescendo of yells the Irish Guards went forward in a rush like a pack of hounds. There was no stopping them. The killing had begun, and they must be in at the death. As they vanished tempestuously into the haze our Ensign heard a sharp cry beside him.

"Oh, sir!"

MacFinnigan was on the ground, his left arm limp, the blood gushing out from his shoulder. Our Ensign plucked his field-dressing from his pocket in the lining of his jacket, and bound the man up as best he could. The orderly was very game, for, though he made no sound, his face showed that he was in pain. Our Ensign gave him a drink out of his water-bottle . . . tea and brandy mixed . . . and turned to the second-in-command, who was speaking to him.

"They've stopped again," he said. "Isn't that Bruce over there by the road? I wonder why they are not going on. I think you'd better go and ask Bruce, and come back here and tell me, so that we can send back word to the commanding officer."

Our Ensign marked the spot where he left the party. The Second-in-command was in a shell hole beside a blackened stump of a telegraph pole, MacFinnigan at his feet. On the crest of the ridge, exposed to the full blast of machine-gun fire and the barrage, there were many dead and wounded. The air was full of bullets, the shells were bursting noisily all over the place, and our Ensign frequently resisted a strong inclination to duck.

Presently he came across two stretcher-bearers of his own battalion. They were bending over a man who was obviously at the point of death.

"He's gone," said the first stretcher-bearer. "Come on now, Michael!" as our Ensign came up. The officer asked them to attend to his orderly, pointing to the place with his stick.

"Sir!" said the first stretcher-bearer, straightening himself up. Our Ensign remembered this little touch of formality afterwards, and recollected that, at the time, this echo of the "square" had not struck him as unusual.

He reached the spot where he thought he should find Bruce, but it turned out to be an officer of another brigade who had strayed a little off the line. The Coldstream had been held up, he told our Ensign, by a couple of unsuspected trenches between them and the first objective, but the line had gone on now.

Our Ensign hastened back to report. As he had gone over to the right the advance had passed on in his absence, and the ground was deserted save for the wounded and the dead. As he hurried over the broken ground a bullet sang past his ear with a loud crack. A man nursing a bleeding leg in a shell-hole called out to him—

"They're sniping from the dugouts, sir. You'll want to mind yourself!"

Our Ensign plunged on. Suddenly out of a shell-hole at his very feet scrambled a tall, wan figure in grey, a bloodstained bandage wound about his head. Our young man had his revolver out in a second. But the stranger made no show of resistance. He was repeating to himself in a sing-song voice—

"*Kamerad! Nicht schiessen! Kamerad! Nicht schiessen!*"

Our Ensign drove the German on in front of him until he came to a sunken road where a Grenadier sergeant and half a dozen men were marshalling a score or so of much-dishevelled German prisoners. He handed over the German, who was still crooning his song, and pursued his way towards the shell-hole by the blackened telegraph pole.

He found it deserted. The second-in-command, MacFinnigan, the rest of the party, all had vanished. On the ground lay a bloodstained whistle and some shreds of field-dressing.

The German shell fire had greatly increased in intensity. They were now laying a barrage over the whole scene of the advance. Our young man found that walking alone over heavy, shell swept ground is a very different thing from sweeping forward with the advancing line, with courage and resolution running, like an electric fluid, from man to man. So he bent his head and started to get over the ground and out of the barrage as hard as he could.

Strange and manifold are the encounters of the battlefield. A brief half an hour before, the brown and furrowed slope, up which our Ensign was painfully making his way to the farther ridge beyond which the Guards had disappeared, had been No Man's Land—the desolate tract at which, from the front trenches, one would peer furtively through a periscope. Now it was the highway of the battlefield, strewn with the wastage of the fight, traversed by the lagging steps of the wounded.

There is this vision in our Ensign's memory, . . . an officer with half his tunic torn to ribbons, one bare arm wrapped in bandages protruding from his shirt, bareheaded, livid of face, besmeared with mud and blood. He staggered like a drunkard as he walked straight ahead, falling into shell-holes, heedless of the enemy fire. On one lapel of his tunic the small grenade of the Royal Engineers had survived intact.

"Blown up with some sappers," he said thickly to our young man, "lookin' for dressin' station . . . terrible . . . terrible, . . ." and he reeled onward over the broken earth.

Then came a hurrying, stumbling herd of German prisoners, abject, dishevelled, hands above their heads, four strapping Guardsmen, each with a helmet hung to his belt, driving them before them, broad grins on their faces.

Now our Ensign had reached the first of those hidden trenches which had brought a burst of unsuspected fire to bear on the advancing Coldstream. The khaki was pretty thick amid the trampled and riven wire, but beyond the *Feldgrauen* lay in heaps, many still wearing the little round caps and the greatcoats in which they had been sleeping, their arms outspread, waxen-faced, limp, and where they lay the brown earth was stained a deeper hue.

A little group came hobbling painfully towards our Ensign as he went up the slope, two grenadiers carrying one of their officers on a rifle slung between them. They stopped in front of our Ensign.

"Are you in pain?" said our young man to the officer.

"Pretty fair," came from the other's lips.

"Where are you hit?" asked our Ensign.

"Stomach . . . do you know anything about it? These men were going to take me to an aid-post."

"I don't know much about it," said our young man, "but I think you ought to lie quiet for a stomach wound. The Huns are barraging pretty hard back there, and I believe you'd be safer here for a bit in one of these shell-holes."

"Got any brandy?" asked the Grenadier.

"Tea and brandy mixed," replied our Ensign; "but really, you know, you oughtn't to drink, though you're welcome to the lot. Will you have a cigarette? . . . that can't hurt you."

The two grenadiers had very gently deposited their load in a shell-hole, and one of them, pulling a haversack off a dead man lying on the lip of the crater, put it under the wounded officer's head. Our Ensign gave the wounded man a cigarette, and lit it for him. The grenadier puffed for a moment in silence, then said—

"How are things going?"

"Everything looks all right," replied our young man; "the whole brigade seems to have walked off the map. I'm trying to catch 'em up . . . there's a devil of a lot of dead Huns lying around . . . that's always a good sign. . . ."

"I suppose you'll have to be going on," said the wounded man; "take care of yourself, and good luck!"

"So long! I hope you'll be all right," said our Ensign, and once more started to clamber up the slope after a glance at his compass to assure himself that he was bearing in the right direction. He kept a sharp look-out ahead to see if he could discern any signs of his own battalion. He thought he must soon be catching up with them now. . . . . . Then, without any warning, he was flung headlong into a shell-hole amid a foul reek of black smoke and a thick cloud of dust.

"That's done it! I'm dead!" was his first thought; but he found himself unwounded at the bottom of the hole, his throat and nose full of dust and his ears singing.

He scrambled out in a panic and dashed on. He caught up with a Guards officer, whose face he seemed to know, leading a party of heavily laden men.

"Are you machine-guns?" he asked the other, as he drew level, . . . his voice sounded very faint in his ears. The other made no reply. Our Ensign repeated his question, and still he got no response. Our young man was feeling dazed and rather cross, and was about to shout his question for the third time, when he observed, greatly to his surprise, that the other officer was speaking to him—that is to say, his lips were moving, but our Ensign heard nothing.

Then the officer put his hands to his mouth and bawled: "I'm . . . stokes mortars . . . you know me . . . you dined with us the other night!" Our Ensign explained that he had just been blown up . . . and realised that he was almost deaf. Presently their ways parted, and our Ensign was once more trudging on alone.

He crossed a trench where Guardsmen were digging in furiously among a lot of German corpses, passed a tank on the extreme left, apparently stranded and looking forlorn but intact, met other troops of German prisoners, each bigger than the last, shuffling along at their brisk, characteristic amble, reached the top of the ridge, and plunged into a network of broken barbed wire. There the bullets were humming, and men were shouting and shooting furiously from a crowded trench just in front of him, while in the distance he heard the "*tack-tack*" of machine-guns and the reverberating explosions of bombs. Bending low our Ensign pelted through the wire, and sprang into a dense throng of men in the trench.

Chapter 14

Then was seen with what majesty the British soldier fights.—Napier.

Once again our Ensign was in the midst of the Guards—Grenadiers, Coldstream, Irish, . . . remains of half a dozen battalions were there, intermingled with a good sprinkling of men from all manner of line regiments. They stood packed close as herrings in a barrel in the deep and narrow trench, so that it was well-nigh impossible to force a passage. Of officers, for the moment, there was no trace.

Our Ensign stood for a moment to regain his breath and to take in the surroundings. The trench was in a hideous mess, showing abundant traces of the appalling pounding it had received during three days' incessant artillery fire. The British shells had blown whole segments bodily out of it, so that here the parapet, there the parados, was blasted clean away—sometimes both in the same place—leaving a broad gap void of all protection.

In its time it had been a good specimen of a German fire-trench—in point of fact it was the German main third line—with a neat fire-step, solid traverses, and deep, timber lined dug outs with many steps leading sheer down into the bowels of the earth. But now the fire-step was broken and crumbling, the traverses were nearly all blown in, and in many of the dugouts part of the framework had collapsed, leaving the entrance either sagging or completely blocked up by fallen earth.

The place was a shambles. There were shapeless masses of field-grey trodden down fast into the soft mud bottom of the trench, and sprawling forms, both khaki and grey, lay all over the place. In a yawning rent in the trench, at our Ensign's very elbow, was the dead body of a lad wearing the black buttons and badges of a Rifle regiment,—a mere boy, with a round bullet-hole in the temple. At his side a figure was sitting, knees drawn up, head resting on the hand, in an attitude of contemplation. Our Ensign recognised a sergeant of his own battalion ... an oldish, steady man whom he had known well.... So tired and utterly weary was the look on his face, that for the moment the young officer fancied that the man had fallen asleep. But the waxen features told a different tale.... Our Ensign's heart sank a little within him as he gazed on the two listless figures: all the morning they remained there, and every time he passed them he felt himself shrinking with horror.

The trench was strewn with "souvenirs"—German helmets and caps and rifles and greatcoats and ammunition pouches, boxes of cigars, loaves of bread, tins of meat and sardines, empty bottles, letters, pay-books, littered about among the prostrate forms. The men in the trench were turning these over; many had rank German cigars in their mouths. But our Ensign had no time to waste in poring over these things—as the only officer present, he felt that it devolved upon him to try and bring a little order into the chaos.

Presently he espied a familiar form, gaunt and tall,—it was Sergeant Jackson, of our Ensign's company. Briefly, the sergeant gave the officer the news. All the officers of our Ensign's company and the acting company sergeant-major had been knocked out ... none of the officers were killed, he thought ... he had seen "the captain" being carried away in all his usual serenity. There were some officers farther along the trench.

Our Ensign bade the sergeant get the men to work in consolidating the position. Now that the trench was in British hands, it had to be reversed, the parapet built up into a parados and a fire-step cut in the parapet.

"The men will have to work like blazes," added our young man; "in a few minutes we shall have every German gun in the place opening on us, and the men will want all the cover they can get."

"And, for Heaven s sake, Sergeant Jackson," he went on, "get some of these bodies put out of the trench!"

Then, with infinite difficulty, our young man started to force himself along the crowded trench. There was no shelling as yet, but there was a lot of machine-gun fire and the air was fairly humming with bullets. He fought his way along desperately hard: the men were willing enough to let him pass, but your Guardsman in full attacking order is a big object that, even edgeways, almost blocks an ordinary trench, and our Ensign had an exhausting time. As he dragged himself round a traverse, he all but stepped on a German lying on the ground. As he passed him, the man caught hold of the officer's legs and shrieked in a broad Bavarian accent—

"*Ach! Herr Leutnant! Ich halt'es nicht aus . . . schiessen Sie mich! Ach! schiessen Sie mich! Ich bitt' Sie!*"

The taking of a man's life in cold blood had never entered into our novice's philosophy, so he shook the man off and passed on, with a horrid picture in his memory of a livid, grimacing mask.

Our Ensign next came to a broad gap blown clean through parados and parapet. As he was about to pass, a young Coldstreamer at his elbow pushed past him into the gap. The next moment the lad cried out "Oh!" a loud, gasping exclamation of utter astonishment, spun round, and fell prone at the officer's feet with a great gush of blood that splashed the other's tunic.

"There's a sniper laying on that gap, sir," said an Irish Guardsman standing by; "for the love of God, kape your head down!"

"This is a bloody business," said our Ensign to himself. These ghastly sights were beginning to get on his nerves. Then, ducking down, he darted across the gap and in a minute or two found himself in the presence of headquarters. The commanding officer told him he was to take command of No. 2 Company, as the only officer surviving, and asked for news of the second-in-command. Our Ensign told his tale.

A group of officers were there: Roderick, tall and quite cool; The Lad, brimming over with excitement, who had drifted in from his battalion, together with his commanding officer, a brigade machine-gun officer, the doctor, the *padre*, a forward observation officer.

Roderick gave our Ensign a brief budget of news. The Don had been shot through the thigh, crossing the ridge; Apollo had got it through the shoulder, and had last been seen volubly explaining to the stretcher bearers carrying him down the exact nature of his wound in highly technical language; Duke was all right. Of the officers of the other companies, two at least were known to be killed—Roderick had heard the men talking about them.

One of these two officers was a friend of our Ensign's, yet he heard of his death quite unmoved. In the heat of battle everything appears unreal—so much is rumour, so little is fact; and even towards the concrete realities under his very eyes a man feels that he will wake up and find it all a dream....

One of the group of officers, who was surveying through his glasses the low brown horizon with its tangle of rusted wire, suddenly pointed to the right.

"That communication trench is full of Huns," he cried; "look! you can see them in their helmets leaning on the parapet!"

Everybody put up their glasses. There, sure enough, was a long line of heads in coal-scuttle helmets lining the trench indicated. They had a machine-gun trained on the trench where the Guards were; they were also busy sniping into all the gaps.

A Lewis gunner was haled forth from the crowded trench, and he lost no time in laying his gun on the line of Germans. But the gun jammed at the first burst of fire. While they were trying another, our Ensign was ordered to take charge of the left of the line, post sentries, and set every man to the task of consolidating the trench. He was briefly told the situation. On the right, the attacking troops had been held up by the strong position known as The Quadrilateral, bristling with machine-guns, the same guns which had caught the Guards in enfilade as they crossed the ridge; what had happened on the left was not clear.

Our Ensign set off back along the way he had come with a light heart. He rejoiced at having a definite job which would keep him from thinking about the horrors piling up on every side of him. With him went the brigade machine-gun officer and a grenadier ensign, from whom our young man had once taken over in the trenches in the salient. Of the three officers, only our Ensign was destined to survive the day, but, of course, he did not know that then.

The German, who had clutched at our Ensign's leg on his passage, lay dead in the bottom of the trench. Our Ensign wondered whether the man had found some one to do the service that he refused him. The dead Coldstreamer in the gap had now three companions prone on their faces in the mud.

As they elbowed their way along, the three officers set every man in the trench to the task of consolidation. The men obeyed willingly enough, and the sergeants, at the officers' bidding, posted sentries at intervals along the trench, with strict injunctions to keep a sharp look-out, right, left, and centre. Thus the three officers forced their way down the trench, leaving a trail of busy diggers in their wake. By mutual arrangement our Ensign pushed on alone to the extreme left, where he found himself among troops of the line, until he met a very youthful subaltern of a Rifle regiment, whom our Ensign informed of the situation, and of the measures they were taking for their protection. This done, our Ensign toiled his way back again along the trench.

And now the long-expected *strafe* began. A German battery that had been shelling over them shortened its range, and the shells, vicious, black "whizz-bangs," began dropping uncomfortably close to the trench. Word had been coming along from the right, "All men of the such-and-such battalion of the Coldstream to the right," "All men of the such-and-such battalion of the Irish Guards to the right," so the trench was a little clearer as the different battalions got sifted out. Some kind of advance was going forward to the extreme right. Our Ensign saw long lines of men advancing through a tornado of great, black shell bursts. Presently a flock of grey figures, hands above their heads, bolted across the open. Shouts rang out all down the trench.

"Shoot the dogs! Lend me your rifle, mate! Let them be! Shoot the ———! Ah, leave them alone!" But no shot fell, and the frightened herd plunged across the broken ground among their own shells, a couple of phlegmatic figures in khaki driving them before them.

The German shell fire was growing in intensity. A 5.9 battery had joined in. The cry of "stretcher bearer!" ran up and down the trench; here and there men lagged at their digging. Our Ensign had to run up and down, "speeding up" the laggards like a negro slave-driver. But he noticed many more limp figures, many more ghastly wounds, and every dugout had its pale and bloodstained occupants....

In all his efforts our Ensign was loyally supported by his own non commissioned officers and men. The sergeants by word, the men by deed, gave a splendid lead to the reluctant. It is in battle that the sterling loyalty of British troops to their officers comes out strongest.

On his knees at the bottom of the trench, scraping vigorously away with his entrenching tool at the parapet to fashion a fire-step, our Ensign found old Lawson, one of the battalion snipers, the sweat glistening on his face, for by now the sun was shining hotly. By his side stood Sergeant Jackson, as dispassionate as ever.

"We're going to catch it hot here, sir," said the sergeant, with a shake of his head, to our Ensign, who sat down beside the couple and wiped his damp brow. Then, with a shrill scream, a salvo of four shells burst right over the group; someone yelled out loud, and a tangle of men fell all over our Ensign as he squatted on the ground, driving his helmet over his eyes. He fought himself clear, and found that all the men about him had stopped working. Some had taken refuge in a low dugout, where three or four wounded men were sheltering. Our Ensign rooted them out and set them again to their task. Then he looked about him.

Old Lawson, the sniper, lay on his face in the trench, breathing stertorously. Our Ensign turned him over on his back, and saw at a glance that the old soldier was hovering on the brink of eternity. A few yards farther along the trench two men lay dead; another, with a staring white face, was opening his jacket with trembling, blood-stained hands. A little movement behind him caught our Ensign's ear. He turned and found Sergeant Jackson, his face running with blood, rocking himself gently two and fro. On the ground beside him was his helmet, with a great jagged rent in the crown.

Our Ensign tore out his last remaining field-dressing and bound up a gaping wound in the sergeant's head. Then he gave him a pull of the famous tea-and-brandy mixture. The sergeant was conscious, but he spoke in a curious, thick fashion.

"I'm all right, sir," he said, "but I don't quite feel up to duty somehow; and I've got a bit of a brow-ache, too!" And then his head fell forward, and with a sharp pang our Ensign thought he was dead. But presently he spoke again, complained that he could not hear, that his eyes were failing; so our Ensign gave him another pull at the water-bottle, and offered him a cigarette, which he took and was able to light alone. The officer left him seated in the trench contentedly puffing, and set off again to keep the men to their task.

And now our Ensign felt the reaction of the morning's excitement coming over him. All the exhilaration he had experienced in the magnificent opening act of the day seemed to have evaporated. He found himself dwelling with loathing on the mere thought of war; his mind toyed with crude pictures he had seen in German papers of Hindenburg, the German Man of Destiny, striding over mounds of corpses—even such corpses as those that lay strewn all around.

Our Ensign felt his gorge rising at the horrors besetting him. He found himself longing fervently for a mad charge, a German attack,— anything to get away from the shambles, the blood, the mud, the dank smell of the earth, the hideous painted sky that mocked their sufferings. Of all the manifold sensations of the day, the hours he spent in that trench left the deepest impress on our Ensign's memory, and ran their span again and again, with horrors intensified, in the battle dreams that came to him in many nights subsequently.

In reality, they were not more than three or four hours in the third German line. To our Ensign the delay seemed endless; the men, too, were chafing to be away "after the Gers.," anything rather than to sit there and be shelled to atoms.

Down the trench our Ensign found the brigade machine-gunner again. The latter told him that apparently the attacking lines, misled by the two trenches which had lain, all unsuspected, between them and their first objective, had believed the trench they were in to be the third objective, whereas it was in reality only the first objective, as far as could be ascertained. In a country from which practically every landmark has been razed, where one trench looks exactly like another, such an error was easily made. Hence the delay. However, the machine-gunner said, the first lines had gone on now, and probably the rest would soon follow.

A charming fellow, this machine-gunner, practical, conscientious, and fearless beyond all praise. He and our Ensign found themselves cordially agreed that the sights in that trench were enough to sicken a man of war for the rest of his life.

Then our Ensign suddenly saw his commanding officer on the parapet above his head. He ordered our young man to collect all the men he could and bring them forward. Our Ensign and the machine-gunner were out of the trench in an instant, bawling to the men to follow them. The men were delighted to get away, and the machine-gunner, surrounded by a knot of his men with guns and tripods and ammunition boxes, led a big batch forward, whilst our Ensign ran up and down the trench beating up the rest. And so presently our young Ensign led the way over a wild chaos of broken wire and shell-ploughed brown earth out into the blue, turning his back for ever on that sinister place where, as it seemed to him, years of his life had been spent. On they went, through a few spasmodic shells, to the top of the low ridge, where an unforgettable sight burst upon their vision.

A broad green valley lay unfolded before them, a beauteous panorama as yet unspoiled by war. Mars had not laid a finger on the long green slopes and smiling valleys. Neat little villages still snuggled intact amid clumps of bosky trees, between them long white ribbons of roads bordered by trim rows of poplars. Here was a pretty hamlet with the glint of red roofs amid the verdant foliage, through which a slender yellow church tower thrust itself up into the azure sky. As though protruding right into the foreground—though in reality it was a mile behind the hamlet—ran a broad white ribbon with a tall fringe of trees,—one of the great national highways of France.

At the first view the whole countryside appeared to slumber in the brilliant sunshine of the Indian summer. Birds were singing in the sky, the trees rustled gently in the breeze, and the pleasant old church towers dotting the horizon, seen through the shimmering heat haze that arose off the green fields, seemed to nod drowsily as they kept their ancient watch over their little villages.

But there, clearly discernible to the naked eye, along the white patches of distant roads, was a flicker of moving dots which, seen through the glasses, resolved themselves into long lines of men on the march, guns, transport waggons, and the like. Then, in the nearer foreground, where the yellow church tower emerged from the trees, the eye caught a glimpse of figures—here a knot of men streaming away across the fields, there a solitary form strained to an attitude of watching. Over to the right, along a distant road running across the slope of a hill, a limber came galloping; and our Ensign's eyes, following the moving vehicle through the glasses, rested upon a German battery drawn up in the open, an officer (our Ensign could see his tightly-waisted greatcoat) in the centre, peering through his glasses.

A voice just behind our Ensign exclaimed—

"By God! we've got them in the open at last!"

Another cried excitedly—

"Jasus, boys, look at Fritz running away!"

But for the most part the men were silent, standing erect in the open, gazing spellbound at the Promised Land which it had taken two years' bitter fighting to attain. Thus Cortes and his little band of adventurers may have stood on the Sierra and contemplated with a thrill of mystery the wonder-city of the Aztecs which lay spread out at their feet. There were many Guardsmen in that little band of men from half a dozen Guards' battalions who had suffered all the bitterness of the retreat from Mons, who had thrilled to the pursuit of the fleeing enemy from the Marne, and then had undergone the long vicissitudes of trench warfare against a better equipped foe. And now they saw him on the run! Those veterans must have felt that now they could die content—and many died that day and the next.

That sight banished all thoughts save one from the minds of that thin brown line. Hardly a man there but had his uniform torn and bloody,—not a man but had lost a friend; since the start at dawn they had had no word from the rear—just a handful of adventurers standing on the fringe of an empty and forsaken stretch of ground. Yet no man heeded any of these things. Operation Orders had said: "The attack will be pushed with the utmost vigour," and the thought dominating every mind was the determination to drive home to its logical conclusion the victory which that spectacle of rout proclaimed they had won. It was a moment such as occurs in all great battles . . . on which the memory afterwards loves to linger in the spirit of "what might have been."

The sun was shining, the sky was blue, the birds were singing, the grass was firm and springy underfoot, and the men went forward joyously, all unconcerned at the shells which fell spasmodically about them. They waded through a field of long rank thistles and dried corn-stalks reaching up to their middles, and came out on the other side to a low shallow trench, which had apparently been constructed to provide a covered way between the guns of a German battery once posted there. The place was littered with the long wickerwork cases in which the Germans carry their shells, and with brass shell-cases innumerable. One Irish Guardsman found on the ground a very delicate and beautiful telescopic sight for use with a 77-millimetre field gun in a brown leathern case, and pounced upon it as a "souvenir."

The machine-gunner and our Ensign had a brief council of war on the edge of the root-field, and decided to put the men into the shallow trench and set them digging themselves in pending further orders. While the Machine Gunner began to install his guns in convenient shell-holes, our Ensign spread the men out along the trench until they came in touch with another party of the Guards who were in the same trench. There were one or two officers with them, a couple of

Coldstreamers, and a grenadier captain.

By this time the shelling was growing distinctly unpleasant. Through his glasses our Ensign could clearly see the German battery he had already observed, in action, the men standing to the guns, two officers in flat caps and greatcoats in the middle. The shells were whizz-bangs—shrapnel and high explosive—and they were bursting with unpleasant regularity and disconcerting accuracy up and down the trench line. Everybody was horribly exposed, and now the disagreeable "*swish* . . . *swish*" of some very active machine-guns on the right (in the Quadrilateral, no doubt) blended with the whistle of the shells. Every man in the trench was now working like a Trojan, scraping and hacking away with his entrenching tool in the soft brown soil, and the narrow trench was quite impassable. To get along one had simply to walk across the open and pay no heed to the bullets snapping in the air.

But the excitement of being "in the open" made everybody amazingly callous. The men never ceased working, though here and there hideously mutilated bodies were gently lifted out of the trench and bedded in the thistles, and in places men were shouting, unanswered, the familiar battlefield cry, "Stretcher-*bearer!*"

Officers were walking about in the open, keeping the men to their task, and on the edge of the root-field three commanding officers of the Guards were talking things over, raising their glasses now and then to their eyes, like spectators at an Army point-to-point. They were our Ensign's commanding officer, that commanding officer of the Coldstream who had that day rallied his men to the note of the silver hunting-horn which our Ensign saw sticking between the buttons of his jacket, and another. Presently, somebody suggested the advisability of taking a little cover, and they adjourned into an adjacent deep shell-hole, where the discussion was resumed. Many days afterwards our Ensign read in a message from *The Times* war correspondent in France how:

> At one point in the advance certain battalion commanders of the Guards held a conference, which will be historic, in a shell-hole to try and locate precisely where they were.

Near the "historic shell-hole" our Ensign met Duke, an ensign of his own battalion, one of his own mess, in a huge trench coat. He informed our Ensign that Roderick had been sniped in the trench and badly wounded.

"You and I," he said to our Ensign, "seem to be the only company officers left. Everybody else has disappeared. My word! it was hot getting up to that last trench!"

He told our Ensign that *El Capitan* (who had been left behind when the battalion went into action) had been sent for after Roderick was hit, and was coming to take over the company.

And here was *El Capitan* himself, rubbing his hands, bristling with fight.

"We're going on," he grinned; "there's another mixed party of Guards and people in shell-holes a bit down the slope, and we're going to try and join up with 'em!"

Our Ensign's recollections of the rest of that afternoon are rather hazy. He remembers sallying out again with a party of Irish Guardsmen over the coarse yellow grass towards a long low slope running across from left to right. There came a perfect tornado of German shells and a steady incessant swish of bullets from the machine-guns enfilading the slope from the Quadrilateral. Still the line went on, but strangely thinned, as our Ensign noticed in wonder. He remembers seeing little spurts of dust about his feet without understanding what they meant, and asking himself whether the curious whistling noises followed by a metallic whirr were rifle grenades. He caught a glimpse of the machine gun officer coming out with his men, standing on the slope behind him. When he looked once more he was gone, and our Ensign never saw him again.

All the men were in shell holes now. Our Ensign toppled breathlessly into one, a shallow crater, where there were two men of the machine-gun team with a gun. The German guns were searching the whole slope with whizz-bangs and those rifle grenades, or whatever they were, that made that whistling noise and that curious metallic whirr (our Ensign afterwards knew them to be H.E. shrapnel). The shells were bursting everywhere; one could *taste* their sulphur reek, and the ears ached with the perpetual detonations.

The machine-gunners scraped vigorously at the bottom of the hole. It was obviously too small to shelter three, so our Ensign scrambled out and, bending low, darted forward. Once more there was a whirr of bullets. He realised that he must be in full view of some one watching that slope. He dropped into another shell-hole, a much bigger one than the last. A solitary Irish Guardsman was sitting there, phlegmatically scooping himself a little trench with his entrenching tool.

Then our Ensign saw *El Capitan* striding across the open, his orderly by his side. As our young man watched, he saw the orderly clap his hand to his leg and drop. *El Capitan* disappeared into a shell hole with him and presently emerged alone. Our Ensign shouted to him: the other waved to him to stay where he was, and went striding on calmly back to the trench.

A man dropped heavily on our Ensign and his companion in the shell-hole. He was an Irish Guardsman, too.

"I was in with two chaps in the hole beyant," he panted, "and a shell is after landing on the edge of the hole. It's a wonder that meself's alive, for thim other two is dead!"

"Well, take a hould on your entrinchin' tool," said the other without sympathy, "and dig this out a bit for th' officer!"

While they scraped away our Ensign chatted to the two men. Their talk was all of the "Gerboys harin' off," the number of prisoners they had seen . . . incidents of the day's fighting; of their present position in a shell-hole on a bullet-swept slope with shells bursting all around them they said nothing.

The slope of the ground in front rather masked the view, so our young man resolved to push on a shell-hole or two and try and discover what was happening at the front of the slope. He crawled for a dozen yards, then he heard a shell "coming at him," as the saying is, and he flung himself into the nearest hole. There he found Duke with an ashen face, his jacket split up the back and drenched in blood. With him was his orderly, a big man wearing the D.C.M. ribbon.

"I'm all right," observed the wounded man; "I've got it in the shoulder, I think. They put a shell—shrapnel, I believe it was—right on top of us. Have you got a cigarette to spare?"

Our Ensign looked at his watch. It was four o'clock, a brilliant autumn afternoon, full of light and colour. He found it quite impossible to realise that it was on the cards that none of them would ever get out of that hole alive. But the oddness of their situation tickled his sense of humour, and he remarked upon it as he handed his fellow ensign his cigarette-case.

Thus they sat for fully an hour and a half. By that time our Ensign and the orderly had dug the shell-hole into quite a respectable trench. They had to work with great circumspection, for the least movement attracted a shower of projectiles in their direction. Otherwise, the enemy seemed loath to waste ammunition; when the surface of the slope was unruffled the guns were silent.

No word came up from the trench behind them, meanwhile, and at half-past five our Ensign thought he had better go back and find out what was happening. He promised to send out the stretcher-bearers to fetch in Duke as soon as darkness fell. Then he crawled cautiously back, noticing on his way that the shell-hole in which he had first taken shelter now held two corpses and a wrecked machine-gun.

Chapter 15

On returning to the trench, our Ensign found that, during his absence, the men had dug a foot or so down and had fashioned a rude kind of fire-step. Their numbers had been increased by the arrival of two more officers of our Ensign's Battalion with mixed parties of Guards. These two officers had been having an exhilarating time bombing the enemy out of the right of the third German line. Our Ensign found all the surviving officers of his battalion—with the commanding officer, the doctor, and the *padre*, seven in all—installed in a sort of small observation trench (probably dug originally for the officers of the German battery installed there). Several of the party were busy deepening the trench with pick and entrenching tool, but others were looking through their glasses at the slopes to the right of the yellow church tower where strange doings were toward.

Word had been brought in from the small party of Guards and other units holding the most advanced line that the Germans were massing for a counter-attack. Through his glasses our Ensign could clearly descry dense parties of men advancing in artillery formation on the distant slopes bathed in the mellow evening sunshine, while on the roads transport waggons, artillery limbers, and even motor-buses were to be seen rolling up. The situation was desperate enough. The Guards were still without word from the rear, without any known support, without any definite connection either right or left, without machine-guns, for the last team had been knocked out that afternoon, without Verey lights for the approach of darkness, or any material to put the trench in a proper state of defence. If the Germans attacked it would have to be a fight to a finish, for, of course, there was no idea of falling back. Our Ensign noticed the commanding officer, who was perfectly cheerful and entirely confident, examining the chamber of his revolver.

Then, over to the right, a sudden German barrage with nasty, black 5.9 shells, began with unexpected violence. Through the high spouting shell bursts a steady line plodded forward and the word flashed along the line—

"The Scots Guards are attacking!" Onward they went in the failing light, tall figures swallowed up in black masses of smoke, men flung this way and that, ducking, stumbling, falling. Suddenly our Ensign, watching through his glasses, saw an officer he knew well topping the skyline,—a shell burst quite close to the familiar figure—he shot up an arm to protect his face, then plunged forward again and was lost to view in the eddying smoke and the gathering dusk. Then the line was slowly swallowed up, and only the shells remained to bar the advance of supports.

The day died reluctantly, sullenly, and the temperature began to sink. Our Ensign, who had been doing his share of the digging, suddenly remembered that he had had no lunch. He looked for his orderly, a man he had got in the last line to take the place of the wounded MacFinnigan, but he was nowhere to be seen, vanished in the smoke of battle together with our Ensign's haversack containing his sandwiches. However, *El Capitan* came to the rescue with a hunk of bread and tongue and a bar of chocolate, which, together with a draught of the famous tea-and-brandy mixture, gave our young man a satisfying meal. As he was eating he saw the stretcher bearers arriving with Duke, with whom the doctor immediately busied himself.

It was almost dark when an Irish Guards sergeant arrived with the news that the Germans were still massing to attack. Our Ensign never forgot the sight of that man, a big Celtic type with fine eyes, a blood-stained bandage round his head, very white against his black hair. He had come from the mixed party still holding out in the most advanced line. Having delivered his message, he went forth once more into the dusk . . . and was never seen again. Thus do men vanish in battle.

The counter-attack never came. Long after the German star-shells had begun spouting, long after the survivors of the party in the most advanced line and of the detachment which had gone forward in the afternoon had been withdrawn, the Guards remained on the *qui vive*. Our Ensign and his brother ensigns divided the night into watches, and took turns to spend three hours in the raw air with the line of outposts which the Guards threw out in front of their trench. That night, at last, they got touch with a line battalion on the left, and on the right with another battalion of Guards.

When our Ensign returned to the trench on being relieved on outpost duty . . . it was about midnight . . . feeling very cold and utterly weary, he found an unwonted stir there. Rations and water had come up and were being distributed among the men. Nor had the officers been forgotten. Three servants had accompanied the ration party and brought food and drink for the officers, also the letters. Loud were the praises of the quartermaster sung that night, for it was a great feat. All day the battalion had been marooned, yet, with the coming of night, the rations arrived in spite of Heaven knows what difficulties to be surmounted on the way up. There were three letters for our Ensign, and the first he opened was a bill from a London florist! That thin sheet of paper, with its elaborately engraved heading, brought home vividly to him the extraordinary contrasts in which war abounds,—at one moment cowering in a shell hole, with death busy all about; the next moment back again in the old routine of life, with letters and newspapers . . . and bills! Thus our Ensign pondered as he devoured cold tongue and bread and biscuits, and sipped some excellent claret out of an enamel mug, at his feet *El Capitan* and the *padre* snoring peaceably.

When the first streaks of another dawn appeared in the sky, the outpost line was withdrawn and the men came trudging back to the trench, muddy, red-eyed with want of sleep, transpierced with cold. Our Ensign watched the morning creeping rosy-fingered into the sky, and idly wondered what the day would bring forth. During the night, apparently, the British artillery had profited by the deep stretch of ground won from the enemy, for, as soon as it was light, some vicious little field-pounders began barking very close up behind the Guardsmen's position. Then a few British aeroplanes hummed out into the clear morning sky and flew away. Not long after a regular covey of German machines sallied out and hovered above the Guards, cramped up in their shallow and altogether unprotected trench.

"Now we shall catch it," thought our Ensign, and catch it they did. It was mostly shrapnel, H.E. shrapnel, black and vile-smelling, with a deafening detonation, that the Hun sent over, reserving his heavier stuff for the little battery behind, which barked incessantly notwithstanding. The German shooting was bad, and the shells fell short of or over the trench. Several shrapnel bursts clanged and whizzed and pattered round the heads of the officers as they sat in the bottom of their corner of the trench, but they had no casualties. In fact, although the shelling went on at intervals all through the day, the casualties were few.

But it was an arduous time. There was no means of proceeding along the trench, for it was far too crowded, and, indeed, there was no object in doing so. One could only sit there and attempt the impossible—namely, to pay no heed to the shells. The little group of officers was strangely isolated, for there was no movement to be observed, either before or behind them. The ground in the rear was in full view of the enemy, so communication with the troops in the line behind was cut off during the daylight hours. It all gave our young man a queer sort of "desert island" sensation, and he kept on thinking of the shipwrecked pleasure party in "The Admirable Crichton."

Some of the officers slept, others ate, others took turns at assisting the orderlies to deepen still further the trench, the bottom of which was found to consist of live German shells in their wicker cases. One of the orderlies, stoutly wielding a pick, made this interesting discovery, upon which the pick was unanimously disqualified, and only very gentle scraping with the entrenching tool allowed. Our Ensign slept a little and ate a little and drank a little, and then did a thing he had never done before, being a strict Tory, . . . he read *The Daily News* from cover to cover—leading articles, Women's Page, advertisements, and all, and then passed it on to somebody else, who did the same. It was the only newspaper in the trench.

But the green panorama stretched out before them was not without its compensations either. Ever since the previous afternoon the British Heavies had played a wonderful game with the pretty little hamlet with the yellow church tower peering forth from among the trees. Huge projectiles whooshed noisily through the air, and hurled destruction among the red roofs and the verdant foliage.

A great pall of smoke, flanked by spouts of black and brown earth, and topped with eddies of coral-pink haze, was the last that our Ensign had seen of the little village by daylight. At night, as he went round the outposts, however, he had still heard the great shells crashing into the village, and watched a house blaze heavenwards with a glare that lit up the surrounding spouts of smoke. In the first light of morning he had seen the yellow church tower but a single ragged stick of broken masonry amid a tangle of broken trees and gaping roofs. And still the shells went pounding in. Ah, the guns of the Somme—they do their work thoroughly!

It is not often in this war of trenches that a man can get a comprehensive view of an attack. To the little group of officers, cooped up in their narrow trench, was vouchsafed that morning as *grandiose* a spectacle as (our Ensign believes) any man has witnessed in this war. Somewhere about the hour of half-past nine a light infantry brigade over on the left attacked, and from their "grand stand," as the men, delighted, called it, the Guards could see every detail of the advance. It was a sight, too, to gladden brave men's eyes! For though the little lines of brown dots that went creeping forward up the distant green slopes were swept away again and again, while across the valley echoed the loud stutter of the German machine-guns, yet the succeeding lines went on. The tiny brown figures seemed literally to be blown down, yet others struggled forward, wave upon wave, until they were lost to view.

Through the glasses one could see the wake they had left—little figures crawling about, hobbling, with the stretcher-bearers darting and ducking and dodging to and fro. Once a figure detached itself from the advancing line, right in the teeth of that whirlwind of death, bent over a prostrate figure, picked it up, and started to struggle along. . . . probably towards the shelter of a shell-hole. But, even as our Ensign watched, with bated breath, the little brown figure and his burden rolled over and lay still.

All the valley now re-echoed to the roar of artillery, and the Germans left the Guards alone while they concentrated on the attacking forces. The British supports were seen coming up through a heavy barrage, then men began to trickle back down the slope strewn with brown figures left in the trail of the advance. What had happened? No one knew. Had the attack failed? None could say. Little by little the artillery fire slackened, some inquisitive aeroplanes came out and hovered over the scene, and, by-and-by, the noise and the smoke subsided. Then, after a pause, the enemy turned his attention to the Guards, and started his intermittent bombardment again.

In the course of the day word at last came up from the rear. The Guards were to maintain their position, and might be called upon to support an attack. In the afternoon the troops on the left went forward again to the attack, but the wind blew the smoke across the field of vision, and the Guards could not exactly see what was going forward. Germans, however, could still be discerned in and about the ruined village.

Towards dusk that evening our Ensign and a grenadier officer took a party of men and raided some *chevaux de frise*—trestles garnished with barbed wire—which the lynx eye of our Ensign's Commanding Officer had noticed in front of a German trench in their rear. This was lifted bodily in sections, and put out in front of the trench to furnish some slight measure of protection in the event of a German attack.

Night fell again, dank and cold, with a menace of rain. Still there was no word of relief. How distant seemed that fresh dawn when, under the paling stars, the Guards had gone forward to the attack! Everybody was worn out. Excitement, fatigue, want of sleep, had done their work. But no respite could be granted. Again, at nightfall, the line of outposts was posted; and again the ensigns, haggard and scrubby, did a shift each in turn. The men were so utterly exhausted that they literally could not keep their eyes open as they lay crouching in their shell-holes in pairs, their faces towards the spouting German lights, their backs towards the blackness of their trench. Our Ensign, moving continually during his turn of duty to keep himself awake, had to go from shell-hole to shell-hole and assure himself that the sentries were watchful by kicking the soles of their boots.

While our Ensign was out during the hours before midnight, in company with one of his sergeants, he managed to get in touch with the troops who had made the gallant attacks that morning and afternoon. In a sunken road which had been wrested from the enemy, and was strewn with German and British dead, he found the wounded laid out in long lines of stretchers, moaning, shivering with cold, pathetically asking for cigarettes—a thing he could not give them. They were waiting their turn to be carried down over the broken and shell-swept ground to the rendezvous of the field ambulances, a mile or so back.

In a German dugout our Ensign found two battalion commanders supping off bread and chocolate and a drain of whisky in a bottle, with them two or three young officers. They were all mud-stained and worn, but they made our Ensign welcome and offered him a share in their drain of whisky. They told our Ensign they were momentarily expecting to be relieved, and promised to inform their successors of the Guards' line of outposts, so that they could join up with the Guards.

When our Ensign got back to the trench, he heard glad tidings: the Guards were to be relieved that night. It was half-past one in the morning, but there were no signs of the relief as yet; and presently our Ensign was sent out again with another party of men to strengthen the outpost line, for there were rumours of a German attack to be delivered at two o'clock.

Once more the weary men, many of whom had already been three hours on outpost duty that night, fared forth into the blackness in a smother of rain. The night was very dark, and it was hard work getting the men out of the trench and lined up, for they were heavy with sleep. Perhaps this operation created an undue amount of noise; but the fact remains that hardly had our Ensign led them into the open than a perfect storm of German bullets came over—machine-guns stuttered loudly, and a great shower of German lights soared up into the sky.

Everybody flung himself flat on his face, our Ensign reflecting that the enemy seemed to anticipate a further British attack rather than to contemplate launching one himself. Presently the storm abated, and our Ensign rose to his feet. But the man at his side did not stir. Bending down, our Ensign shaded his lamp with his hand and flashed the light for an instant on to the prostrate figure. It was our Ensign's orderly—his third since the attack started—lying dead on his back with a bullet through the head. He was the only casualty.

******

The cold night was all but spent, and the sky was slowly changing to the play of the approaching day, when, from out of a scene of some bustle about the trench, word came to our Ensign to bring the outposts in . . . the reliefs had arrived. Never was relief effected more swiftly. It went at a whirlwind pace. Stiff and aching, the outposts stumbled in and were pushed by their comrades into their places in the sadly shrunk companies of the battalion; a blur of figures groped their way into the trench, a couple of infantry subalterns emerged and reported to the Commanding Officer, . . . how fresh they looked, thought our Ensign. . . .

Then a German shell screamed over and burst noisily, scattering a pailful of shrapnel about: another followed, and another. The sky is flushing with the coming of the sun: every moment the light grows brighter. Hurry, hurry, or the Huns will finish off even that wasted shadow of a battalion before it clears the ridge. What are they waiting for in front? *Clang . . . whee . . . ee ... oo ... oo!* goes the shrapnel. Why the devil don't they move on? *Crash!* there falls another shell. . . .

But the leading company is off at a good steady amble, the rest of the battalion at its heels, each company commander taking the shortest way that will bring his men out of the zone of visibility behind the shelter of the ridge. Away they go, across the German third line, where the only Guards left now are the dead, and muffled figures are frying bacon over little wood fires,—past shell-holes tenanted by stiff forms, over roads strewn with field-grey corpses and littered with the jumble of the battlefield, down the slope back to life and air and safety, where the larks are singing in the pellucid sky, where the gunners are clinking dixies as they come and go about their breakfast—past a smashed gun here and a wrecked horse ambulance there, and so on to a road where signallers and sappers and R.A.M.C. orderlies, washing and shaving and breakfasting in the bright sunshine, wave an encouraging hand as the Guards go by.

There, in an open space by a wood, spruce figures—the officers and non-commissioned officers who had been left behind—are moving in and out of the muddy, dishevelled Guardsmen grouped about the smoking cookers. Peter is there, and all the others; and there, too, is the faithful Johnson, waiting with our Ensign's cap and a discreetly murmured "Glad to see you all right, sir!" There also the mess sergeant, pink and perspiring, darting to and fro among a cloud of servants busy over a white cloth spread on the ground ready for breakfast. The grateful smell of breakfast is in the air and the buzz of many voices— but all the movement stops, all the voices are hushed, as the battalion, much reduced in strength, marches in, forms up, and is dismissed by the commanding officer. Then the buzz of voices breaks forth again, hearty greetings are exchanged, there is much hand shaking, while the company officers, their company sergeant-majors by their sides, run about and see that the men get their breakfast.

Half an hour later our Ensign sank down beside the white tablecloth. The craving for warm food was uppermost, stronger even than the desire to sleep, ... it was a Gargantuan meal in the sunshine. Whilst he ate, he heard of the fortunes of the fight, the fine advance made, the numbers of prisoners captured, the success of the French, the losses, the death of this friend and of that, the condition of the wounded, ... but it made no impression on his mind at the time. He was too tired, his mind was too benumbed by the sensations he had experienced, to grasp or to realise anything.

Then, finally, came the march back to camp, the drums of the battalion at the head. They followed that self-same road by which our Ensign had seen the remnants of the Irish Division coming out of action a week or so before. The men held themselves erect, and stepped out well to the roll of the drums and the squeal of the fifes, which brought out on to the roadside banks men from batteries, bivouacs, and horse-lines all around. Near the camp the brigadier met them and walked a part of the way beside the commanding officer, sitting his horse at the head of the column.

And so, to the lilt of the regimental quickstep, they came to a great city of canvas spread out upon a breezy hillside, and marched in to rest through lines of other Guardsmen, like them, just out of action, who smiled them a welcome through the grime on their faces.

Chapter 16

The moving finger writes; and, having writ,
Moves on: nor all thy piety nor wit
Shall lure it back to cancel half a line,
Nor all thy tears wash out a word of it.
— Omar Khayyám.

The morrow of battle is worse than battle itself, worse even than the eve. For, when the weary body has been rested, the dazed brain begins to reassert itself, and the flood of realisation pains like the rush of blood to a numbed limb. The empty messes, the missing faces, the shrunken appearance of the battalion when the roll is called, the pile of kits lying ownerless outside the quartermaster's store . . . each of these visible signs of the battalion having passed through the fire the mind takes in, reluctantly and recoiling from each fresh shock. In sleep it revives shudderingly every phase of the fight, and, liberated from the shackles of the will, lying powerless in the ban of slumber, suffers unresisting, a thousand times intensified, every torment of fear and horror which the waking mind has suppressed. For dreams—so the psychologists tell us—are but the expression of emotions consciously or subconsciously held in restraint in the waking hours.

Tents, as far as the eye could see, pitched in a sea of mud, ruffled by chill gusts of rain and wind sweeping across the slopes; a mammoth gun belching forth green fire and yellow smoke a few hundred yards away, the thunder of distant cannon, blending with the stir of the camp; drums beating, pipes skirling from the lines of the Scots Guards, the solemn harmony of men's voices singing hymns (only the Welsh Guards possessed a choir like that !) . . . these were the sights and sounds to which our Ensign awoke from his first troubled sleep after getting back to camp.

He came to his senses with a start of terror that sent him flying to the tent door. Hideous nightmare shapes were haunting the tents and huts where officers and men of the Guards slept the sleep of utter exhaustion, physical and mental, the terrifying spectres that drift through the battle dreams of men who have been in action. Until our Ensign had gazed long upon the lines of tents swaying in the wind, and had seen the familiar khaki figures, wrapped in their waterproof capes, passing to and fro in the mud, his mind remained in the grip of a nameless terror: he did not know who or where he was, whether he were alive or dead, on earth or in space. Thus do men awake from their first sleep after coming out of battle.

For a few instants he felt like one raised from the dead. Slowly and painfully his mind picked up, one by one, the threads of his life where it seemed to have left off on that sunny morning—surely it was years ago?—when the whistles had sounded, the hurricane din had broken loose, and the Guards had moved forward into battle.

But there across the tent lay Peter's sleeping valise and things: there, on the tent pole, hung the little mirror they shared in common. The tent was dry and clean: the yellow light diffused through its canvas sides was bright and comforting. And here was the faithful Johnson, getting ready his bath and a complete change of clothing, and collecting his torn and bloodstained uniform for the battalion tailor to mend and scour.

Lazily our Ensign fished a box of cigarettes from his kit spread out beside him, lit one, and lying back in his warm sleeping-bag, watched the smoke curl upwards towards the peaked dome of the tent. He was stiff all over, every bone in his body was aching, but he was conscious of a deep sense of thanksgiving; he was overpoweringly glad to be back in the world again. They had to carry on. He had a pang when he found all those joyous company messes he had known shrunk to a group of officers small enough to take their meals together at one short table. He would not let himself think of the old double-company mess, for only he and two others survived—all the rest were casualties. "*Der Mann stirbt,*" says the old German maxim, "*das Regiment bleibt*" and the old battalion routine continued unbroken.

The battalion had to be remade, companies re-shuffled, new non commissioned officers appointed, casualty lists made up, names sent in for decorations, and with it all the old duties to be done—rifle inspections and rum issues and all the rest. The very matter-of-factness of this resumption of the old life hurt a little sometimes, but the work of the army, like the government of the realm, brooks no interruption.

Drafts arrived to fill up the gaps in the ranks of the battalion. They saw the first batch of these parading one angry and lowering autumn evening as they trooped back through the mud and rain from the little cemetery in the centre of the camp, where they had laid to rest a brother officer ... a plain rite with no other ceremonial than that with which the simple majesty of the Burial Service invests the humblest obsequies, with the rain blowing damp upon their bare heads, and the guns of the Somme growling in the distance.

Truly the regiment is a thing immortal.

✶✶✶✶✶✶

But even in the midst of the work of reorganising the battalion, rumours began to circulate that the Guards, like other divisions, were going to have "a second helping" of the great offensive. There was a plain hint of this intention in the very stirring message of congratulation which the brigadier sent to the battalion for their achievements on September 15, the passage ran:

"You maybe called upon in the near future to carry out similar work, and I know that you will not fail."

Of course they would not, but the news created something akin to dismay amid the little band of survivors of the great advance—not from any reluctance to play a man's part again, but from apprehension as to how the strong leaven of untried recruits in their ranks would withstand the fury of a modern battle as their first taste of active service. Events were to prove how utterly groundless these apprehensions were, but there was a pretty general feeling at the time that it was hard luck for the battalion's fine fighting reputation to be thus staked on the untested quality of new drafts.

Moreover, this time it was the turn of our Ensign's battalion to lead the attack. Everybody was going in: and our Ensign found himself back with his company, as second in command to Peter and the only other officer in the company. Nos. 1 and 2 companies were to furnish the first "waves" of the assault.

One afternoon the corps commander rode over to the camp, and from his horse told the officers of our Ensign's battalion, assembled in a semicircle, what was expected of the battalion, and why. In a few very brief but very lucid words he explained the higher strategy of the Somme offensive, which the general public was to learn three months' later from Sir Douglas Haig's memorable despatch, and assured them that what the great British artillery superiority on the Somme could do to lighten their task would be done in a measure that should surpass anything the Germans had yet experienced in the way of bombardments. Then, wishing them all good luck, he rode away, and in simple language, such as soldiers understand, addressed the non-commissioned officers to the same effect. And that simple, straightforward talk was like a searchlight that picked out and held in its bright beam the word "Duty," which is engraved in every soldier's mind.

★★★★★★

So, on a wet, dark evening, the battalion marched back again to that little copse where in the dugout "The Last Supper of the Girondins" had taken place. The roads had suffered terribly from the combined effects of the rain and the heavy traffic of the recent advance. They had been churned into deep quagmires of glutinous mud, where guns and limbers and G.S. waggons kept on getting bogged, where the men sank in above the middle of their *puttees* at every step.

What with the darkness and the mud and the frequent blocks owing to vehicles sticking fast in the slime, the traffic was in a state of chaos. The rain pelted down unmercifully, and it was so dark that a man could not distinguish the features of his neighbour in the ranks. Reliefs and fatigue parties, passing to and from the front line, got inextricably mixed up. Men lost touch, and amid the curses of the drivers as they urged their exhausted horses or mules through the deep bog of the road, echoed cries such as: "Fatigue party this way!" "All Welsh Guards to move forward"; "Make way there! Stretcher-bearers!" while the rain splashed sorrowfully down and the air trembled to the thundering crash of the guns all around.

The battalion took about four hours to march the few miles separating their last camp from the copse, and when they finally got in they were all drenched and liberally besmeared with mud. A rum issue warmed them a little, and then once more the men set about scraping themselves dry spots in the crumbling shell-holes and building shelters out of the litter of branches and shell-baskets and corrugated iron sheeting scattered about the copse.

Their labours proved to be in vain, for at luncheon the next day a baby-faced infantry subaltern walked up to the officers' mess and very diffidently suggested that the battalion was occupying his battalion's billet. The brigade was consulted and gave the verdict in favour of the line, so that afternoon the battalion moved to another portion of the wood, where, in a number of German dugouts, all more or less battered, and in shell-holes, they managed to make themselves fairly comfortable. With the aid of the mess-servants, the officers managed to put a fairly large dugout into a state of repair, thatching the holes in the roof with sandbags filled with earth, laid across iron girders, and building up the gaps in the back of the shelter with sheets of corrugated iron which one of the orderlies found lying in the wood. The floor was carpeted with clean sandbags, a table was knocked together and a line of seats constructed out of filled sandbags. A brazier of glowing coals was placed in the doorway, for the nights were very cold, and thus they managed to install themselves with some measure of comfort.

The men displayed extraordinary ingenuity in the little bivouacs and earths they constructed out of their waterproof sheets and all kinds of odd material. Fortunately the weather improved, and the sun came out hot in the daytime, though the air got very cold after nightfall.

Early each morning the companies were taken out by an officer and given half an hour's physical drill in the bright sunshine—either a little doubling (which was a matter of some difficulty, as the slopes on which they exercised were pitted with shell-holes) or leap-frog or follow-my-leader. In the afternoons there were fatigues to be done, mostly salvage fatigues, to clear that littered brown slope over which the Guards had advanced.

Until he had superintended one of these salvage parties, our Ensign had had no idea of the extraordinary quantity and variety of articles with which a battlefield is strewn. The men of the party—generally 100 strong—were spread out over the area designated by the brigade to be cleared, and ordered to bring in every single article they found, no matter what it was, and deposit their burdens at a salvage-dump which had been formed by the roadside. At the dump lay in huge piles rusty rifles, both British and German, bayonets and equipment and greatcoats the same, khaki caps and German helmets, boxes of ammunition and bombs, thousands of rounds of ammunition, parts of machine- and Lewis guns and trench mortars, field-dressings in their neat brown cases, and all kinds of unused rations. All the dead that had strewn the slope had, by this time, been covered in, and the articles which the salvage parties brought by the hundred to the dump were merely the superficial litter of the battlefield.

Altogether the battalion spent four days in the wood. For the greater part of the time they were shelled—an utterly haphazard, sporadic bombardment, with large black 5.9 shells. In comparison with their noise and number, the projectiles did very little damage, but they gave the survivors of the 15th of September an insight into the quality of the new drafts. One of these shells exploded in the middle of the night, with a crash that shook the wood, within a score of yards of a leafy shelter beneath which three of the recruits were sleeping. But, as the company sergeant-major informed our Ensign in accents of admiration afterwards, the three recruits merely turned over on their sides and went to sleep again.

It was 9 o'clock in the evening of September 24 when the battalion started out for the trenches from which the attack was to be delivered the next day, at 12.35 p.m. instead of the more customary early hour. Our Ensign's company led off, and as both officers had been over the route they found their way safely to the rendezvous, a tank stranded on the plain, where the guides sent by the battalion they were relieving met them. The night was as dark as pitch and the German guns most unpleasantly active; in fact, as soon as they had topped the ridge—a long winding caterpillar of silent marching figures—high explosive shrapnel began to burst about them with unpleasant force and in dangerous proximity.

Our Ensign marked down their experiences of that night in his diary as "the most beastly night I ever remember." Men marching at night are always inclined to hurry the pace when they come under shell fire, and as the going was very bad over the loose and crumbling shell-holes, the rear of the company, where our Ensign was, had considerable difficulty in keeping touch with the head. Night after night parties of Germans walked into the British lines, for in the devastated country where most trenches were merely lines of shell-holes connected up, there were no landmarks to guide one. Once touch were lost with the head of the column and the guide, our Ensign knew that he and his men stood a very good chance of landing themselves in the German lines.

There was a communication trench, but it was full of water, so the companies went up over the open. Several times they had to cross the trench in its windings, and each time our Ensign had to help his heavily-laden men to leap the yawning gulf, and then urge them forward at the double to catch up with the rest of the party disappearing into the gloom.

At length they reached their destination—a very narrow, shallow trench dug in the soft brown earth on the grassy downward slope of a low ridge, the German star-shells spouting from the flat ground below them. The trench was so narrow that the reliefs had to stand on the edge until the battalion occupying it had scrambled out. There were no dugouts or shelters of any kind—save that, here and there, men had scraped long shelves in the back wall. The only fire-step was a series of rough embrasures scooped at intervals in the forward wall; parapet there was none, for the edge of the trench was practically flush with the ground.

The relief was accomplished with remarkable alacrity, as reliefs in such circumstances generally are, and the outgoing battalion hurried helter-skelter away into the darkness amid a rain of shells. The only means of communication between one end of that crowded trench and the other was by walking along the top. Luckily, as the night advanced, the Hun became quieter, so Peter and our Ensign made their way to the end of their section of the trench and verified their connection with the other Guards battalion which was to attack the next day on their right, and got back unscathed to the officers' corner of the trench.

There they found *El Capitan* and his ensign who were to take No. 1 Company "over the top" in the morning. The only accommodation was a long shelf cut in the wall of the trench which would shelter two sitting or one lying, and a niche, scooped out of the back wall about level with their waists, which they used as a table.

Throughout the long cold hours until daylight the officers took it turn and turn about to watch, whilst the remaining three sought slumber in the sand-hole or on the floor of the trench. But sleep was out of the question, for once below the level of the ground, by some trick of acoustics, the air trembled so violently with the crash of the guns that the ear-drums positively ached. All night the Germans shelled them in desultory fashion, the shells ploughing up and down the trench but never in it, and the only casualties they sustained were in a luckless water fatigue party. All night the British artillery pounded away at the German lines, cleaving a passage by which the Guards would advance in the noonday hours.

Morning broke—the morning of September 25—pearly and fresh and delightful, and from the shallow trench the officers surveyed the objectives of the coming attack set in a landscape whose perfect serenity was marred only by the gleaming shell-bursts that dotted it everywhere. They saw the long gash in the brown shell-ploughed soil which marked the trench, their first objective; beyond it the village, embowered in foliage, swathed in coral pink and saffron smoke ... a yellow, jagged fragment of church tower, a glimpse of long skeleton roofs and of gaping white walls . . . with the capture of which their day's work would be done.

By some miracle of organisation servants turned up with breakfast, and the four officers munched cold bacon and bread-and-butter and hard boiled eggs, and drank scalding hot tea whilst they studied the scene before them. Aeroplanes—British, of course: the Hun variety was a rarity on the Somme in those days—soared out into the cloudless sky, and fussed about over the German lines amid woolly-white shell-bursts, whilst the German trenches broke their silence with the vicious stutter of machineguns.

All the time the British shells screamed overhead and burst with vast brown earth-spouts and creamy belches of smoke about the trench and the village. Up and down that first objective they went, now flinging high into the air great beams of wood and other dark objects that might have been human limbs, now sending up merely a low billow of dust and smoke, showing that the projectile had fallen plumb into the trench.

In the village the shells crashed and thundered and sent great masses of masonry and woodwork flying, and once, after a burst of pink smoke had cleared away, our Ensign saw that the jagged finger of church tower had vanished.

Chapter 17

But, by the Mass! our hearts are in the trim!—Henry V.

The noonday sun was high overhead. The long hand of the watch was passing the half-hour mark after noon. The first wave of Guards was waiting for the whistle-blast that would launch them to the attack, rifle and bayonet in their hands, helmets strapped on tight, and one foot in the little steps they had cut in the forward wall of the trench. The men of the second wave stood, likewise ready, leaning with their backs to the parados, to let the first wave get clear.

Peter and our Ensign were in the middle of the trench, girt about with revolvers and lamps and compasses, helmets back to front so as to hide their regimental crest that would proclaim them as officers, coat collars turned up, and rifles by their sides. Peter was on the firestep, for he was to lead the first wave: a spin of the coin had decided it: our Ensign leant against the back of the trench, and both had their eyes glued to their left wrists, watching the long hand of their watches crawling forward to the appointed hour.

"Now!" cried Peter.

"Now!" echoed the other, and even as the first wave scrambled out, the roar of the guns increased to whirlwind intensity, and all the stretch of No Man's Land in front of them began to seethe yet more madly with the bursting shells.

Away the solid brown line goes, a zigzagging line of figures, diminishing to right and left into mere dots, slowly, slowly, for they must not walk into that creeping hurricane which is sweeping the ground as they go forward. The noise is terrific, a vast cascade of reverberating crashes blending with the swift, incessant, winged scream of heavy metal hurtling through space, the only ingredient sound distinguishable, the high-pitched whinny and spit of bullets in the air.

No whistle could be heard in such a din, and with the drill-book signal for "Advance"—the right arm stretched forward and dropped—our Ensign got his second wave out of the trench into the screaming, vibrating atmosphere of No Man's Land.

How the men responded to that signal! Never a laggard was there. Out they scrambled and staggered and hopped,—it is no easy thing for a big man, heavily laden, to get out of a narrow trench,—eager and willing and determined, one helping the other, spreading out to the proper extended distance, and dressing by the right as calmly as if they were out on a company training day at home. Out they came with a will, thankful to exchange their narrow quarters in the trench for the freedom of the advance.

Over the top! Has any man's life ever offered such a thrill, such a sensation of freedom, such a bursting from incarceration into liberty, from darkness into light, as that inspiriting leap into the open? Gone the uneasiness, the doubtings of the eve—only the great moral uplifting, which the din of battle brings, remains.

Slowly the line surged forward across the broken ground towards the long ragged fringe of red-rusted wire running in front of the German trench. The second wave soon caught up with and merged in the first, and the whole line went on together, Peter and our Ensign and the company sergeant-major darting to and fro to restrain the eagerness of the men, and prevent them from plunging into that maelstrom of fire that crept forward yard by yard in front of them.

The advance was so leisurely that our Ensign had plenty of time to look about him. He saw with some surprise—so slow is the mind to take in the reality of death—how here a man and there a man would suddenly stop and throw himself down with a deliberation that would have excited the ire of a stage manager rehearsing a death scene. He gazed with astonishment on the secrets which that serene and silent stretch of ground, as viewed from their trench, now abruptly revealed,—waxen and sorrowful corpses in clean field-grey overcoats sprawling in shell-holes, the victims of that morning's bombardment; wounded Guardsmen waiting, with that dumb apathy which is such a fine characteristic of our British wounded, for the stolid and dauntless stretcher-bearers.

A brace of partridge suddenly whirred up from the broken and splintered festoons of wire at their very feet. Our Ensign watched them fly off to the left, and noted that they came unscathed through the torrent of fire. The men laughed uproariously at the appearance of the birds,—it takes but very little to set men laughing in battle.

Now they were at the wire which reached to the very lip of the German trench, all battered and pounded. Already frightened faces appeared, mouthing from under the ugly German coal-scuttle helmets their cry of *"Kamerad! Kamerad!"* The whole line burst into a wild "whoroo": the yell echoed up and down the line, and even rang out above the din of the fight. Then, like a torrent, the khaki flood poured into the trench.

From the top of the trench our Ensign surveyed its length. Germans scuttled out of dugouts, running this way and that uncertainly, like trapped rats—then seeing the khaki surging down upon them, flung away their rifles and threw up their hands, bleating *"Kamerad! Kamerad!"*

What a sight that trench was! The dead were lying everywhere—stamped or blown into the soft mud bottom, sprawling at the mouths of the dugouts, prone upon the parapet; and amongst the flaccid forms others yet alive, with ghastly wounds, shuddering, gibbering, slavering, groaning, whimpering for mercy, for food, for water.

There, in a tiny unfinished shelter, cowered a youth with a shattered jaw, slobbering blood; here, in the bottom of the trench, lay another field-grey with one foot blown clean away—mud-stained, unshaven, filthy—sobbing in a sing-song voice, *"Ach, bitte! ach, bitte!"* and all around the shells screamed through the air or crashed with hideous reverberation and clouds of dust and stifling reek into the crumbling ground. Our Ensign took his orderly and a couple of men and pushed along to the right into a bare and apparently unoccupied stretch of trench. He wanted to link up with the Guards attacking on their right, so as to form an unbroken front.

The German barrage had begun, and the shells were bursting freely about the newly captured position. Behind them they could see the supports swarming out across the ground over which they had just advanced. Our Ensign caught a glimpse of a gross German, fat and unwieldy, sprawling dead on the parapet, his face to the ground. Our young man found himself wondering fearfully if a shell would come and hideously dissipate that mass of flesh. With a shudder he hurried on.

They joined hands with the Guards on their right, and heard from the hot and grimy men a hurried tale of uncut wire and heavy losses. Our Ensign was told the story of the heroic death of a friend, an officer, who had adventured forth alone to cut the wire that barred their progress, and had met his death with his face to the enemy, the cutters in his hand. Then a man came up to our Ensign,—there was a German officer in a dugout who demanded to speak to "th' officer."

Our Ensign followed the private, who led him back along the trench to a dugout, at the entrance of which an officer stood facing a ring of Guardsmen. He was the old type of Prussian officer—none of your upstart, counter-jumper, pot-bellied, bespectacled, "I-surrender-and-let's-call-it-a-draw" sort of special reservist, such as we have all met on the Somme, but a tall well-groomed figure, reticent and coldly hostile. He was wearing a Prussian military cap and a well-fitting grey overcoat. In his hand he held his shrapnel helmet. He introduced himself in good German fashion, with a little bow and click of heels, as a Lieutenant of the 240th Infantry Regiment. He came from the Rhine, where our Ensign had learnt his language.

"There are none but wounded men here with me," he said in German, "and we shall make no further resistance."

"You'd better not," observed the British officer.

"I myself am also wounded," the German went on, protruding his leg and showing his trouser ripped up to the thigh, which was wrapped in bloodstained bandages, "and I will give you my word of honour that there shall be no act of aggression on our part. Will you be good enough to see that there is no killing?"

He used the German expression "*Totmachen*" infinitely grimmer, our Ensign thought, than the English equivalent.

"Nobody is going to touch you if you don't get up to any tricks," our Ensign answered. In exchange for the German's blunt expression he gave him a blunter. "*Nur keine Schweinerei Ihrerseits!*" were the words he used. A German best understands plain speaking. But our young man felt himself strangely moved at the spectacle of this Prussian, who walked surrounded by a halo in his own country, pleading so humbly for his life and that of his men's, with his besotted German conviction that as they had done, so they would be done by.

Thus the *pourparlers* of surrender were conducted in a circle of big and gentle British soldiers. The conditions were that all the wounded who were able to walk should come out of the dug out and be sent down to the rear under escort, and that the rest should remain where they were under guard until they could be removed by the stretcher bearers. Our Ensign posted a couple of sentries at the dugout with instructions to shoot anybody who tried to come out. He carefully explained these orders to the officer.

"You'd better go too," our Ensign added, "for this trench is going to be very unhealthy presently, and you'll be sorry you stayed!"

But the officer protested that he could not walk, so he stayed where he was under guard. He offered our Ensign his helmet, but our young man declined it.

"We're too busy to go collecting souvenirs!" he said, and went off to help his company commander get the men to work on the consolidation of the position.

Presently, while the shells spouted on in front of them in a steady stream, and German shells screamed back barraging all the slope behind, the advance went forward again, the supports coming up to hold the newly-won trench, and the attacking waves going forward to the next objective, a sunken road skirting the village. Here they found a rudimentary fire-position with several deep dugouts and massively constructed shelters, into which they dropped a few bombs to make all safe within. But there was no living sign of the enemy.

A few hundred yards across to the right lay the centre of the village, a wild wreck of crumbling ruins, bathed in the mellow afternoon sunshine which gilded the smoke-clouds drifting in and out of the gaunt roofs. The din of battle raged unabated, for in addition to the crash of the mighty projectiles exploding in the village, German shells burst noisily from time to time about their position on the road. But the shooting was poor. The enemy, deprived of the high ground and driven from the air, was shooting by the map and he was guessing badly.

It was very hot. The officers got the men strung out along the road until they were in touch with both flanks. The men lay down and wiped the sweat from their eyes and foreheads and drained their water-bottles, and chatted eagerly about their experiences of the day. Peter and our Ensign sat on a fallen tree-trunk and discussed the exact location of their next objective, a slope on the far side of the village, and debated the possibility of trouble in the forthcoming assault on the village, which was known to be very strongly fortified.

All this time the hamlet showed no sign of life. Scan it as they would, their glasses showed them nothing more than the scatter of splintered rooftrees, the litter of red tiles, the torn white masonry of the houses,—of the enemy no trace. The next advance would take the Battalion right through the extreme left of the village—first through the orchards behind some houses lining a road leading into the main street; then across the road, through the houses on the other side and through more orchards to a sunken road, and across that to the slope beyond. Certainly the place had had an exemplary pounding from the artillery; but German machine-guns have a way of surviving the most ruthless artillery bombardment—especially in these villages of the Somme, which are honeycombed with old quarries and subterranean passages. It was quite on the cards, therefore, that the battalion might be blown off the map before it reached its final objective.

But they did not bother their heads much about that. The men were in the best of spirits. The old hands were delighted with the stout bearing of the young recruits, while the new-comers, if a trifle more sober, were well buoyed up by the excitement of the advance. The company sergeant-major gave our Ensign a Gold Flake cigarette, and our Ensign offered in return his water-bottle, which had again been filled with the famous tea-and-brandy mixture.

It was time to move on again. The officers ran up and down the line getting the men up. They needed no encouragement: they were frantic to get on. So the line swept forward into the village.

They plunged into a tangle of long grass and shell-holes and broken stumps of gnarled apple-trees, and through a great farmyard surrounded by big barns and outhouses smashed and torn by the shells, showing lines of bunks and blankets tossed aside as though the place had been forsaken in a hurry. Somewhere on the right the loud *tacktack* of machine-guns resounded, and the swish of bullets brushed along their front. The officers checked the line a moment. On the right they saw a string of Guardsmen doubling into a house which spat fire from the first storey and basement windows. Abruptly the swish of bullets ceased, and the stream of figures tumbled out of the house again and followed in the wake of the advance.

In its day the village must have been a charming spot, its comfortable white houses with their red roofs embowered in ancient trees: in the spring, when the fruit-trees, clustering so thickly round every farmstead, were in blossom, it must have been rarely beautiful. Our Ensign had seen it in its prime, for on September 15 he had taken a compass-bearing on its yellow church tower, now battered to a blunt and crumbling stump by the British bombardment.

They pressed on through the tangle of ruins, clambering over palings and jumping ditches like a party of boys out for a day in the country, past the ravaged houses and the broken trees, with the smell of singeing cloth and charred beams in their nostrils. They burst from the last orchard into the sunken road with a vision before their eyes of field-grey figures darting away across the fields. Then the men yelled their battle-cry and rifles rang out, and they all poured into the road and up the bank on the other side, and so out upon a wide grassy slope commanding a great green plain, where the British shells were bursting in a long, white, fleecy line.

Our Ensign looked at his watch. It was a quarter to three in the afternoon, and already the day was won. But he knew the hardest part was coming. Now they had to hold what they had gained.

Men are always inclined to rest on their laurels, to sit down in the final objective and light their fags and stretch their legs and talk over their experiences with their pals. But Peter, radiating his satisfaction at their success, chased up and down the line, setting every man to dig the new trench.

They dug in on the fringe of a potato field. The men turned up potatoes by the score, and laid them carefully on one side, saying they would do for supper. The sun burnt down hotly upon them out of a clear blue sky as they dug and burrowed and scraped. The German shells screamed noisily over their heads, but none fell near the diggers. The British barrage still seethed and danced all over the plain in front of them.

That steady rain of shells was too much for the Huns, who had fled from the village to take refuge in shell holes in the open. By twos or threes, and by larger packets, they kept bursting into view, running like men possessed, their hands above their heads, while the Guards, looking up from their digging, cheered derisively. Several parties thus broke cover and rushed hell-for-leather into the midst of our Ensign's battalion, where they meekly, almost gratefully, submitted to be searched, and were marched off at a good round pace to the rear through the raging German barrage.

But now the Germans seemed to have located the new line. Their guns shortened their range, and whizz bangs and 5.9 shells began bursting about the digging Guardsmen. The officers went to and fro encouraging the men, sometimes lending a hand with pick or spade to give a good example. The shell fire was getting hotter every minute, and there was absolutely no cover save such as the shallow shell-holes afforded. There were casualties, and the cry of "Stretcher-*bearer!*" echoed up and down the line.

El Capitan sat on a corn-stook writing his report for the commanding officer; Peter was in conference with the company sergeant-major. The men had buckled to their work with a will and were digging feverishly, the sweat pouring down their faces. A British aeroplane soared, shrilly tooting, above their heads.

Lord, how hot it was! Our Ensign doffed his heavy helmet and wiped his brow. His rifle, which he had carried round with him all day, was planted, bayonet downwards, in the ground beside him. In a shell hole, a few yards away, sat a brother officer whom he had not seen since the previous evening. The latter called out to him to come over and sit down. Our Ensign walked across and dropped on to the edge of the shell hole, at the bottom of which a man was scraping with his entrenching tool.

He filled his pipe and got out his matchbox to light it. Then, from behind, something struck him a tremendous blow and lifted him high in the air with a mighty force, against which he struggled in vain with mind and body, desperately fighting to remain on the ground, striving to retain the mastery over himself. . . .

It was during his convalescence that this narrative came to be written.

ALSO FROM LEONAUR
AVAILABLE IN SOFTCOVER OR HARDCOVER WITH DUST JACKET

THE FALL OF THE MOGHUL EMPIRE OF HINDUSTAN *by H. G. Keene*—By the beginning of the nineteenth century, as British and Indian armies under Lake and Wellesley dominated the scene, a little over half a century of conflict brought the Moghul Empire to its knees.

LADY SALE'S AFGHANISTAN *by Florentia Sale*—An Indomitable Victorian Lady's Account of the Retreat from Kabul During the First Afghan War.

THE CAMPAIGN OF MAGENTA AND SOLFERINO 1859 *by Harold Carmichael Wylly*—The Decisive Conflict for the Unification of Italy.

FRENCH'S CAVALRY CAMPAIGN *by J. G. Maydon*—A Special Correspondent's View of British Army Mounted Troops During the Boer War.

CAVALRY AT WATERLOO *by Sir Evelyn Wood*—British Mounted Troops During the Campaign of 1815.

THE SUBALTERN *by George Robert Gleig*—The Experiences of an Officer of the 85th Light Infantry During the Peninsular War.

NAPOLEON AT BAY, 1814 *by F. Loraine Petre*—The Campaigns to the Fall of the First Empire.

NAPOLEON AND THE CAMPAIGN OF 1806 *by Colonel Vachée*—The Napoleonic Method of Organisation and Command to the Battles of Jena & Auerstädt.

THE COMPLETE ADVENTURES IN THE CONNAUGHT RANGERS *by William Grattan*—The 88th Regiment during the Napoleonic Wars by a Serving Officer.

BUGLER AND OFFICER OF THE RIFLES *by William Green & Harry Smith*—With the 95th (Rifles) during the Peninsular & Waterloo Campaigns of the Napoleonic Wars.

NAPOLEONIC WAR STORIES *by Sir Arthur Quiller-Couch*—Tales of soldiers, spies, battles & sieges from the Peninsular & Waterloo campaingns.

CAPTAIN OF THE 95TH (RIFLES) *by Jonathan Leach*—An officer of Wellington's sharpshooters during the Peninsular, South of France and Waterloo campaigns of the Napoleonic wars.

RIFLEMAN COSTELLO *by Edward Costello*—The adventures of a soldier of the 95th (Rifles) in the Peninsular & Waterloo Campaigns of the Napoleonic wars.

AVAILABLE ONLINE AT **www.leonaur.com**
AND FROM ALL GOOD BOOK STORES

ALSO FROM LEONAUR
AVAILABLE IN SOFTCOVER OR HARDCOVER WITH DUST JACKET

THE 9TH—THE KING'S (LIVERPOOL REGIMENT) IN THE GREAT WAR 1914 - 1918 *by Enos H. G. Roberts*—Mersey to mud—war and Liverpool men.

THE GAMBARDIER *by Mark Severn*—The experiences of a battery of Heavy artillery on the Western Front during the First World War.

FROM MESSINES TO THIRD YPRES *by Thomas Floyd*—A personal account of the First World War on the Western front by a 2/5th Lancashire Fusilier.

THE IRISH GUARDS IN THE GREAT WAR - VOLUME 1 *by Rudyard Kipling*—Edited and Compiled from Their Diaries and Papers—The First Battalion.

THE IRISH GUARDS IN THE GREAT WAR - VOLUME 1 *by Rudyard Kipling*—Edited and Compiled from Their Diaries and Papers—The Second Battalion.

ARMOURED CARS IN EDEN *by K. Roosevelt*—An American President's son serving in Rolls Royce armoured cars with the British in Mesopotamia & with the American Artillery in France during the First World War.

CHASSEUR OF 1914 *by Marcel Dupont*—Experiences of the twilight of the French Light Cavalry by a young officer during the early battles of the great war in Europe.

TROOP HORSE & TRENCH *by R.A. Lloyd*—The experiences of a British Lifeguardsman of the household cavalry fighting on the western front during the First World War 1914-18.

THE EAST AFRICAN MOUNTED RIFLES *by C.J. Wilson*—Experiences of the campaign in the East African bush during the First World War.

THE LONG PATROL *by George Berrie*—A Novel of Light Horsemen from Gallipoli to the Palestine campaign of the First World War.

THE FIGHTING CAMELIERS *by Frank Reid*—The exploits of the Imperial Camel Corps in the desert and Palestine campaigns of the First World War.

STEEL CHARIOTS IN THE DESERT *by S. C. Rolls*—The first world war experiences of a Rolls Royce armoured car driver with the Duke of Westminster in Libya and in Arabia with T.E. Lawrence.

WITH THE IMPERIAL CAMEL CORPS IN THE GREAT WAR *by Geoffrey Inchbald*—The story of a serving officer with the British 2nd battalion against the Senussi and during the Palestine campaign.

AVAILABLE ONLINE AT **www.leonaur.com**
AND FROM ALL GOOD BOOK STORES

www.ingramcontent.com/pod-product-compliance
Lightning Source LLC
Chambersburg PA
CBHW031625160426
43196CB00006B/277